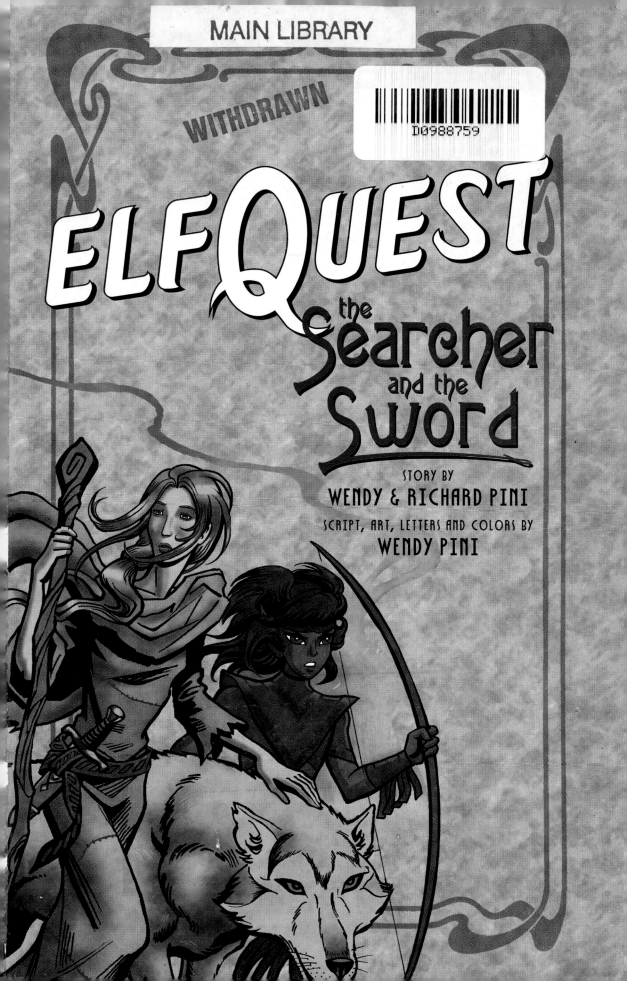

ELFQUEST

the Searcher and the Sword

STORY BY
WENDY & RICHARD PINI

SCRIPT, ART, LETTERS AND COLORS BY
WENDY PINI

ELFQUEST: THE SEARCHER AND THE SWORD

DC Comics, 1700 Broadway, New York, NY 10019
A Warner Bros. Entertainment Company

Printed in Canada. First Printing.
Cover illustration by Wendy Pini.
Hardcover ISBN: 1-4012-0183-0
Softcover ISBN: 1-4012-0184-9
Publication design by Peter Hamboussi.

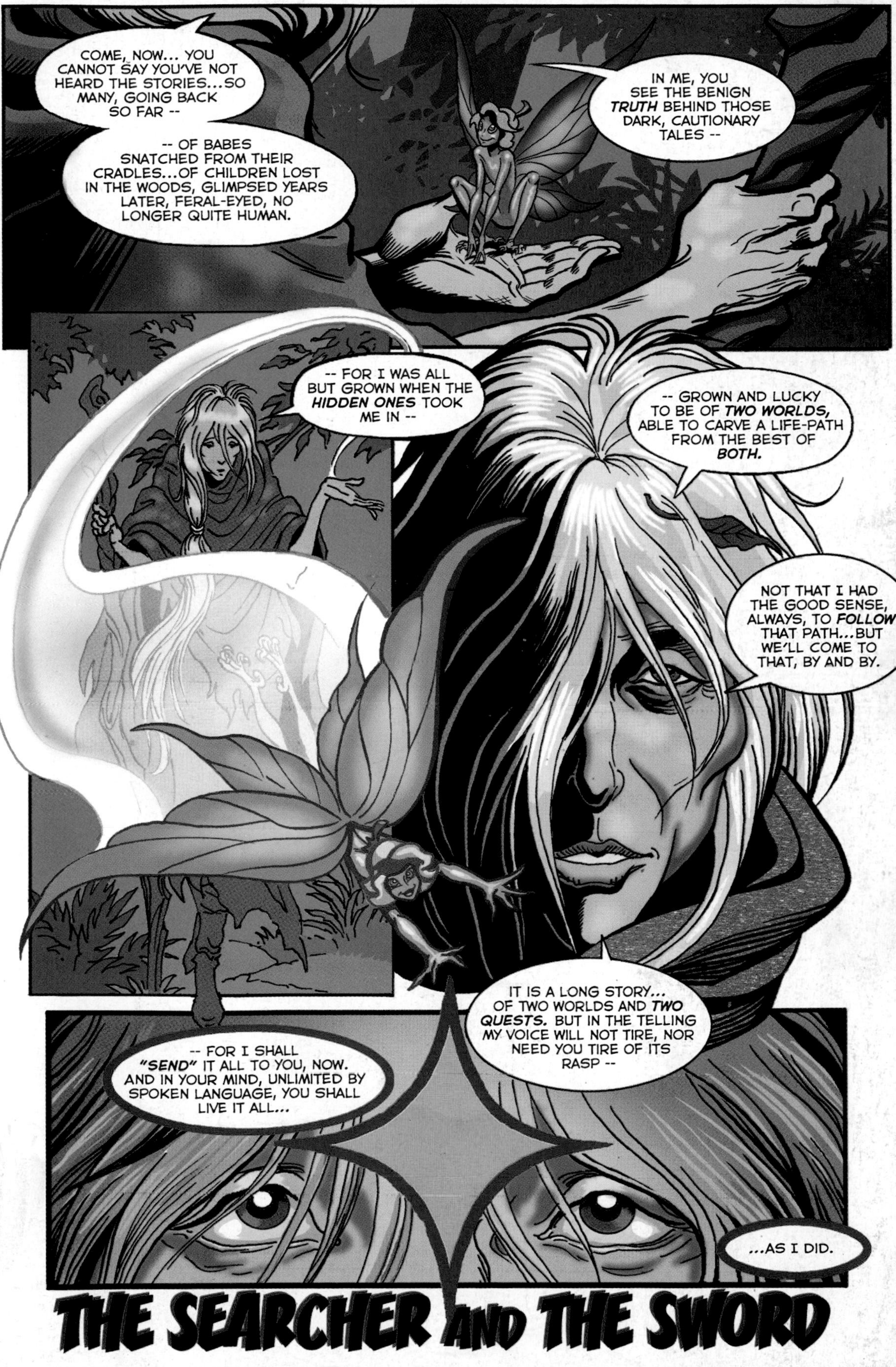
COME, NOW... YOU CANNOT SAY YOU'VE NOT HEARD THE STORIES...SO MANY, GOING BACK SO FAR --
-- OF BABES SNATCHED FROM THEIR CRADLES...OF CHILDREN LOST IN THE WOODS, GLIMPSED YEARS LATER, FERAL-EYED, NO LONGER QUITE HUMAN.
IN ME, YOU SEE THE BENIGN *TRUTH* BEHIND THOSE DARK, CAUTIONARY TALES --
-- FOR I WAS ALL BUT GROWN WHEN THE *HIDDEN ONES* TOOK ME IN --
-- GROWN AND LUCKY TO BE OF *TWO WORLDS,* ABLE TO CARVE A LIFE-PATH FROM THE BEST OF *BOTH.*
NOT THAT I HAD THE GOOD SENSE, ALWAYS, TO *FOLLOW* THAT PATH...BUT WE'LL COME TO THAT, BY AND BY.
IT IS A LONG STORY... OF TWO WORLDS AND *TWO QUESTS.* BUT IN THE TELLING MY VOICE WILL NOT TIRE, NOR NEED YOU TIRE OF ITS RASP --
-- FOR I SHALL *"SEND"* IT ALL TO YOU, NOW. AND IN YOUR MIND, UNLIMITED BY SPOKEN LANGUAGE, YOU SHALL LIVE IT ALL...
...AS I DID.
THE SEARCHER AND THE SWORD

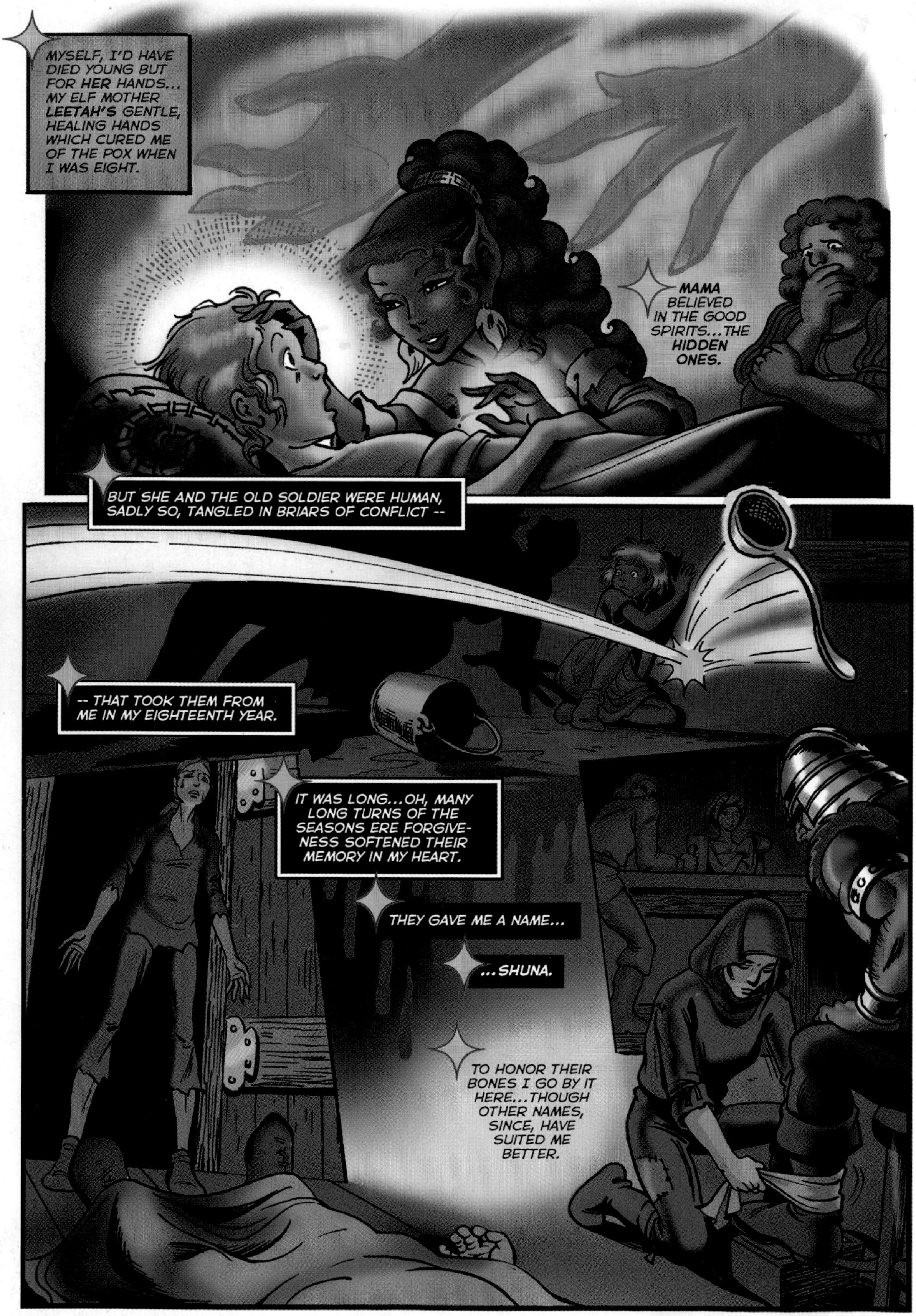
MYSELF, I'D HAVE DIED YOUNG BUT FOR HER HANDS... MY ELF MOTHER LEETAH'S GENTLE, HEALING HANDS WHICH CURED ME OF THE POX WHEN I WAS EIGHT.
MAMA BELIEVED IN THE GOOD SPIRITS...THE HIDDEN ONES.
BUT SHE AND THE OLD SOLDIER WERE HUMAN, SADLY SO, TANGLED IN BRIARS OF CONFLICT --
-- THAT TOOK THEM FROM ME IN MY EIGHTEENTH YEAR.
IT WAS LONG...OH, MANY LONG TURNS OF THE SEASONS ERE FORGIVENESS SOFTENED THEIR MEMORY IN MY HEART.
THEY GAVE ME A NAME...
...SHUNA.
TO HONOR THEIR BONES I GO BY IT HERE...THOUGH OTHER NAMES, SINCE, HAVE SUITED ME BETTER.

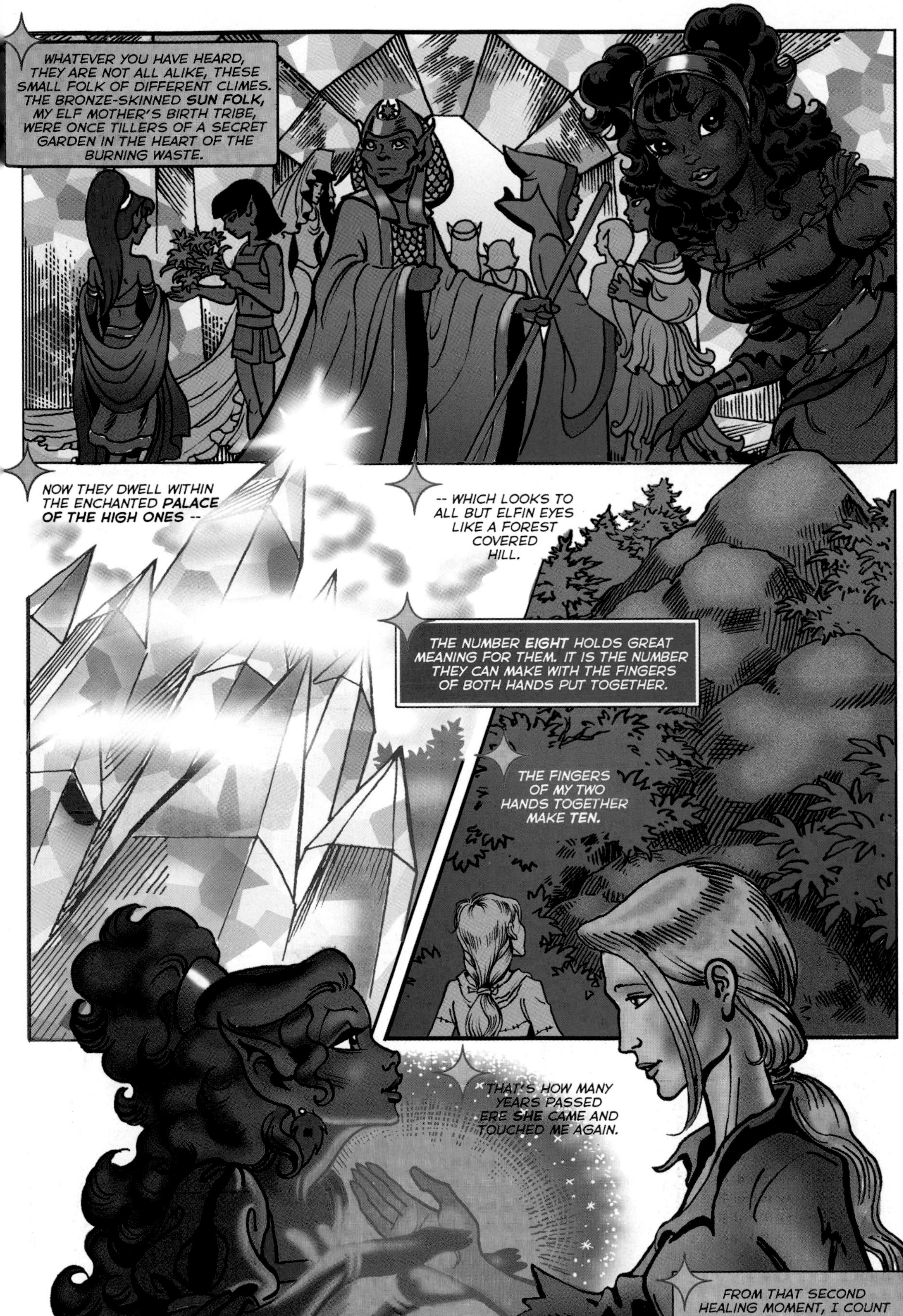
WHATEVER YOU HAVE HEARD, THEY ARE NOT ALL ALIKE, THESE SMALL FOLK OF DIFFERENT CLIMES. THE BRONZE-SKINNED SUN FOLK, MY ELF MOTHER'S BIRTH TRIBE, WERE ONCE TILLERS OF A SECRET GARDEN IN THE HEART OF THE BURNING WASTE.
NOW THEY DWELL WITHIN THE ENCHANTED PALACE OF THE HIGH ONES --
-- WHICH LOOKS TO ALL BUT ELFIN EYES LIKE A FOREST COVERED HILL.
THE NUMBER EIGHT HOLDS GREAT MEANING FOR THEM. IT IS THE NUMBER THEY CAN MAKE WITH THE FINGERS OF BOTH HANDS PUT TOGETHER.
THE FINGERS OF MY TWO HANDS TOGETHER MAKE TEN.
THAT'S HOW MANY YEARS PASSED ERE SHE CAME AND TOUCHED ME AGAIN.
FROM THAT SECOND HEALING MOMENT, I COUNT MYSELF TRULY BORN.

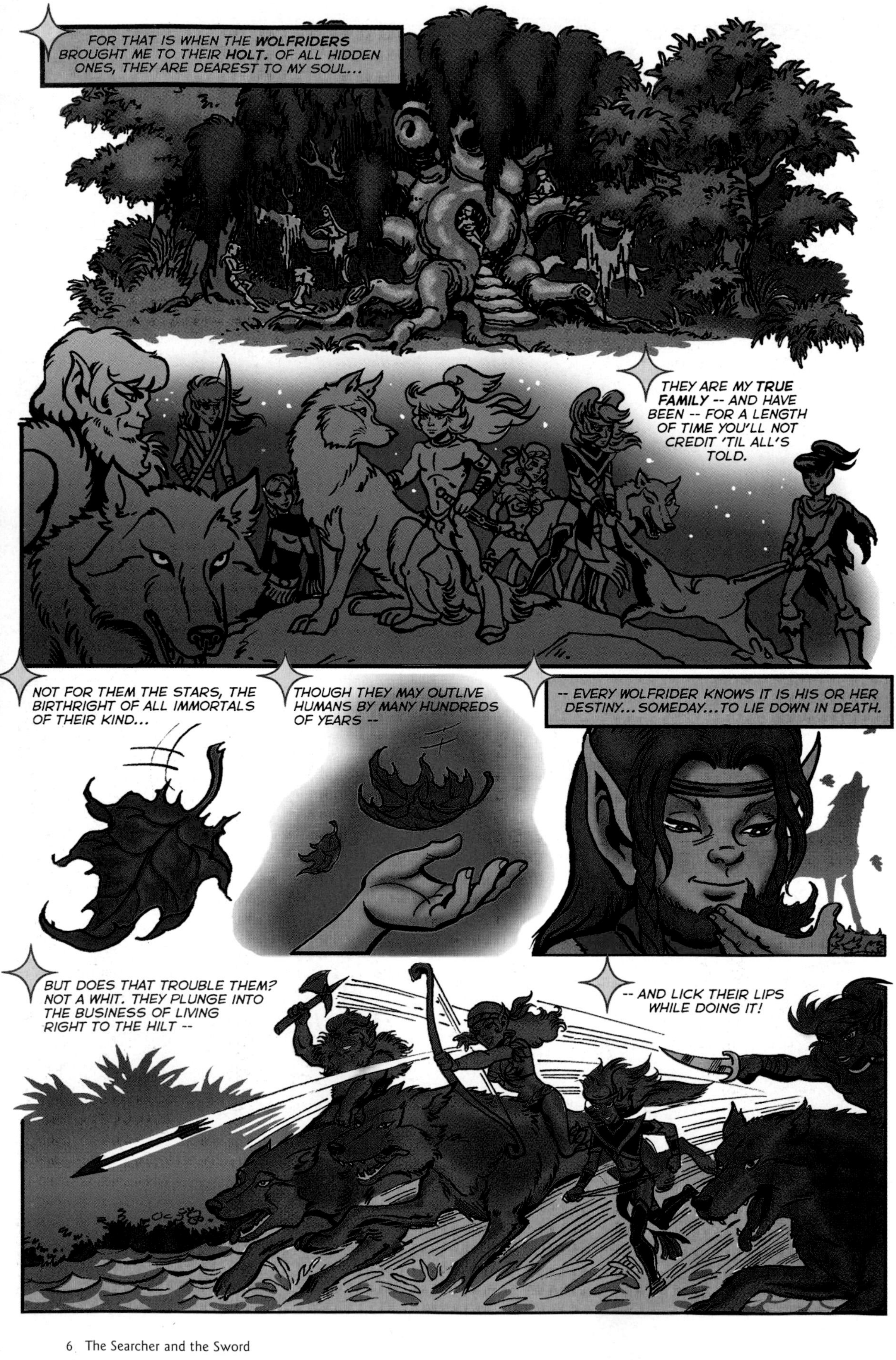
FOR THAT IS WHEN THE WOLFRIDERS BROUGHT ME TO THEIR HOLT. OF ALL HIDDEN ONES, THEY ARE DEAREST TO MY SOUL...
THEY ARE MY TRUE FAMILY -- AND HAVE BEEN -- FOR A LENGTH OF TIME YOU'LL NOT CREDIT 'TIL ALL'S TOLD.
NOT FOR THEM THE STARS, THE BIRTHRIGHT OF ALL IMMORTALS OF THEIR KIND...
THOUGH THEY MAY OUTLIVE HUMANS BY MANY HUNDREDS OF YEARS --
-- EVERY WOLFRIDER KNOWS IT IS HIS OR HER DESTINY... SOMEDAY... TO LIE DOWN IN DEATH.
BUT DOES THAT TROUBLE THEM? NOT A WHIT. THEY PLUNGE INTO THE BUSINESS OF LIVING RIGHT TO THE HILT --
-- AND LICK THEIR LIPS WHILE DOING IT!

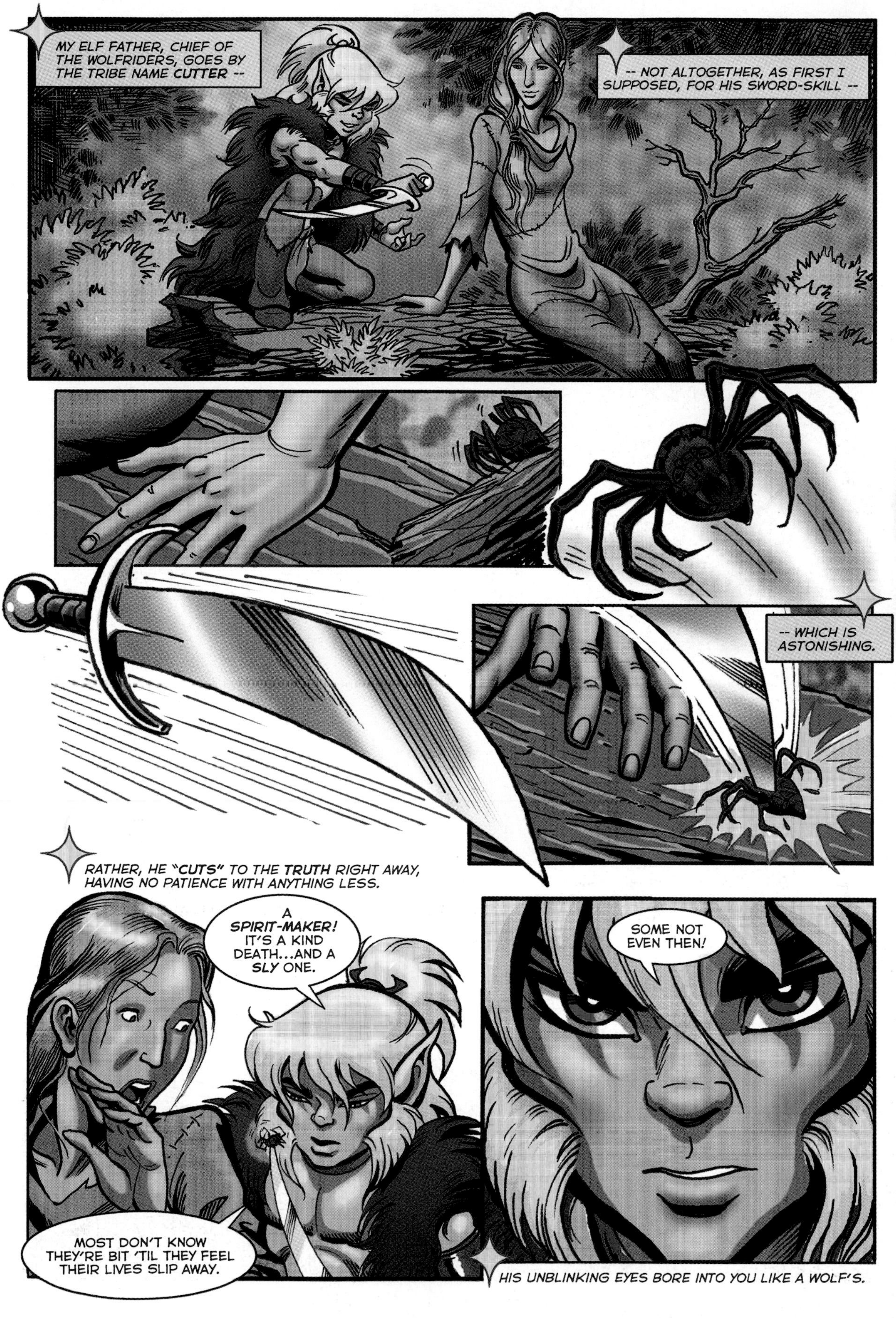
MY ELF FATHER, CHIEF OF THE WOLFRIDERS, GOES BY THE TRIBE NAME CUTTER --
-- NOT ALTOGETHER, AS FIRST I SUPPOSED, FOR HIS SWORD-SKILL --
-- WHICH IS ASTONISHING.
RATHER, HE "CUTS" TO THE TRUTH RIGHT AWAY, HAVING NO PATIENCE WITH ANYTHING LESS.
A SPIRIT-MAKER! IT'S A KIND DEATH...AND A SLY ONE.
MOST DON'T KNOW THEY'RE BIT 'TIL THEY FEEL THEIR LIVES SLIP AWAY.
SOME NOT EVEN THEN!
HIS UNBLINKING EYES BORE INTO YOU LIKE A WOLF'S.

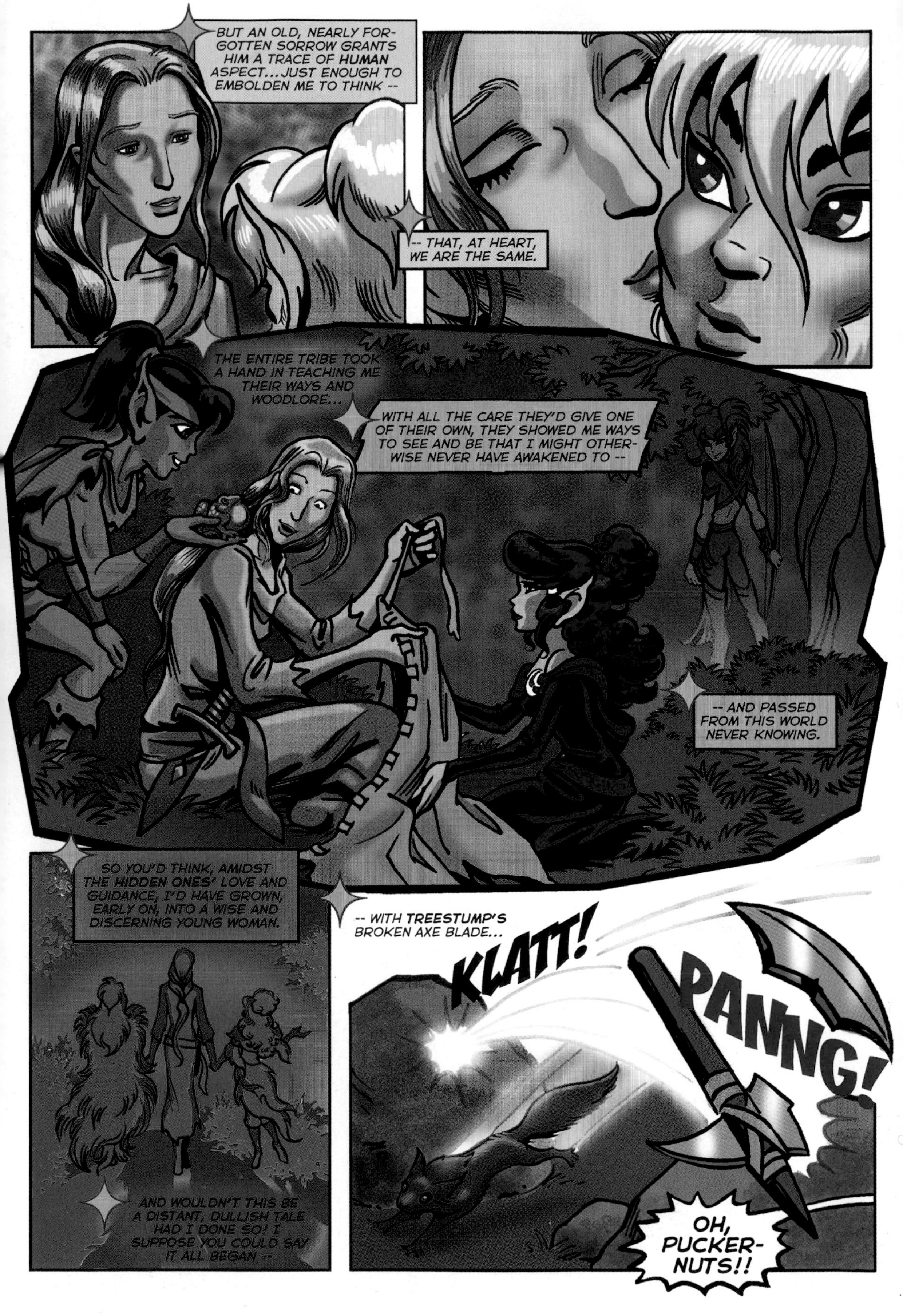
BUT AN OLD, NEARLY FOR-GOTTEN SORROW GRANTS HIM A TRACE OF HUMAN ASPECT... JUST ENOUGH TO EMBOLDEN ME TO THINK --
-- THAT, AT HEART, WE ARE THE SAME.
THE ENTIRE TRIBE TOOK A HAND IN TEACHING ME THEIR WAYS AND WOODLORE...
WITH ALL THE CARE THEY'D GIVE ONE OF THEIR OWN, THEY SHOWED ME WAYS TO SEE AND BE THAT I MIGHT OTHER-WISE NEVER HAVE AWAKENED TO --
-- AND PASSED FROM THIS WORLD NEVER KNOWING.
SO YOU'D THINK, AMIDST THE HIDDEN ONES' LOVE AND GUIDANCE, I'D HAVE GROWN, EARLY ON, INTO A WISE AND DISCERNING YOUNG WOMAN.
AND WOULDN'T THIS BE A DISTANT, DULLISH TALE HAD I DONE SO! I SUPPOSE YOU COULD SAY IT ALL BEGAN --
-- WITH TREESTUMP'S BROKEN AXE BLADE...
KLATT!
PANNG!
OH, PUCKER-NUTS!!

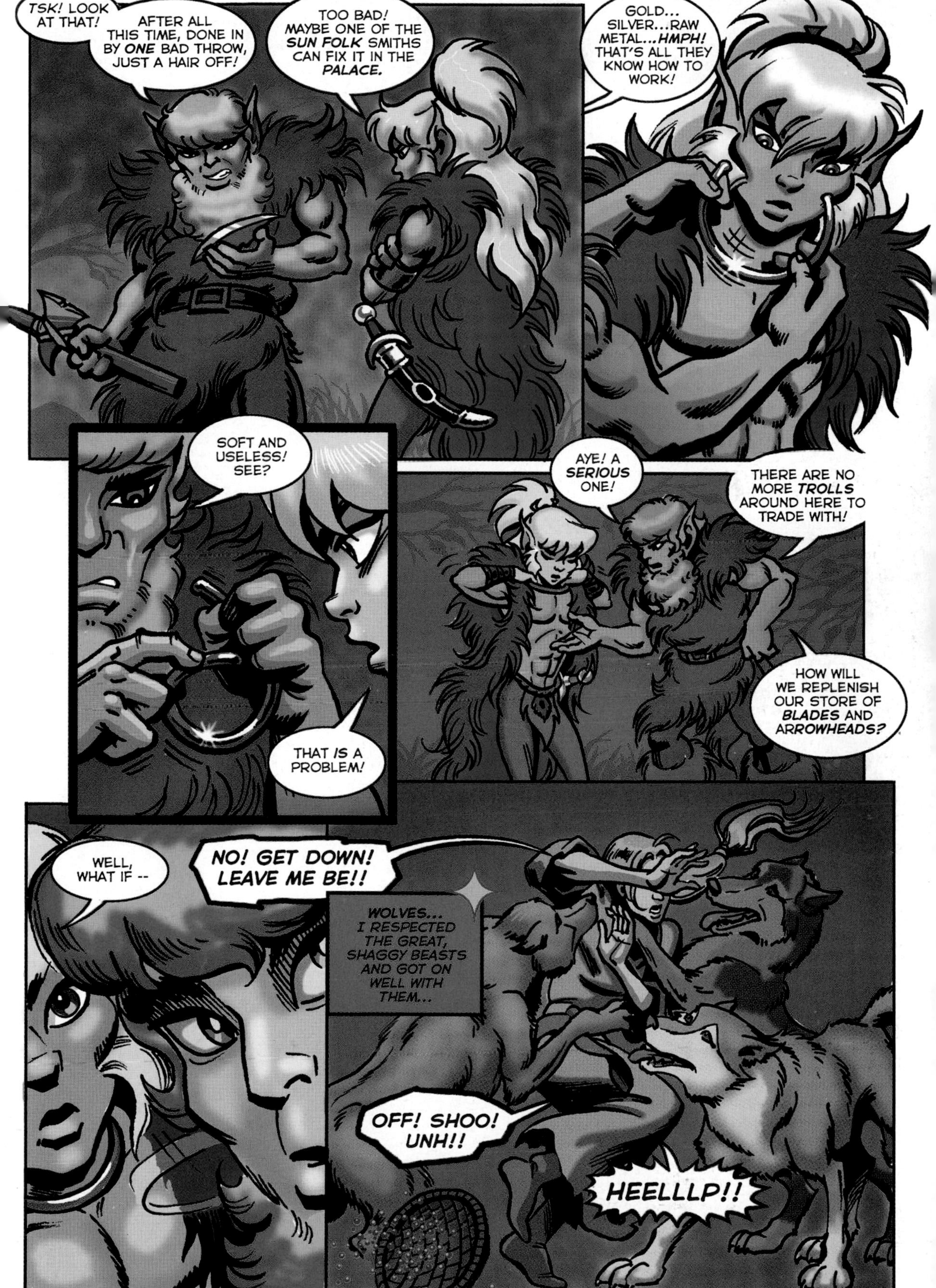
TSK! LOOK AT THAT!
AFTER ALL THIS TIME, DONE IN BY ONE BAD THROW, JUST A HAIR OFF!
TOO BAD! MAYBE ONE OF THE SUN FOLK SMITHS CAN FIX IT IN THE PALACE.
GOLD... SILVER...RAW METAL...HMPH! THAT'S ALL THEY KNOW HOW TO WORK!
SOFT AND USELESS! SEE?
THAT IS A PROBLEM!
AYE! A SERIOUS ONE!
THERE ARE NO MORE TROLLS AROUND HERE TO TRADE WITH!
HOW WILL WE REPLENISH OUR STORE OF BLADES AND ARROWHEADS?
WELL, WHAT IF --
NO! GET DOWN! LEAVE ME BE!!
WOLVES... I RESPECTED THE GREAT, SHAGGY BEASTS AND GOT ON WELL WITH THEM...
OFF! SHOO! UNH!!
HEELLLP!!

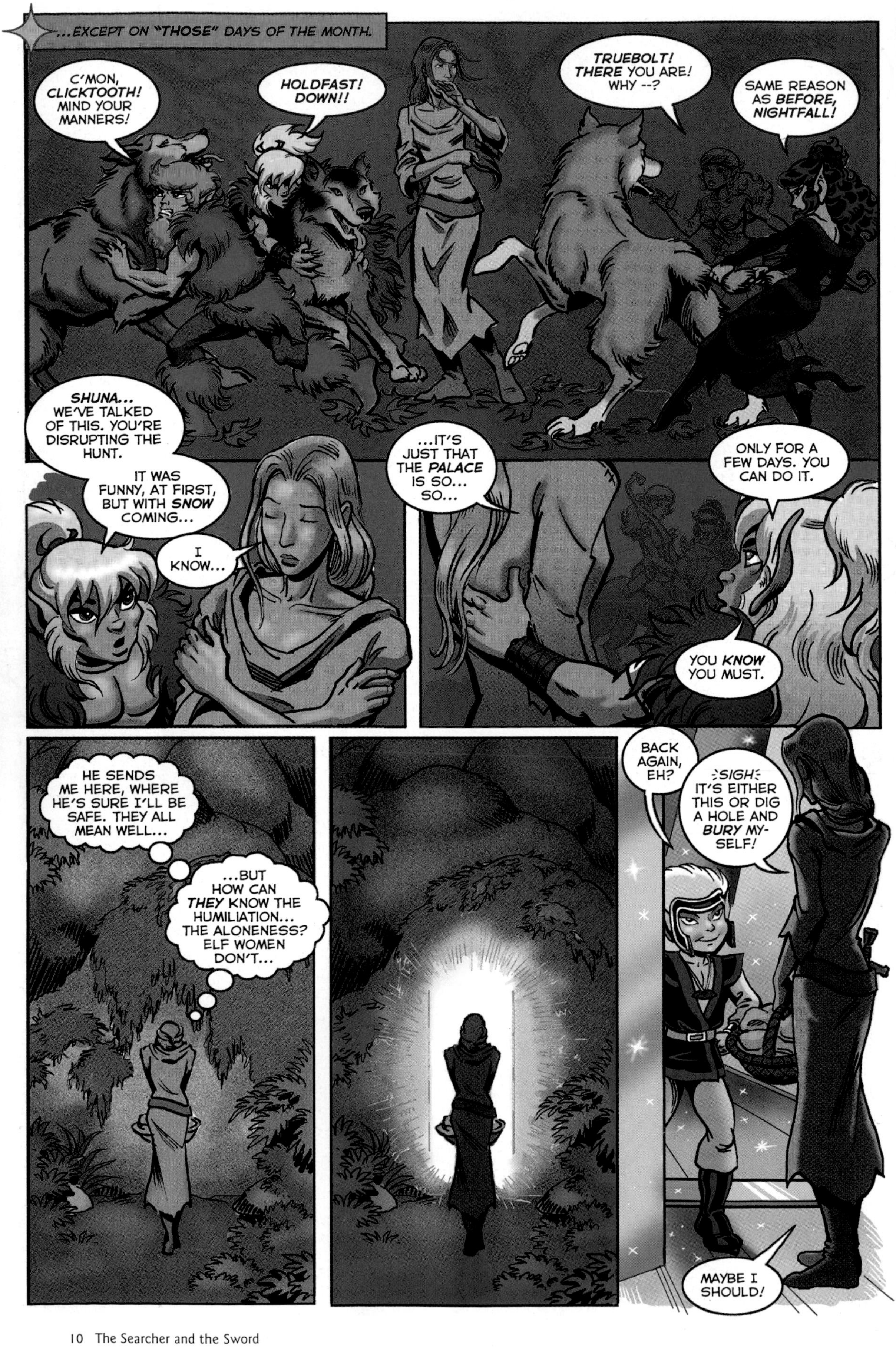
...EXCEPT ON "THOSE" DAYS OF THE MONTH.
C'MON, CLICKTOOTH! MIND YOUR MANNERS!
HOLDFAST! DOWN!!
TRUEBOLT! THERE YOU ARE! WHY --?
SAME REASON AS BEFORE, NIGHTFALL!
SHUNA... WE'VE TALKED OF THIS. YOU'RE DISRUPTING THE HUNT.
IT WAS FUNNY, AT FIRST, BUT WITH SNOW COMING...
I KNOW...
...IT'S JUST THAT THE PALACE IS SO... SO...
ONLY FOR A FEW DAYS. YOU CAN DO IT.
YOU KNOW YOU MUST.
HE SENDS ME HERE, WHERE HE'S SURE I'LL BE SAFE. THEY ALL MEAN WELL...
...BUT HOW CAN THEY KNOW THE HUMILIATION... THE ALONENESS? ELF WOMEN DON'T...
BACK AGAIN, EH?
SIGH
IT'S EITHER THIS OR DIG A HOLE AND BURY MY-SELF!
MAYBE I SHOULD!

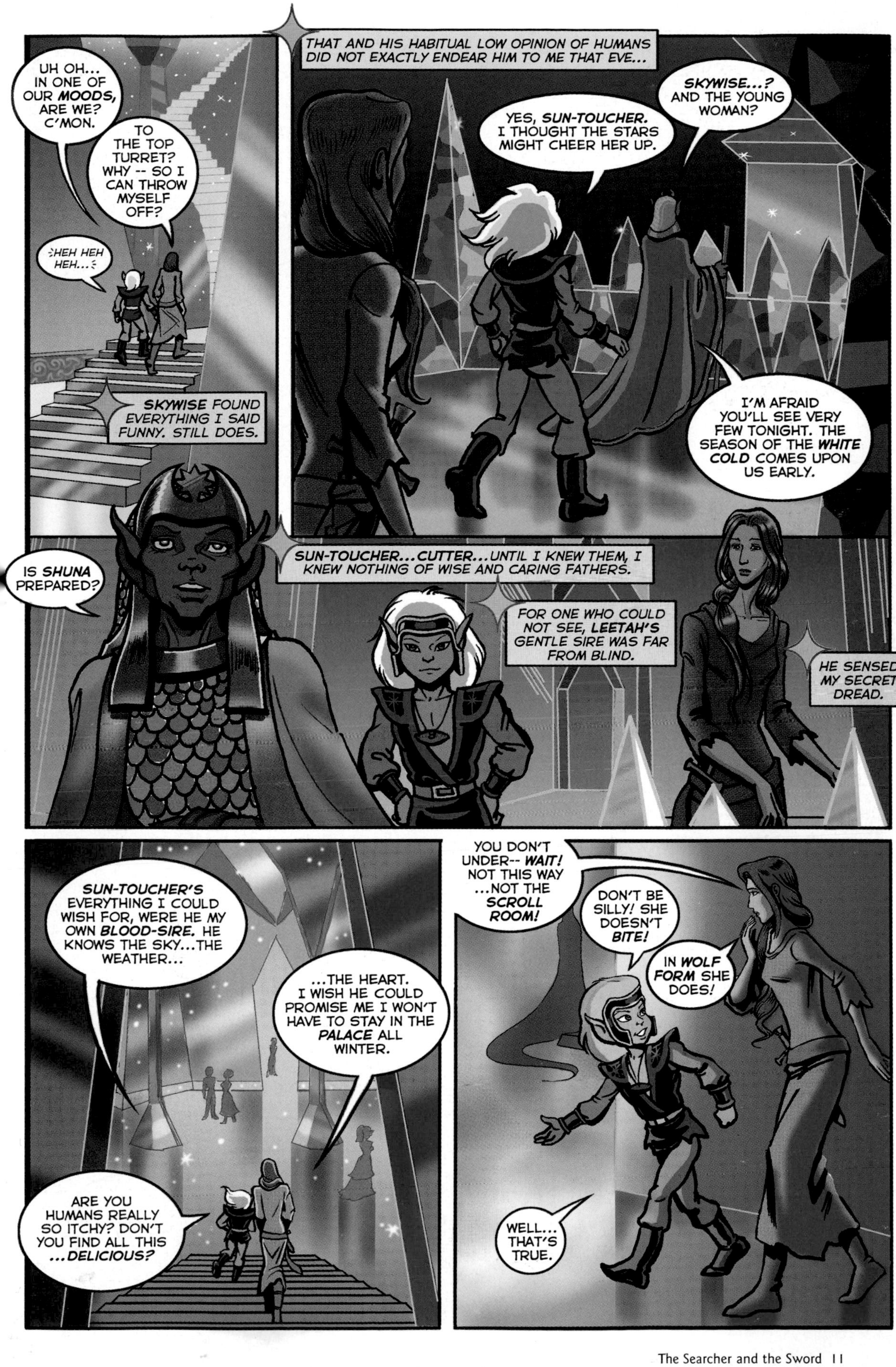
UH OH... IN ONE OF OUR MOODS, ARE WE? C'MON.
TO THE TOP TURRET? WHY -- SO I CAN THROW MYSELF OFF?
HEH HEH HEH...
SKYWISE FOUND EVERYTHING I SAID FUNNY. STILL DOES.
THAT AND HIS HABITUAL LOW OPINION OF HUMANS DID NOT EXACTLY ENDEAR HIM TO ME THAT EVE...
YES, SUN-TOUCHER. I THOUGHT THE STARS MIGHT CHEER HER UP.
SKYWISE...? AND THE YOUNG WOMAN?
I'M AFRAID YOU'LL SEE VERY FEW TONIGHT. THE SEASON OF THE WHITE COLD COMES UPON US EARLY.
IS SHUNA PREPARED?
SUN-TOUCHER...CUTTER...UNTIL I KNEW THEM, I KNEW NOTHING OF WISE AND CARING FATHERS.
FOR ONE WHO COULD NOT SEE, LEETAH'S GENTLE SIRE WAS FAR FROM BLIND.
HE SENSED MY SECRET DREAD.
SUN-TOUCHER'S EVERYTHING I COULD WISH FOR, WERE HE MY OWN BLOOD-SIRE. HE KNOWS THE SKY...THE WEATHER...
...THE HEART. I WISH HE COULD PROMISE ME I WON'T HAVE TO STAY IN THE PALACE ALL WINTER.
ARE YOU HUMANS REALLY SO ITCHY? DON'T YOU FIND ALL THIS ...DELICIOUS?
YOU DON'T UNDER-- WAIT! NOT THIS WAY ...NOT THE SCROLL ROOM!
DON'T BE SILLY! SHE DOESN'T BITE!
IN WOLF FORM SHE DOES!
WELL... THAT'S TRUE.

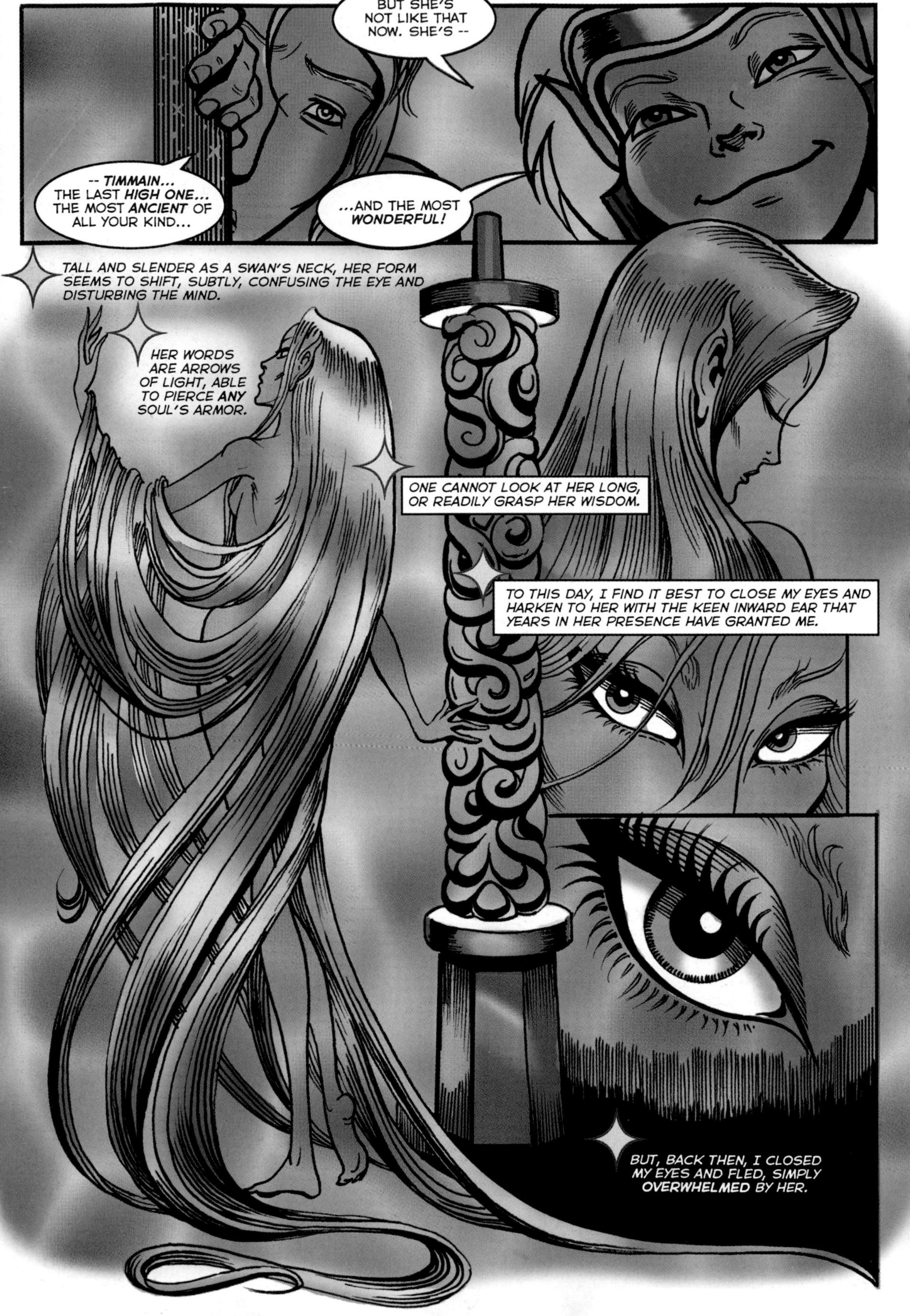
BUT SHE'S NOT LIKE THAT NOW. SHE'S --
-- TIMMAIN... THE LAST HIGH ONE... THE MOST ANCIENT OF ALL YOUR KIND...
...AND THE MOST WONDERFUL!
TALL AND SLENDER AS A SWAN'S NECK, HER FORM SEEMS TO SHIFT, SUBTLY, CONFUSING THE EYE AND DISTURBING THE MIND.
HER WORDS ARE ARROWS OF LIGHT, ABLE TO PIERCE ANY SOUL'S ARMOR.
ONE CANNOT LOOK AT HER LONG, OR READILY GRASP HER WISDOM.
TO THIS DAY, I FIND IT BEST TO CLOSE MY EYES AND HARKEN TO HER WITH THE KEEN INWARD EAR THAT YEARS IN HER PRESENCE HAVE GRANTED ME.
BUT, BACK THEN, I CLOSED MY EYES AND FLED, SIMPLY OVERWHELMED BY HER.

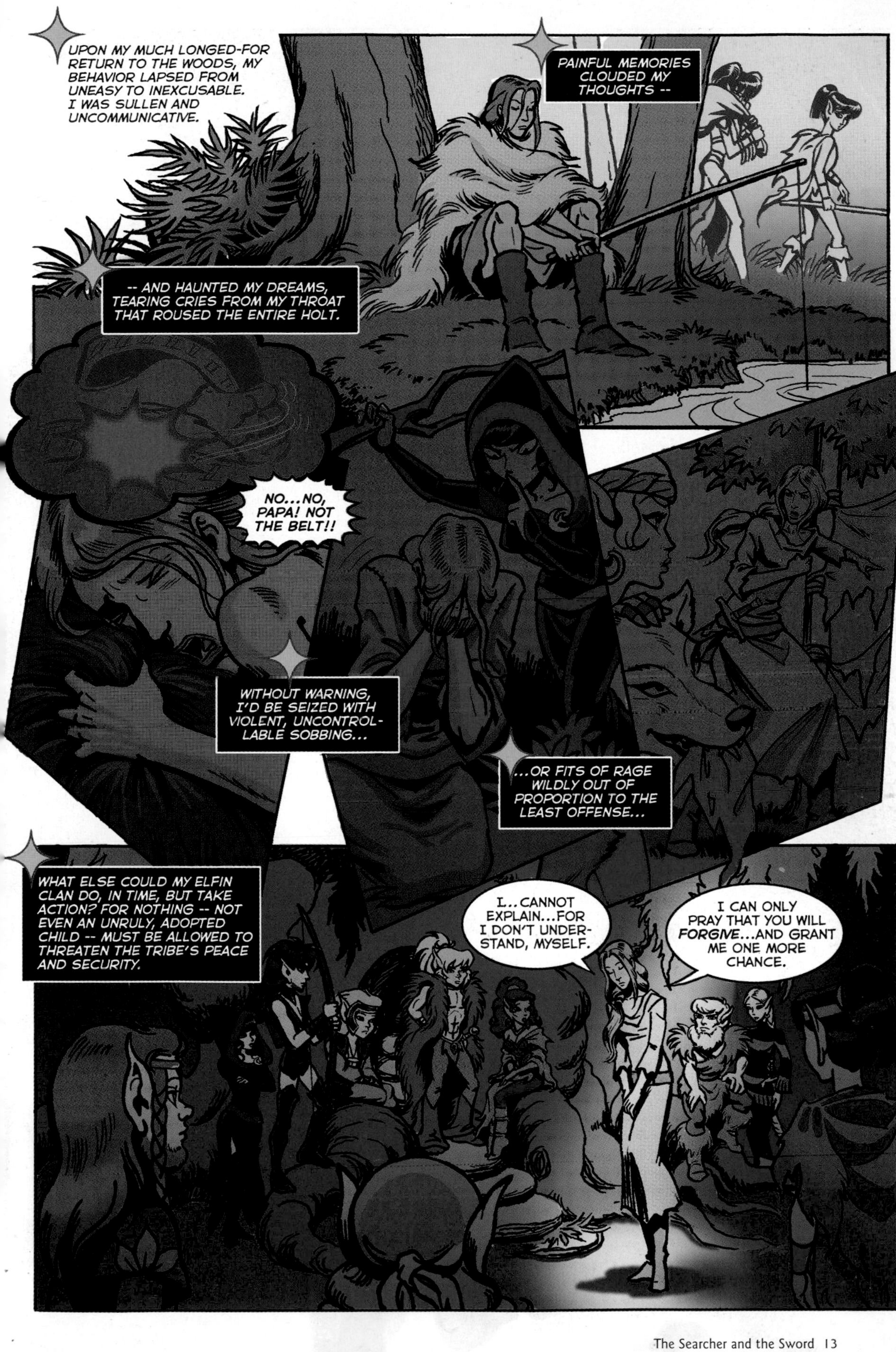
UPON MY MUCH LONGED-FOR RETURN TO THE WOODS, MY BEHAVIOR LAPSED FROM UNEASY TO INEXCUSABLE. I WAS SULLEN AND UNCOMMUNICATIVE.
PAINFUL MEMORIES CLOUDED MY THOUGHTS --
-- AND HAUNTED MY DREAMS, TEARING CRIES FROM MY THROAT THAT ROUSED THE ENTIRE HOLT.
NO...NO, PAPA! NOT THE BELT!!
WITHOUT WARNING, I'D BE SEIZED WITH VIOLENT, UNCONTROL-LABLE SOBBING...
...OR FITS OF RAGE WILDLY OUT OF PROPORTION TO THE LEAST OFFENSE...
WHAT ELSE COULD MY ELFIN CLAN DO, IN TIME, BUT TAKE ACTION? FOR NOTHING -- NOT EVEN AN UNRULY, ADOPTED CHILD -- MUST BE ALLOWED TO THREATEN THE TRIBE'S PEACE AND SECURITY.
I...CANNOT EXPLAIN...FOR I DON'T UNDER-STAND, MYSELF.
I CAN ONLY PRAY THAT YOU WILL FORGIVE...AND GRANT ME ONE MORE CHANCE.

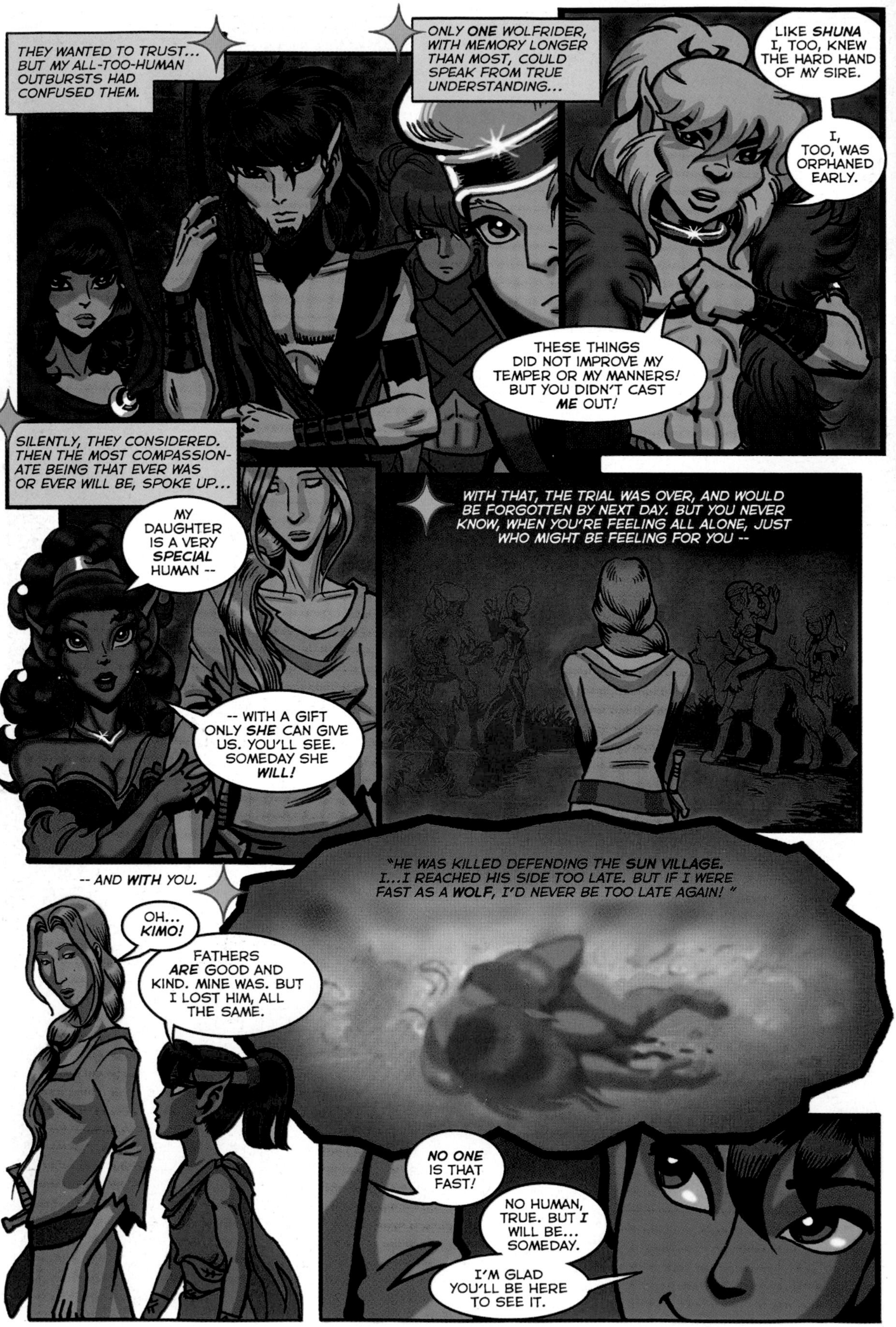
THEY WANTED TO TRUST... BUT MY ALL-TOO-HUMAN OUTBURSTS HAD CONFUSED THEM.
ONLY ONE WOLFRIDER, WITH MEMORY LONGER THAN MOST, COULD SPEAK FROM TRUE UNDERSTANDING...
LIKE SHUNA I, TOO, KNEW THE HARD HAND OF MY SIRE.
I, TOO, WAS ORPHANED EARLY.
THESE THINGS DID NOT IMPROVE MY TEMPER OR MY MANNERS! BUT YOU DIDN'T CAST ME OUT!
SILENTLY, THEY CONSIDERED. THEN THE MOST COMPASSIONATE BEING THAT EVER WAS OR EVER WILL BE, SPOKE UP...
MY DAUGHTER IS A VERY SPECIAL HUMAN --
-- WITH A GIFT ONLY SHE CAN GIVE US. YOU'LL SEE. SOMEDAY SHE WILL!
WITH THAT, THE TRIAL WAS OVER, AND WOULD BE FORGOTTEN BY NEXT DAY. BUT YOU NEVER KNOW, WHEN YOU'RE FEELING ALL ALONE, JUST WHO MIGHT BE FEELING FOR YOU --
-- AND WITH YOU.
OH... KIMO!
FATHERS ARE GOOD AND KIND. MINE WAS. BUT I LOST HIM, ALL THE SAME.
"HE WAS KILLED DEFENDING THE SUN VILLAGE. I...I REACHED HIS SIDE TOO LATE. BUT IF I WERE FAST AS A WOLF, I'D NEVER BE TOO LATE AGAIN!"
NO ONE IS THAT FAST!
NO HUMAN, TRUE. BUT I WILL BE... SOMEDAY.
I'M GLAD YOU'LL BE HERE TO SEE IT.

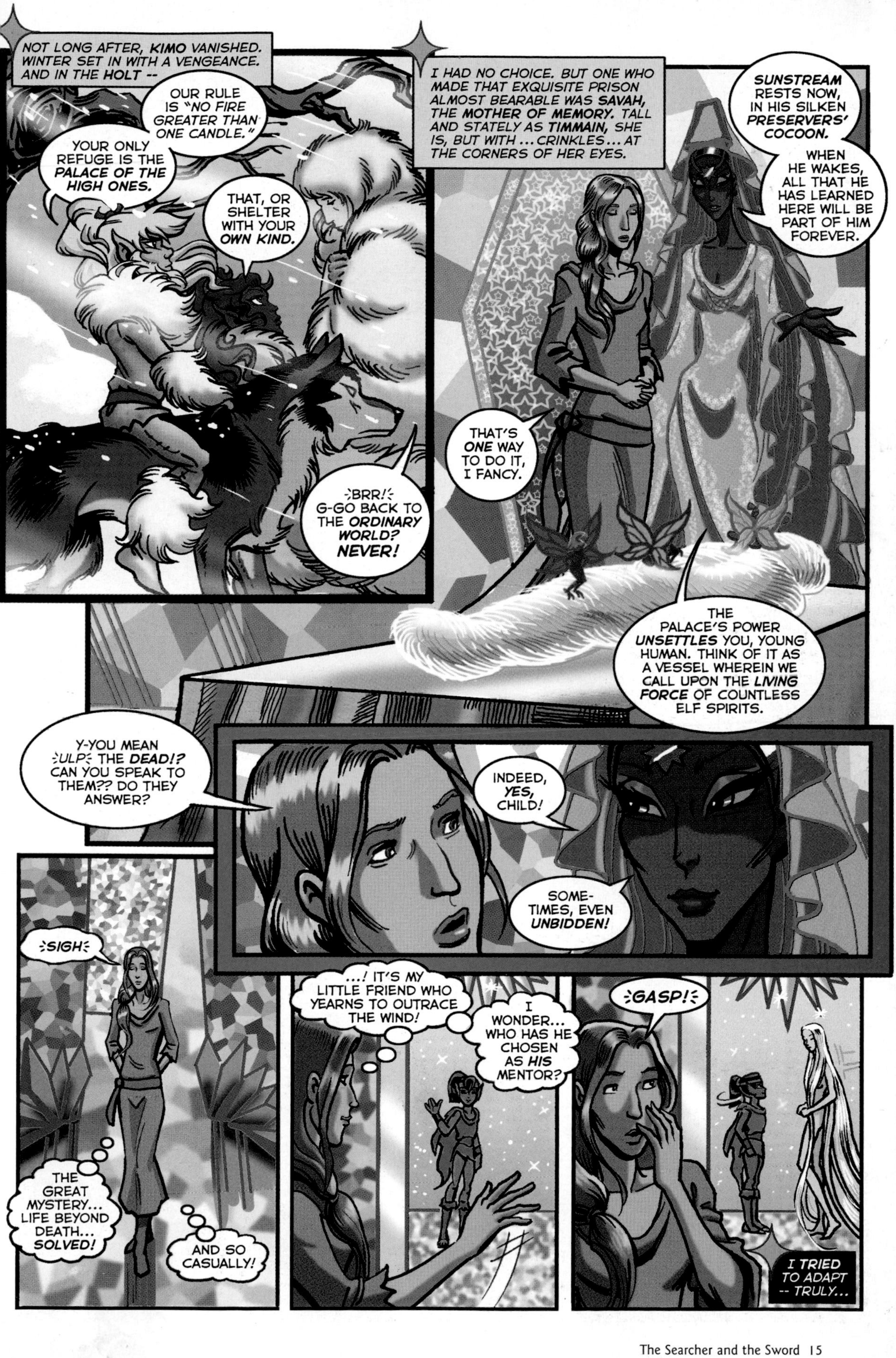

NOT LONG AFTER, KIMO VANISHED. WINTER SET IN WITH A VENGEANCE. AND IN THE HOLT --
OUR RULE IS "NO FIRE GREATER THAN ONE CANDLE."
YOUR ONLY REFUGE IS THE PALACE OF THE HIGH ONES.
THAT, OR SHELTER WITH YOUR OWN KIND.
BRR! G-GO BACK TO THE ORDINARY WORLD? NEVER!
I HAD NO CHOICE. BUT ONE WHO MADE THAT EXQUISITE PRISON ALMOST BEARABLE WAS SAVAH, THE MOTHER OF MEMORY. TALL AND STATELY AS TIMMAIN, SHE IS, BUT WITH ... CRINKLES ... AT THE CORNERS OF HER EYES.
SUNSTREAM RESTS NOW, IN HIS SILKEN PRESERVERS' COCOON.
WHEN HE WAKES, ALL THAT HE HAS LEARNED HERE WILL BE PART OF HIM FOREVER.
THAT'S ONE WAY TO DO IT, I FANCY.
THE PALACE'S POWER UNSETTLES YOU, YOUNG HUMAN. THINK OF IT AS A VESSEL WHEREIN WE CALL UPON THE LIVING FORCE OF COUNTLESS ELF SPIRITS.
Y-YOU MEAN ULP THE DEAD!? CAN YOU SPEAK TO THEM?? DO THEY ANSWER?
INDEED, YES, CHILD!
SOME-TIMES, EVEN UNBIDDEN!
SIGH
THE GREAT MYSTERY... LIFE BEYOND DEATH... SOLVED!
AND SO CASUALLY!
...! IT'S MY LITTLE FRIEND WHO YEARNS TO OUTRACE THE WIND!
I WONDER... WHO HAS HE CHOSEN AS HIS MENTOR?
GASP!
I TRIED TO ADAPT -- TRULY...

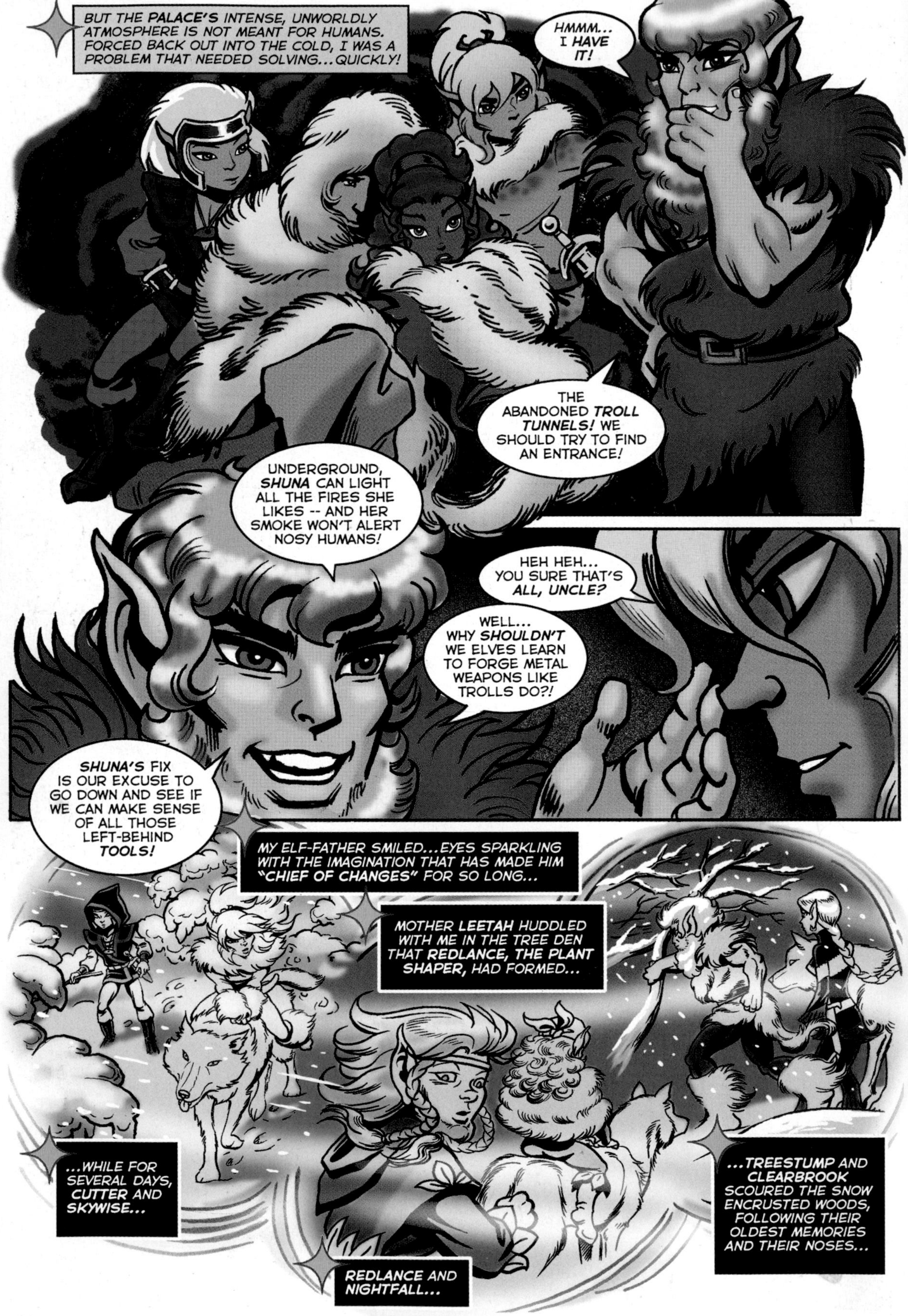
BUT THE PALACE'S INTENSE, UNWORLDLY ATMOSPHERE IS NOT MEANT FOR HUMANS. FORCED BACK OUT INTO THE COLD, I WAS A PROBLEM THAT NEEDED SOLVING...QUICKLY!
HMMM... I HAVE IT!
THE ABANDONED TROLL TUNNELS! WE SHOULD TRY TO FIND AN ENTRANCE!
UNDERGROUND, SHUNA CAN LIGHT ALL THE FIRES SHE LIKES -- AND HER SMOKE WON'T ALERT NOSY HUMANS!
HEH HEH... YOU SURE THAT'S ALL, UNCLE?
WELL... WHY SHOULDN'T WE ELVES LEARN TO FORGE METAL WEAPONS LIKE TROLLS DO?!
SHUNA'S FIX IS OUR EXCUSE TO GO DOWN AND SEE IF WE CAN MAKE SENSE OF ALL THOSE LEFT-BEHIND TOOLS!
MY ELF-FATHER SMILED...EYES SPARKLING WITH THE IMAGINATION THAT HAS MADE HIM "CHIEF OF CHANGES" FOR SO LONG...
MOTHER LEETAH HUDDLED WITH ME IN THE TREE DEN THAT REDLANCE, THE PLANT SHAPER, HAD FORMED...
...WHILE FOR SEVERAL DAYS, CUTTER AND SKYWISE...
REDLANCE AND NIGHTFALL...
...TREESTUMP AND CLEARBROOK SCOURED THE SNOW ENCRUSTED WOODS, FOLLOWING THEIR OLDEST MEMORIES AND THEIR NOSES...

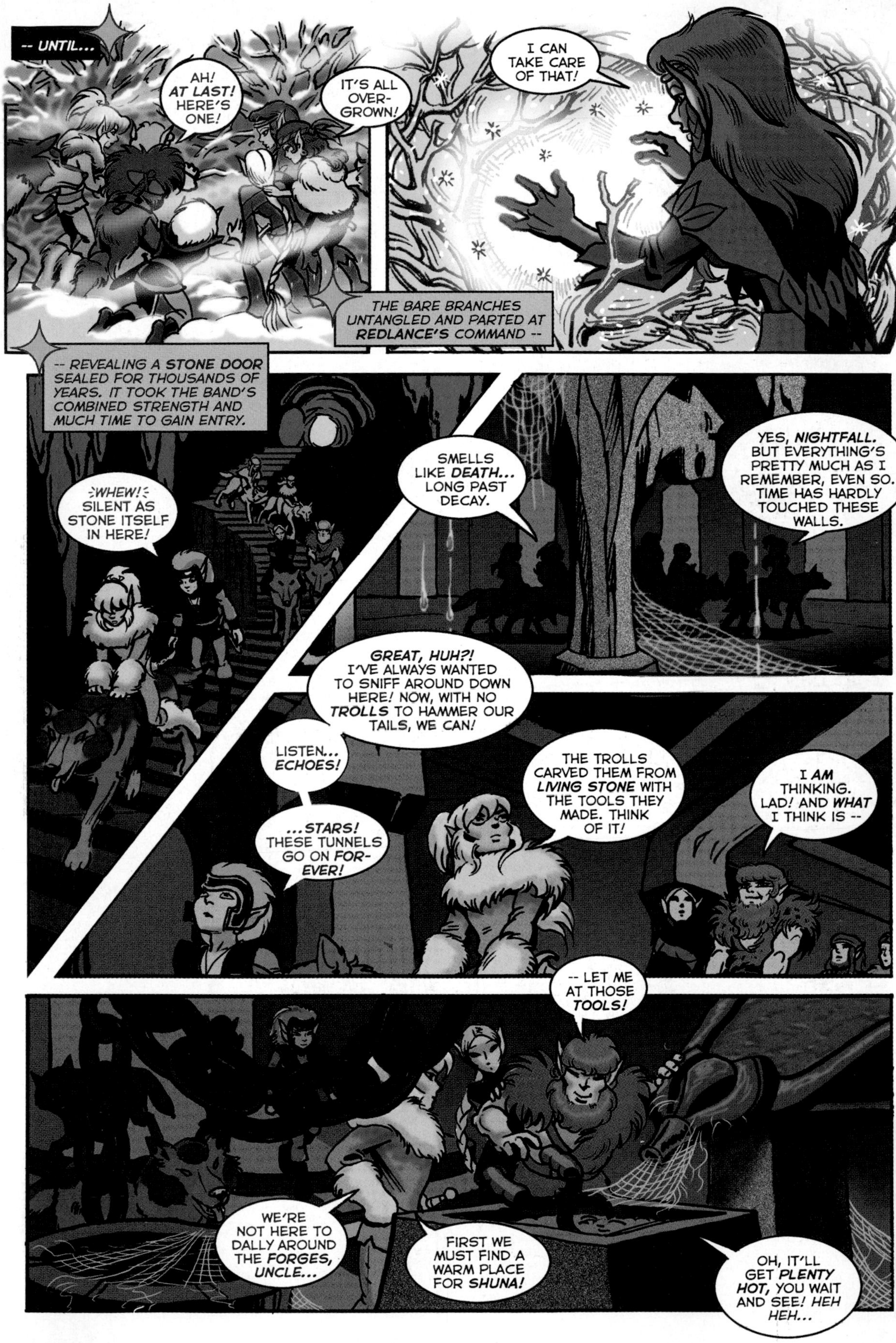
-- UNTIL...
AH! AT LAST! HERE'S ONE!
IT'S ALL OVER-GROWN!
I CAN TAKE CARE OF THAT!
THE BARE BRANCHES UNTANGLED AND PARTED AT REDLANCE'S COMMAND --
-- REVEALING A STONE DOOR SEALED FOR THOUSANDS OF YEARS. IT TOOK THE BAND'S COMBINED STRENGTH AND MUCH TIME TO GAIN ENTRY.
WHEW! SILENT AS STONE ITSELF IN HERE!
SMELLS LIKE DEATH... LONG PAST DECAY.
YES, NIGHTFALL. BUT EVERYTHING'S PRETTY MUCH AS I REMEMBER, EVEN SO. TIME HAS HARDLY TOUCHED THESE WALLS.
GREAT, HUH?! I'VE ALWAYS WANTED TO SNIFF AROUND DOWN HERE! NOW, WITH NO TROLLS TO HAMMER OUR TAILS, WE CAN!
LISTEN... ECHOES!
...STARS! THESE TUNNELS GO ON FOR-EVER!
THE TROLLS CARVED THEM FROM LIVING STONE WITH THE TOOLS THEY MADE. THINK OF IT!
I AM THINKING. LAD! AND WHAT I THINK IS --
-- LET ME AT THOSE TOOLS!
WE'RE NOT HERE TO DALLY AROUND THE FORGES, UNCLE...
FIRST WE MUST FIND A WARM PLACE FOR SHUNA!
OH, IT'LL GET PLENTY HOT, YOU WAIT AND SEE! HEH HEH...

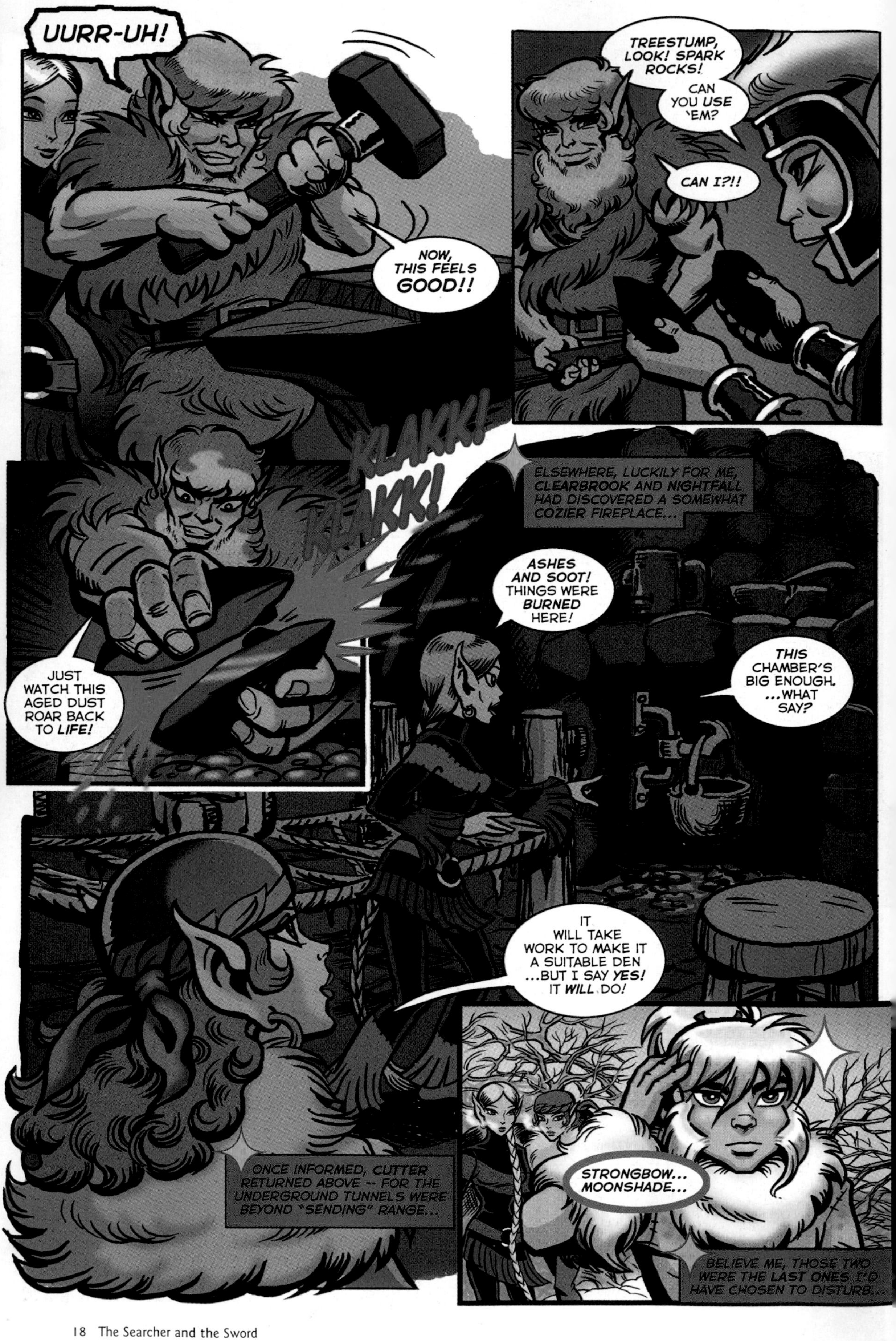
UURR-UH!
NOW, THIS FEELS GOOD!!
TREESTUMP, LOOK! SPARK ROCKS!
CAN YOU USE 'EM?
CAN I?!!
KLAKK! KLAKK!
JUST WATCH THIS AGED DUST ROAR BACK TO LIFE!
ELSEWHERE, LUCKILY FOR ME, CLEARBROOK AND NIGHTFALL HAD DISCOVERED A SOMEWHAT COZIER FIREPLACE...
ASHES AND SOOT! THINGS WERE BURNED HERE!
THIS CHAMBER'S BIG ENOUGH. ...WHAT SAY?
IT WILL TAKE WORK TO MAKE IT A SUITABLE DEN ...BUT I SAY YES! IT WILL DO!
ONCE INFORMED, CUTTER RETURNED ABOVE -- FOR THE UNDERGROUND TUNNELS WERE BEYOND "SENDING" RANGE...
STRONGBOW... MOONSHADE...
BELIEVE ME, THOSE TWO WERE THE LAST ONES I'D HAVE CHOSEN TO DISTURB...

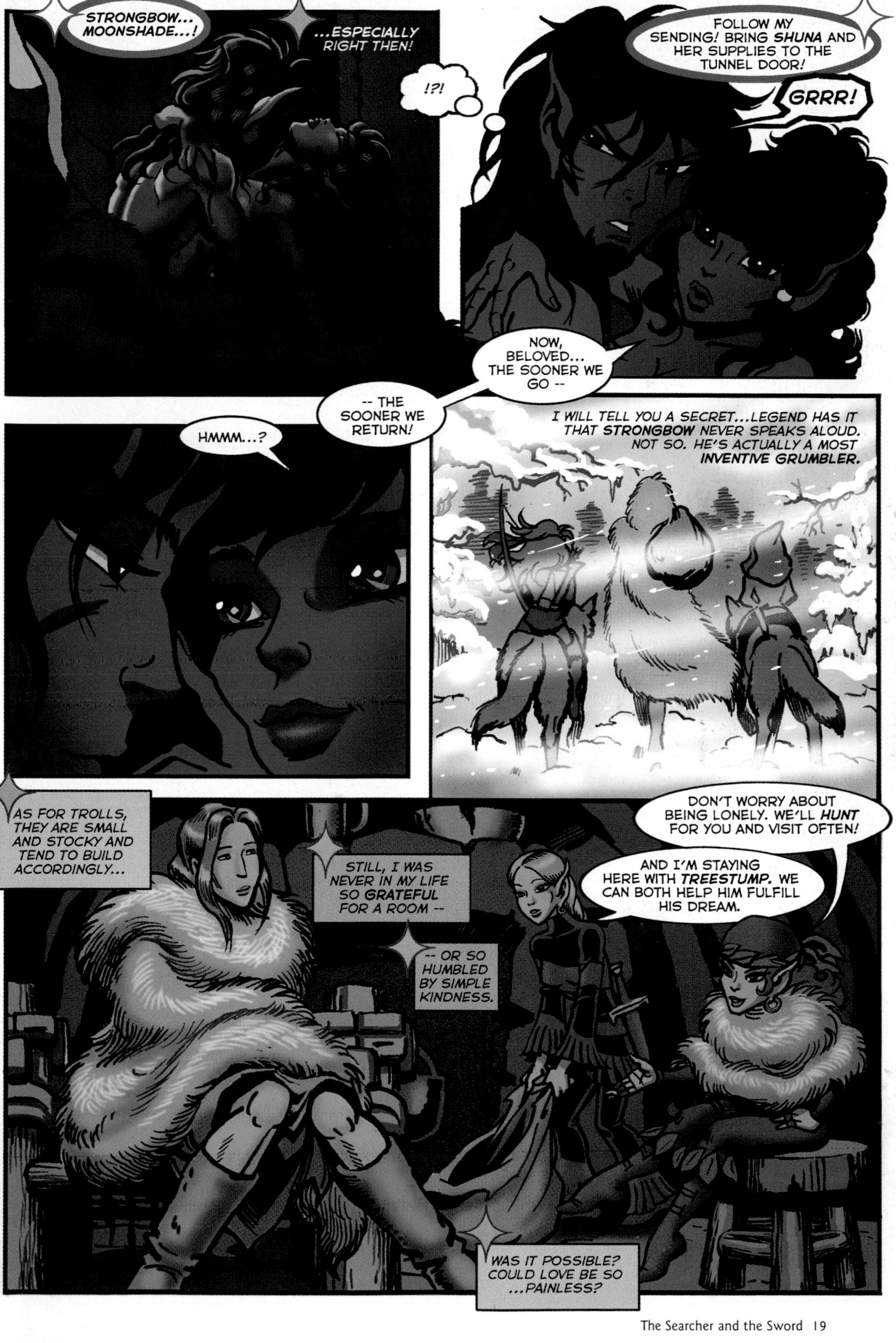

STRONGBOW... MOONSHADE...!
...ESPECIALLY RIGHT THEN!
!?!
FOLLOW MY SENDING! BRING SHUNA AND HER SUPPLIES TO THE TUNNEL DOOR!
GRRR!
NOW, BELOVED... THE SOONER WE GO --
-- THE SOONER WE RETURN!
HMMM...?
I WILL TELL YOU A SECRET...LEGEND HAS IT THAT STRONGBOW NEVER SPEAKS ALOUD. NOT SO. HE'S ACTUALLY A MOST INVENTIVE GRUMBLER.
AS FOR TROLLS, THEY ARE SMALL AND STOCKY AND TEND TO BUILD ACCORDINGLY...
STILL, I WAS NEVER IN MY LIFE SO GRATEFUL FOR A ROOM --
-- OR SO HUMBLED BY SIMPLE KINDNESS.
DON'T WORRY ABOUT BEING LONELY. WE'LL HUNT FOR YOU AND VISIT OFTEN!
AND I'M STAYING HERE WITH TREESTUMP. WE CAN BOTH HELP HIM FULFILL HIS DREAM.
WAS IT POSSIBLE? COULD LOVE BE SO ...PAINLESS?

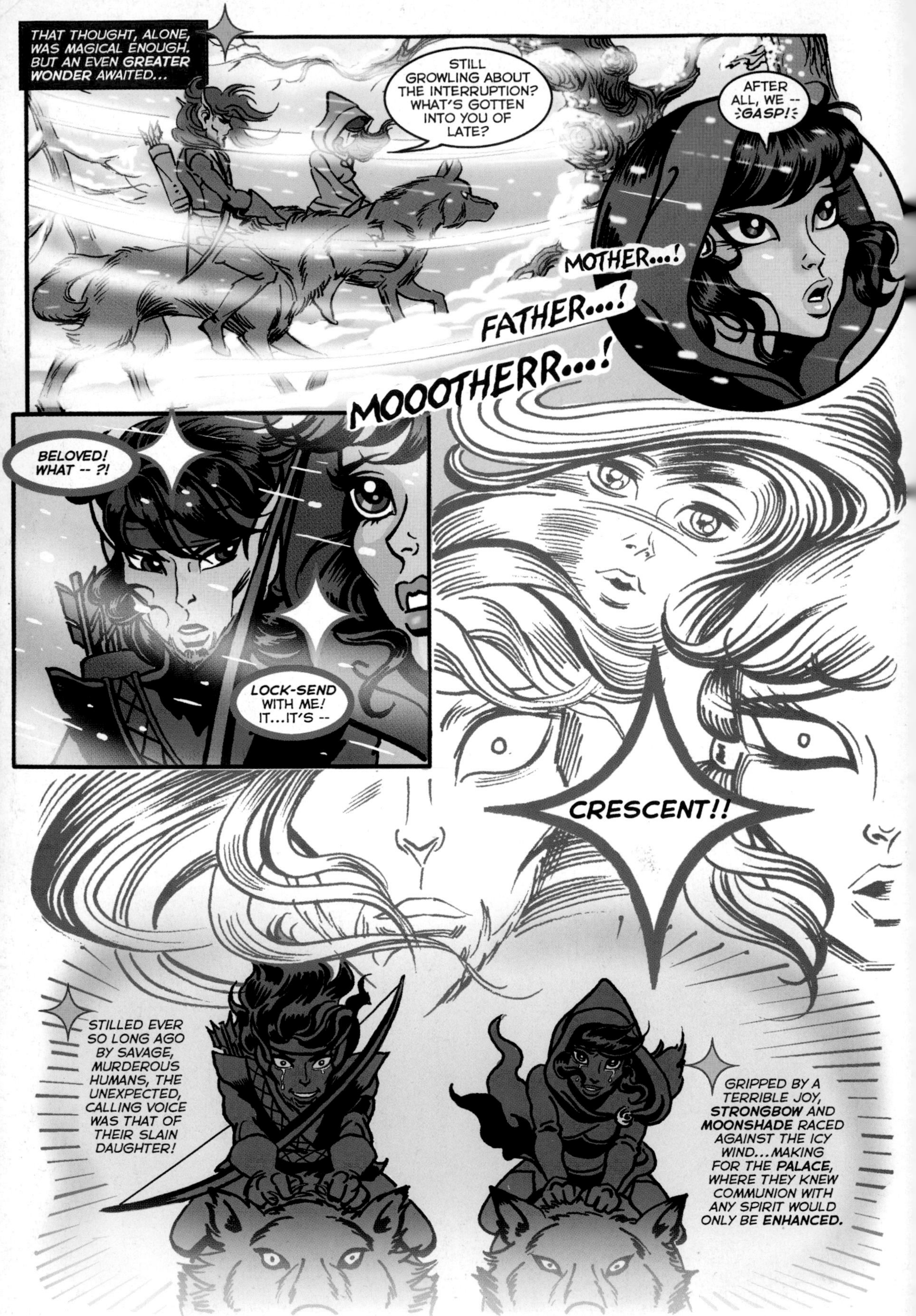
THAT THOUGHT, ALONE, WAS MAGICAL ENOUGH. BUT AN EVEN GREATER WONDER AWAITED...
STILL GROWLING ABOUT THE INTERRUPTION? WHAT'S GOTTEN INTO YOU OF LATE?
AFTER ALL, WE -- GASP!
MOTHER...!
FATHER...!
MOOOTHERR...!
BELOVED! WHAT -- ?!
LOCK-SEND WITH ME! IT...IT'S --
CRESCENT!!
STILLED EVER SO LONG AGO BY SAVAGE, MURDEROUS HUMANS, THE UNEXPECTED, CALLING VOICE WAS THAT OF THEIR SLAIN DAUGHTER!
GRIPPED BY A TERRIBLE JOY, STRONGBOW AND MOONSHADE RACED AGAINST THE ICY WIND...MAKING FOR THE PALACE, WHERE THEY KNEW COMMUNION WITH ANY SPIRIT WOULD ONLY BE ENHANCED.

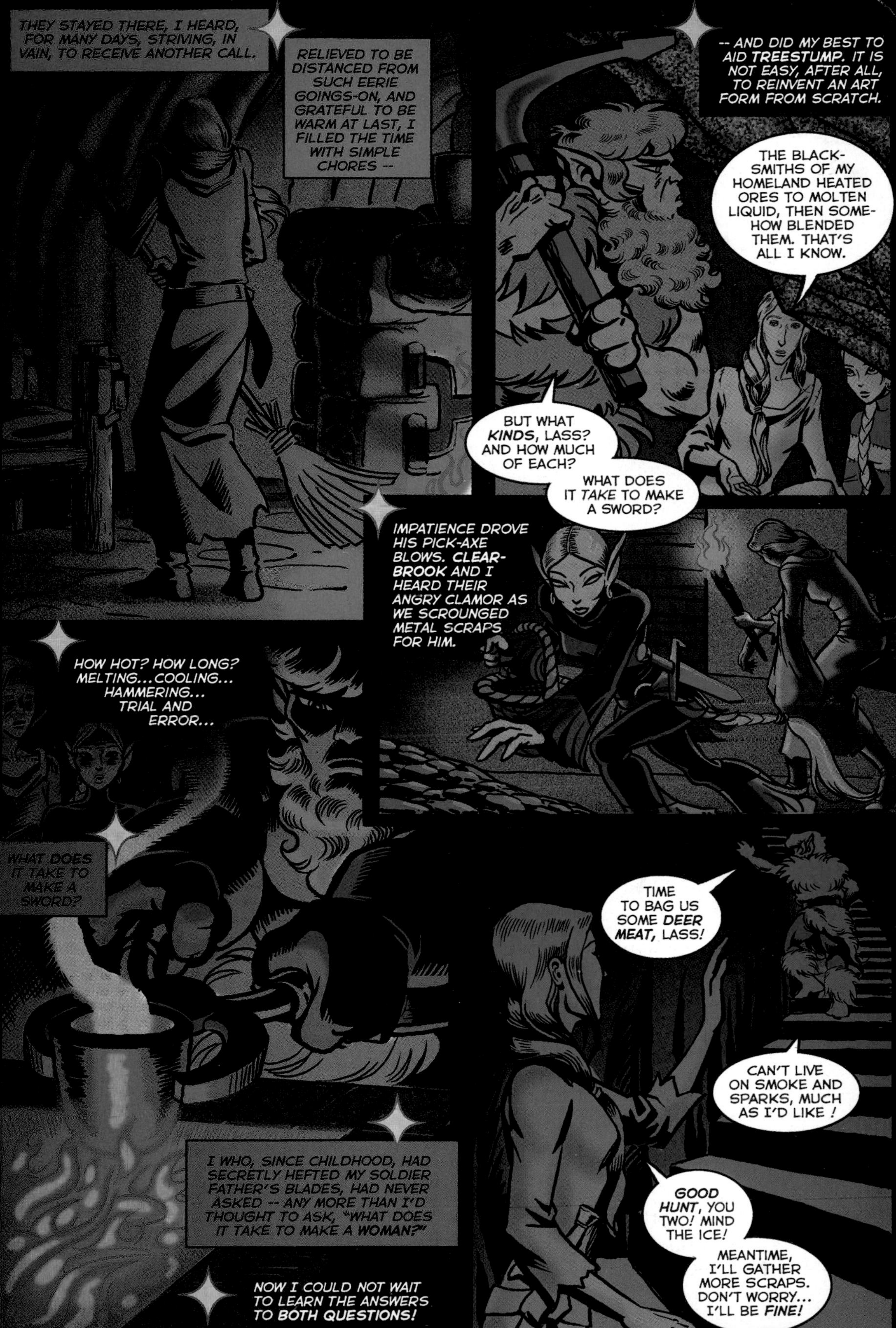
THEY STAYED THERE, I HEARD, FOR MANY DAYS, STRIVING, IN VAIN, TO RECEIVE ANOTHER CALL.
RELIEVED TO BE DISTANCED FROM SUCH EERIE GOINGS-ON, AND GRATEFUL TO BE WARM AT LAST, I FILLED THE TIME WITH SIMPLE CHORES --
-- AND DID MY BEST TO AID TREESTUMP. IT IS NOT EASY, AFTER ALL, TO REINVENT AN ART FORM FROM SCRATCH.
THE BLACKSMITHS OF MY HOMELAND HEATED ORES TO MOLTEN LIQUID, THEN SOMEHOW BLENDED THEM. THAT'S ALL I KNOW.
BUT WHAT KINDS, LASS? AND HOW MUCH OF EACH?
WHAT DOES IT TAKE TO MAKE A SWORD?
IMPATIENCE DROVE HIS PICK-AXE BLOWS. CLEARBROOK AND I HEARD THEIR ANGRY CLAMOR AS WE SCROUNGED METAL SCRAPS FOR HIM.
HOW HOT? HOW LONG? MELTING... COOLING... HAMMERING... TRIAL AND ERROR...
WHAT DOES IT TAKE TO MAKE A SWORD?
TIME TO BAG US SOME DEER MEAT, LASS!
CAN'T LIVE ON SMOKE AND SPARKS, MUCH AS I'D LIKE!
I WHO, SINCE CHILDHOOD, HAD SECRETLY HEFTED MY SOLDIER FATHER'S BLADES, HAD NEVER ASKED -- ANY MORE THAN I'D THOUGHT TO ASK, "WHAT DOES IT TAKE TO MAKE A WOMAN?"
GOOD HUNT, YOU TWO! MIND THE ICE!
MEANTIME, I'LL GATHER MORE SCRAPS. DON'T WORRY... I'LL BE FINE!
NOW I COULD NOT WAIT TO LEARN THE ANSWERS TO BOTH QUESTIONS!

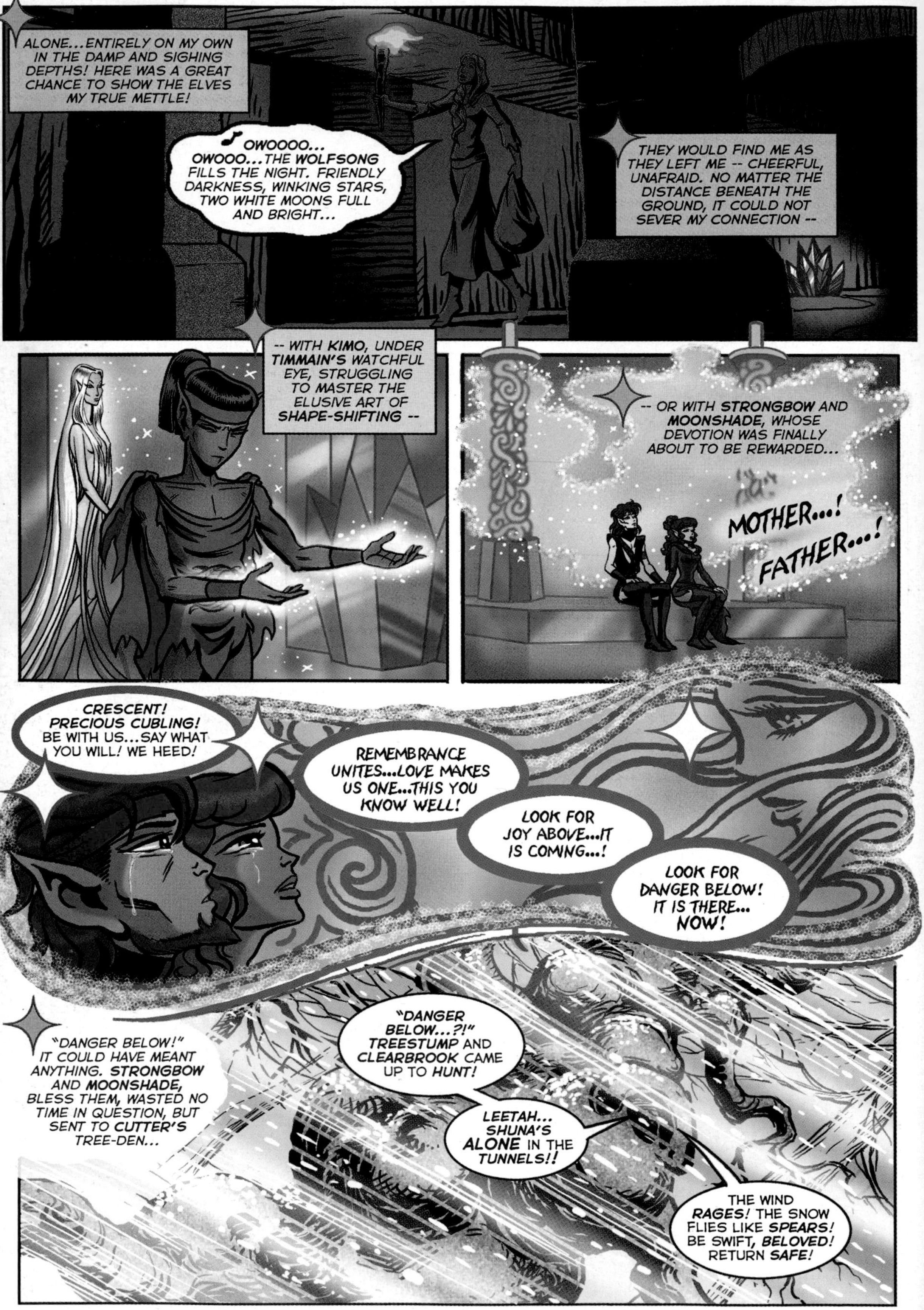
ALONE...ENTIRELY ON MY OWN IN THE DAMP AND SIGHING DEPTHS! HERE WAS A GREAT CHANCE TO SHOW THE ELVES MY TRUE METTLE!
OWOOOO... OWOOO...THE WOLFSONG FILLS THE NIGHT. FRIENDLY DARKNESS, WINKING STARS, TWO WHITE MOONS FULL AND BRIGHT...
THEY WOULD FIND ME AS THEY LEFT ME -- CHEERFUL, UNAFRAID. NO MATTER THE DISTANCE BENEATH THE GROUND, IT COULD NOT SEVER MY CONNECTION --
-- WITH KIMO, UNDER TIMMAIN'S WATCHFUL EYE, STRUGGLING TO MASTER THE ELUSIVE ART OF SHAPE-SHIFTING --
-- OR WITH STRONGBOW AND MOONSHADE, WHOSE DEVOTION WAS FINALLY ABOUT TO BE REWARDED...
MOTHER...!
FATHER...!
CRESCENT! PRECIOUS CUBLING! BE WITH US...SAY WHAT YOU WILL! WE HEED!
REMEMBRANCE UNITES...LOVE MAKES US ONE...THIS YOU KNOW WELL!
LOOK FOR JOY ABOVE...IT IS COMING...!
LOOK FOR DANGER BELOW! IT IS THERE... NOW!
"DANGER BELOW!" IT COULD HAVE MEANT ANYTHING. STRONGBOW AND MOONSHADE, BLESS THEM, WASTED NO TIME IN QUESTION, BUT SENT TO CUTTER'S TREE-DEN...
"DANGER BELOW...?!" TREESTUMP AND CLEARBROOK CAME UP TO HUNT!
LEETAH... SHUNA'S ALONE IN THE TUNNELS!!
THE WIND RAGES! THE SNOW FLIES LIKE SPEARS! BE SWIFT, BELOVED! RETURN SAFE!

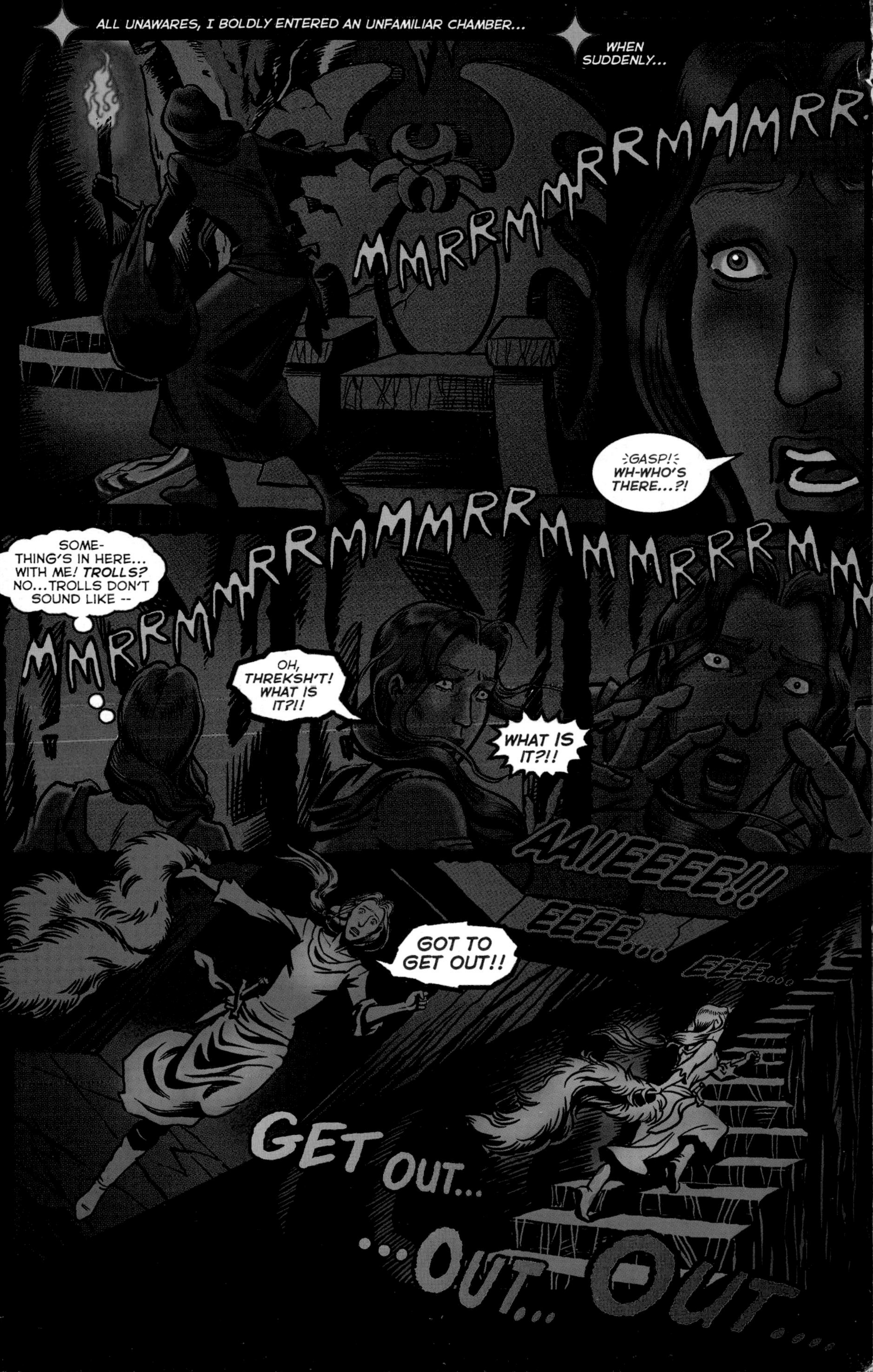

ALL UNAWARES, I BOLDLY ENTERED AN UNFAMILIAR CHAMBER...
WHEN SUDDENLY...
MMRRMMRRMMMMRR
GASP! WH-WHO'S THERE...?!
SOME-THING'S IN HERE... WITH ME! TROLLS? NO...TROLLS DON'T SOUND LIKE --
MMRRMMRRMMMMRRMMMRRRMM
OH, THREKSH'T! WHAT IS IT?!!
WHAT IS IT?!!
AAIIEEEEE!!
EEEE...
EEEE...
GOT TO GET OUT!!
GET OUT...
...OUT...OUT...

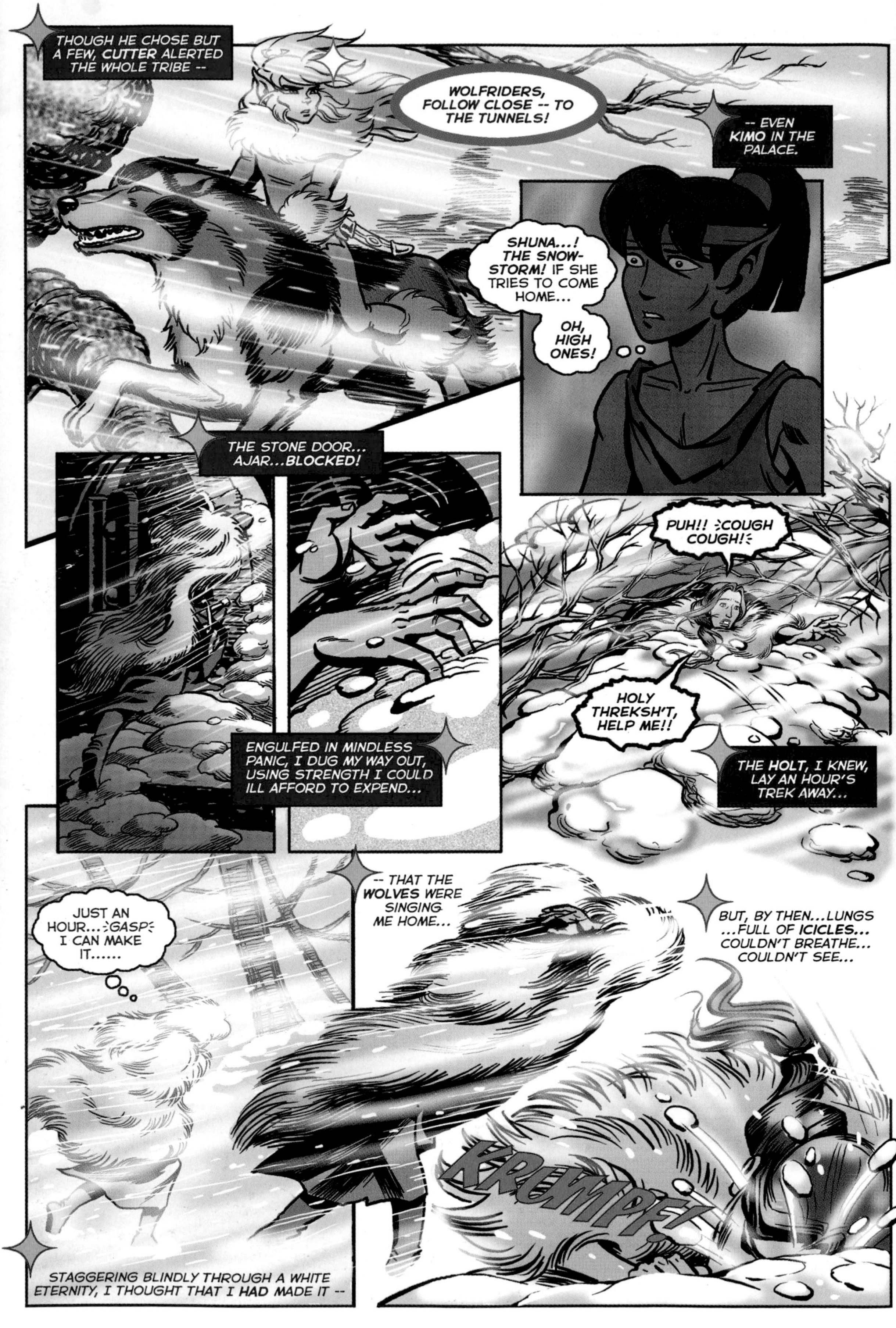
THOUGH HE CHOSE BUT A FEW, CUTTER ALERTED THE WHOLE TRIBE --
WOLFRIDERS, FOLLOW CLOSE -- TO THE TUNNELS!
-- EVEN KIMO IN THE PALACE.
SHUNA...! THE SNOW-STORM! IF SHE TRIES TO COME HOME...
OH, HIGH ONES!
THE STONE DOOR... AJAR...BLOCKED!
PUH!! COUGH COUGH!
HOLY THREKSH'T, HELP ME!!
ENGULFED IN MINDLESS PANIC, I DUG MY WAY OUT, USING STRENGTH I COULD ILL AFFORD TO EXPEND...
THE HOLT, I KNEW, LAY AN HOUR'S TREK AWAY...
JUST AN HOUR... GASP I CAN MAKE IT......
-- THAT THE WOLVES WERE SINGING ME HOME...
BUT, BY THEN...LUNGS ...FULL OF ICICLES... COULDN'T BREATHE... COULDN'T SEE...
KRUMPF!
STAGGERING BLINDLY THROUGH A WHITE ETERNITY, I THOUGHT THAT I HAD MADE IT --

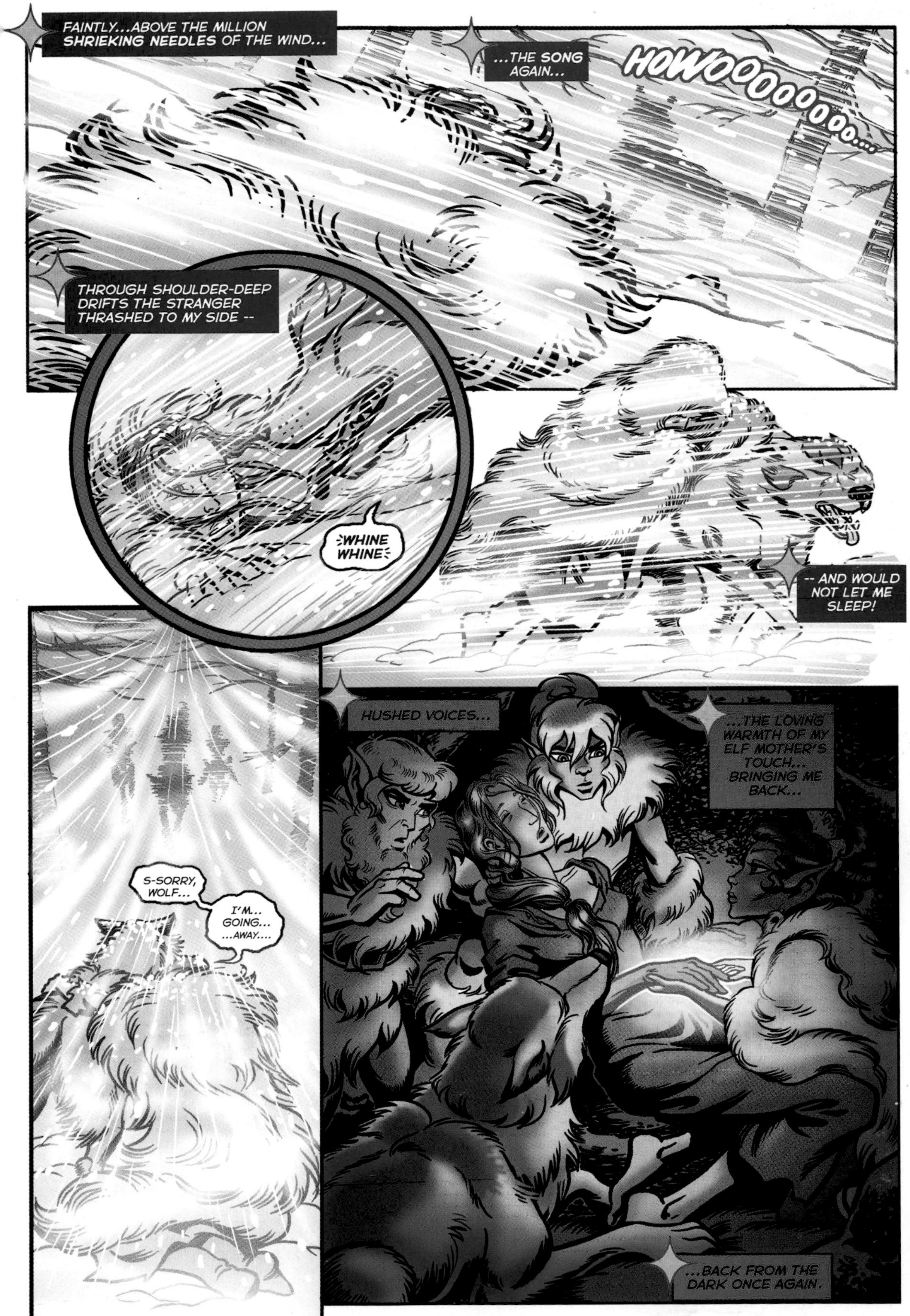
FAINTLY...ABOVE THE MILLION SHRIEKING NEEDLES OF THE WIND...
...THE SONG AGAIN...
HOWOOOOOOOOo...
THROUGH SHOULDER-DEEP DRIFTS THE STRANGER THRASHED TO MY SIDE --
WHINE WHINE
-- AND WOULD NOT LET ME SLEEP!
S-SORRY, WOLF...
I'M... GOING... ...AWAY....
HUSHED VOICES...
...THE LOVING WARMTH OF MY ELF MOTHER'S TOUCH... BRINGING ME BACK...
...BACK FROM THE DARK ONCE AGAIN.

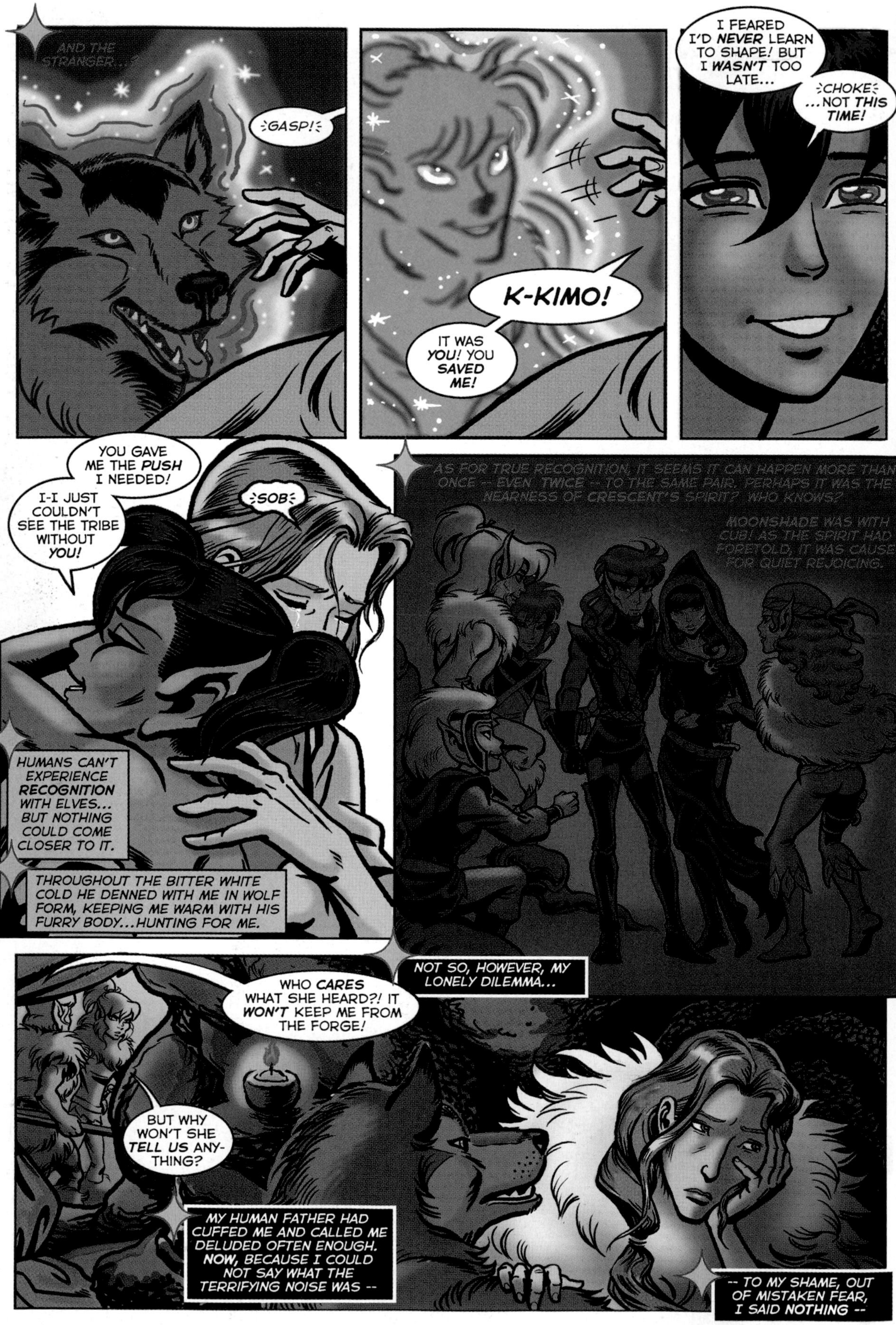
AND THE STRANGER...?
GASP!
K-KIMO!
IT WAS YOU! YOU SAVED ME!
I FEARED I'D NEVER LEARN TO SHAPE! BUT I WASN'T TOO LATE...
CHOKE
...NOT THIS TIME!
YOU GAVE ME THE PUSH I NEEDED!
I-I JUST COULDN'T SEE THE TRIBE WITHOUT YOU!
SOB
HUMANS CAN'T EXPERIENCE RECOGNITION WITH ELVES... BUT NOTHING COULD COME CLOSER TO IT.
THROUGHOUT THE BITTER WHITE COLD HE DENNED WITH ME IN WOLF FORM, KEEPING ME WARM WITH HIS FURRY BODY...HUNTING FOR ME.
AS FOR TRUE RECOGNITION, IT SEEMS IT CAN HAPPEN MORE THAN ONCE -- EVEN TWICE -- TO THE SAME PAIR. PERHAPS IT WAS THE NEARNESS OF CRESCENT'S SPIRIT? WHO KNOWS?
MOONSHADE WAS WITH CUB! AS THE SPIRIT HAD FORETOLD, IT WAS CAUSE FOR QUIET REJOICING.
NOT SO, HOWEVER, MY LONELY DILEMMA...
WHO CARES WHAT SHE HEARD?! IT WON'T KEEP ME FROM THE FORGE!
BUT WHY WON'T SHE TELL US ANYTHING?
MY HUMAN FATHER HAD CUFFED ME AND CALLED ME DELUDED OFTEN ENOUGH. NOW, BECAUSE I COULD NOT SAY WHAT THE TERRIFYING NOISE WAS --
-- TO MY SHAME, OUT OF MISTAKEN FEAR, I SAID NOTHING --

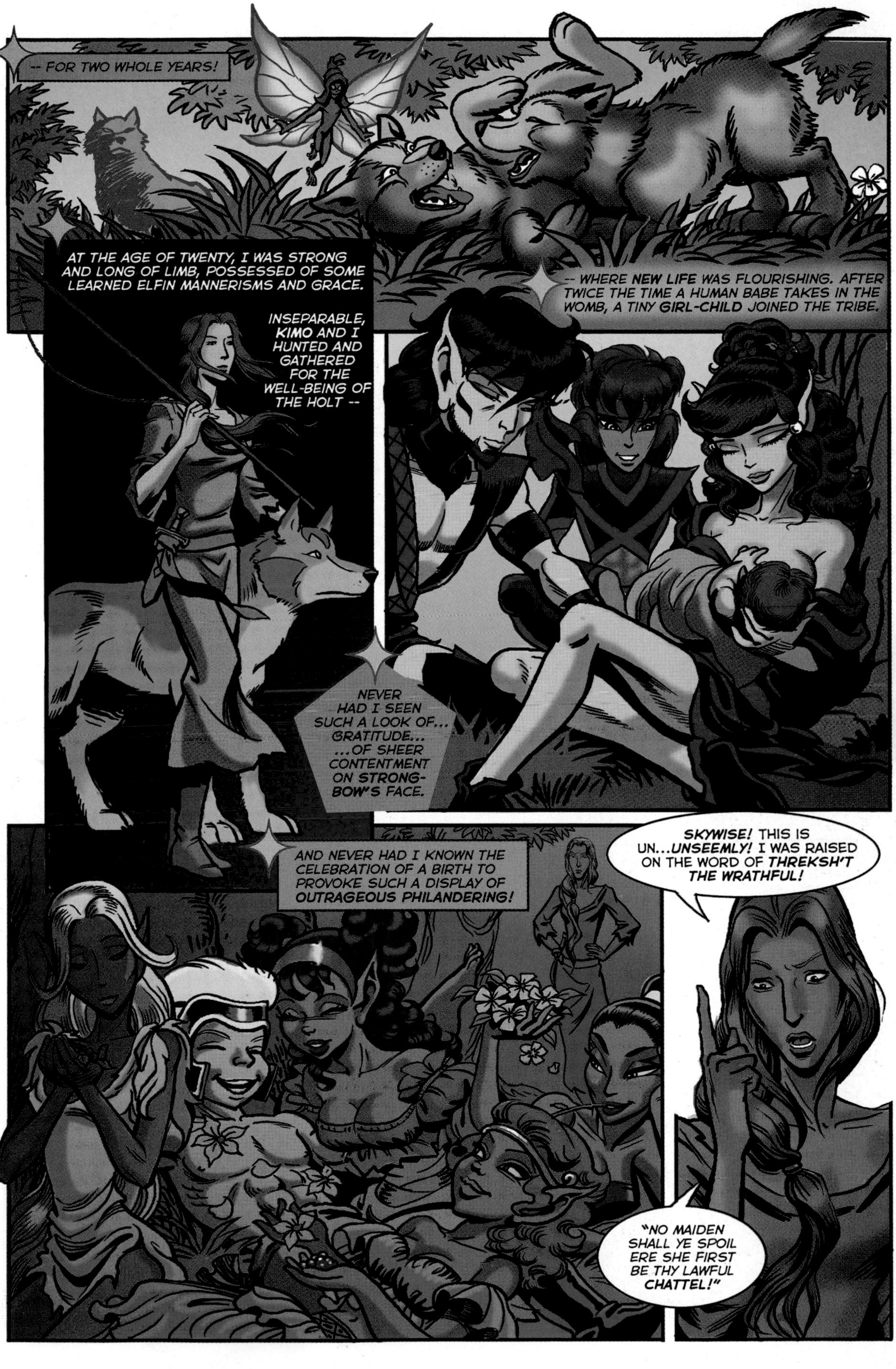
-- FOR TWO WHOLE YEARS!
AT THE AGE OF TWENTY, I WAS STRONG AND LONG OF LIMB, POSSESSED OF SOME LEARNED ELFIN MANNERISMS AND GRACE.
INSEPARABLE, KIMO AND I HUNTED AND GATHERED FOR THE WELL-BEING OF THE HOLT --
-- WHERE NEW LIFE WAS FLOURISHING. AFTER TWICE THE TIME A HUMAN BABE TAKES IN THE WOMB, A TINY GIRL-CHILD JOINED THE TRIBE.
NEVER HAD I SEEN SUCH A LOOK OF... GRATITUDE... ...OF SHEER CONTENTMENT ON STRONG-BOW'S FACE.
AND NEVER HAD I KNOWN THE CELEBRATION OF A BIRTH TO PROVOKE SUCH A DISPLAY OF OUTRAGEOUS PHILANDERING!
SKYWISE! THIS IS UN...UNSEEMLY! I WAS RAISED ON THE WORD OF THREKSH'T THE WRATHFUL!
"NO MAIDEN SHALL YE SPOIL ERE SHE FIRST BE THY LAWFUL CHATTEL!"

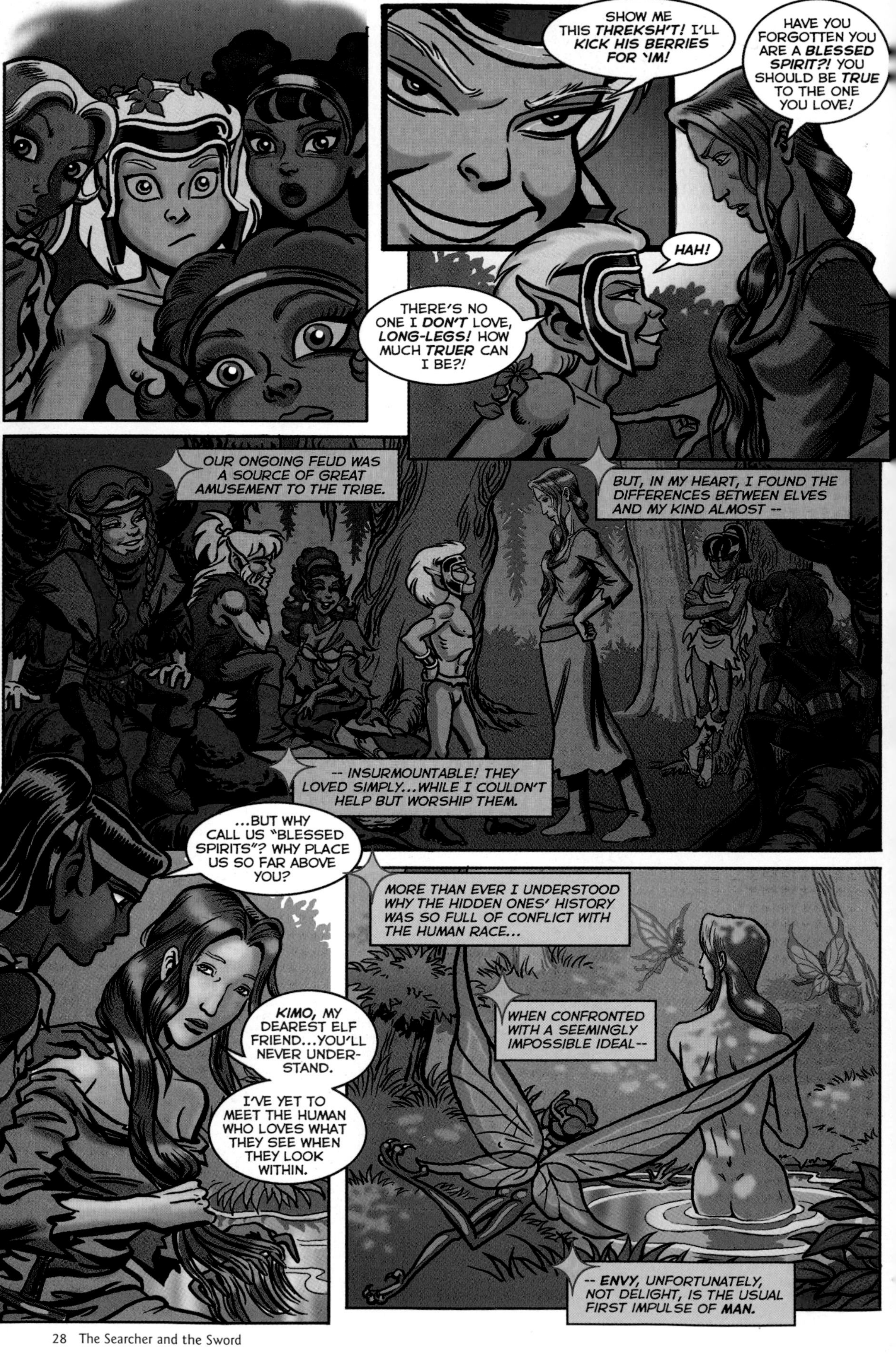
SHOW ME THIS THREKSH'T! I'LL KICK HIS BERRIES FOR 'IM!
HAVE YOU FORGOTTEN YOU ARE A BLESSED SPIRIT?! YOU SHOULD BE TRUE TO THE ONE YOU LOVE!
HAH!
THERE'S NO ONE I DON'T LOVE, LONG-LEGS! HOW MUCH TRUER CAN I BE?!
OUR ONGOING FEUD WAS A SOURCE OF GREAT AMUSEMENT TO THE TRIBE.
BUT, IN MY HEART, I FOUND THE DIFFERENCES BETWEEN ELVES AND MY KIND ALMOST --
-- INSURMOUNTABLE! THEY LOVED SIMPLY...WHILE I COULDN'T HELP BUT WORSHIP THEM.
...BUT WHY CALL US "BLESSED SPIRITS"? WHY PLACE US SO FAR ABOVE YOU?
KIMO, MY DEAREST ELF FRIEND...YOU'LL NEVER UNDERSTAND.
I'VE YET TO MEET THE HUMAN WHO LOVES WHAT THEY SEE WHEN THEY LOOK WITHIN.
MORE THAN EVER I UNDERSTOOD WHY THE HIDDEN ONES' HISTORY WAS SO FULL OF CONFLICT WITH THE HUMAN RACE...
WHEN CONFRONTED WITH A SEEMINGLY IMPOSSIBLE IDEAL--
-- ENVY, UNFORTUNATELY, NOT DELIGHT, IS THE USUAL FIRST IMPULSE OF MAN.

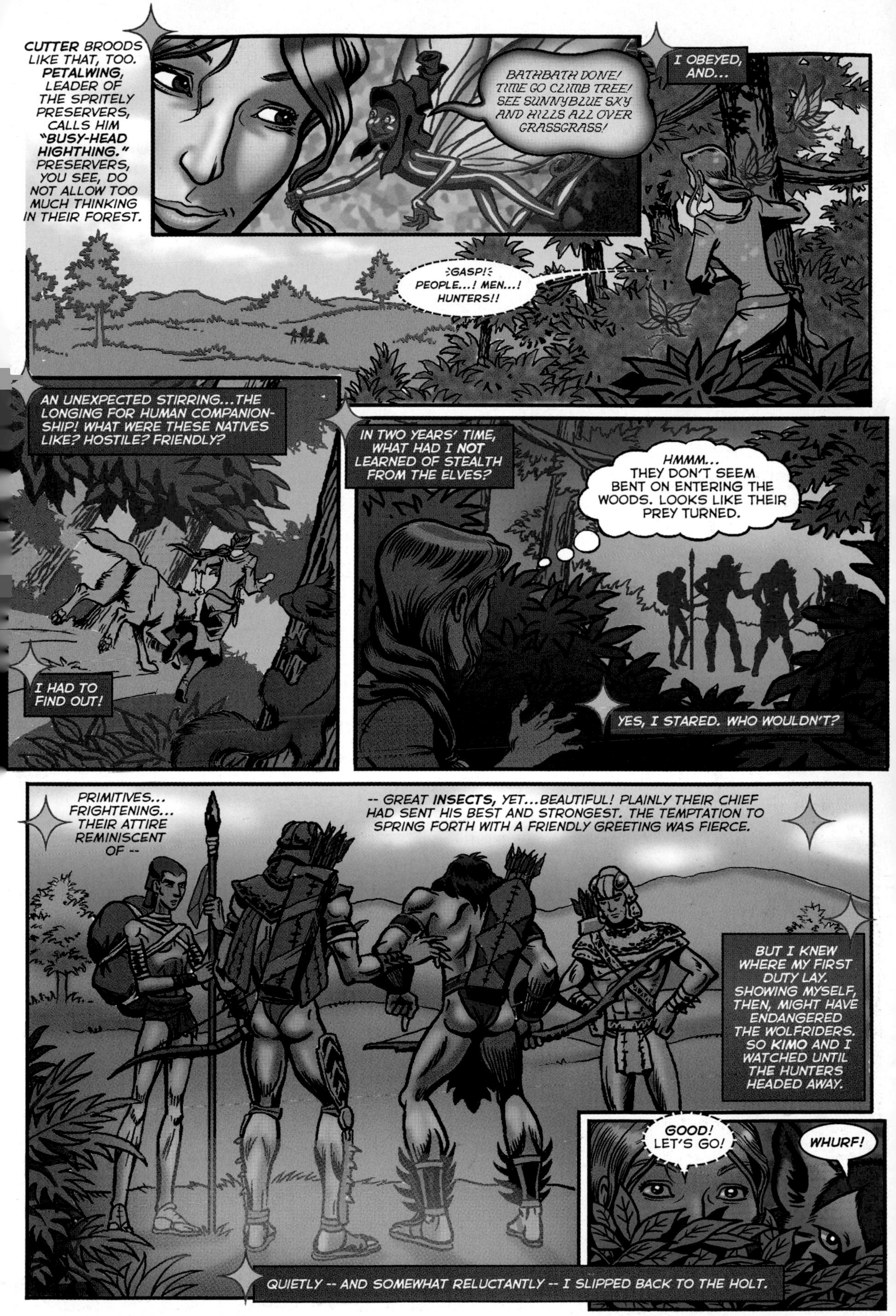
CUTTER BROODS LIKE THAT, TOO. PETALWING, LEADER OF THE SPRITELY PRESERVERS, CALLS HIM "BUSY-HEAD HIGHTHING." PRESERVERS, YOU SEE, DO NOT ALLOW TOO MUCH THINKING IN THEIR FOREST.
BATHBATH DONE! TIME GO CLIMB TREE! SEE SUNNYBLUE SKY AND HILLS ALL OVER GRASSGRASS!
I OBEYED, AND...
GASP! PEOPLE...! MEN...! HUNTERS!!
AN UNEXPECTED STIRRING...THE LONGING FOR HUMAN COMPANIONSHIP! WHAT WERE THESE NATIVES LIKE? HOSTILE? FRIENDLY?
I HAD TO FIND OUT!
IN TWO YEARS' TIME, WHAT HAD I NOT LEARNED OF STEALTH FROM THE ELVES?
HMMM... THEY DON'T SEEM BENT ON ENTERING THE WOODS. LOOKS LIKE THEIR PREY TURNED.
YES, I STARED. WHO WOULDN'T?
PRIMITIVES... FRIGHTENING... THEIR ATTIRE REMINISCENT OF --
-- GREAT INSECTS, YET...BEAUTIFUL! PLAINLY THEIR CHIEF HAD SENT HIS BEST AND STRONGEST. THE TEMPTATION TO SPRING FORTH WITH A FRIENDLY GREETING WAS FIERCE.
BUT I KNEW WHERE MY FIRST DUTY LAY. SHOWING MYSELF, THEN, MIGHT HAVE ENDANGERED THE WOLFRIDERS. SO KIMO AND I WATCHED UNTIL THE HUNTERS HEADED AWAY.
GOOD! LET'S GO!
WHURF!
QUIETLY -- AND SOMEWHAT RELUCTANTLY -- I SLIPPED BACK TO THE HOLT.

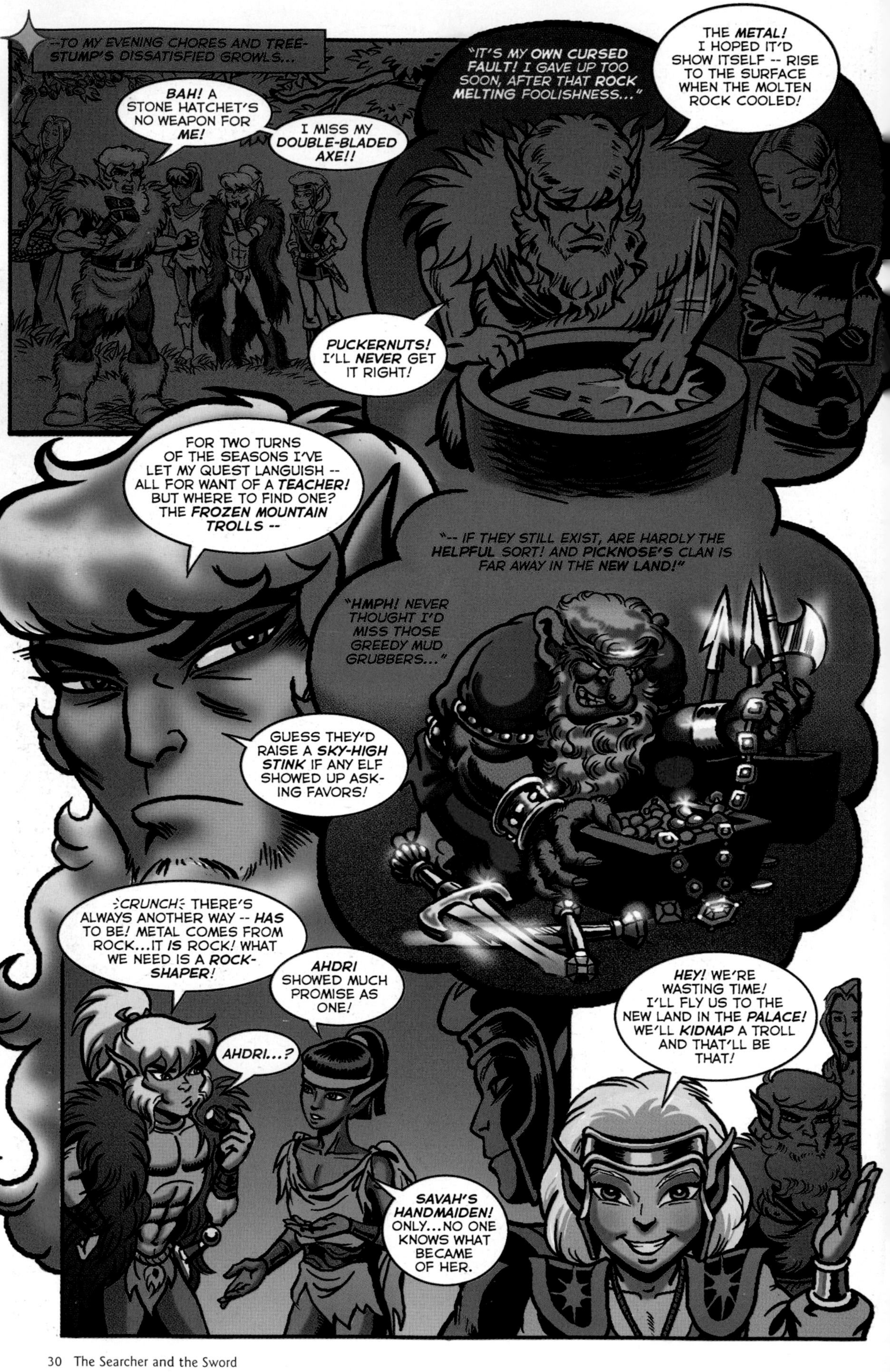
--TO MY EVENING CHORES AND TREE-STUMP'S DISSATISFIED GROWLS...
BAH! A STONE HATCHET'S NO WEAPON FOR ME!
I MISS MY DOUBLE-BLADED AXE!!
"IT'S MY OWN CURSED FAULT! I GAVE UP TOO SOON, AFTER THAT ROCK MELTING FOOLISHNESS..."
THE METAL! I HOPED IT'D SHOW ITSELF -- RISE TO THE SURFACE WHEN THE MOLTEN ROCK COOLED!
PUCKERNUTS! I'LL NEVER GET IT RIGHT!
FOR TWO TURNS OF THE SEASONS I'VE LET MY QUEST LANGUISH -- ALL FOR WANT OF A TEACHER! BUT WHERE TO FIND ONE? THE FROZEN MOUNTAIN TROLLS --
"-- IF THEY STILL EXIST, ARE HARDLY THE HELPFUL SORT! AND PICKNOSE'S CLAN IS FAR AWAY IN THE NEW LAND!"
"HMPH! NEVER THOUGHT I'D MISS THOSE GREEDY MUD GRUBBERS..."
GUESS THEY'D RAISE A SKY-HIGH STINK IF ANY ELF SHOWED UP ASKING FAVORS!
CRUNCH THERE'S ALWAYS ANOTHER WAY -- HAS TO BE! METAL COMES FROM ROCK...IT IS ROCK! WHAT WE NEED IS A ROCK-SHAPER!
AHDRI SHOWED MUCH PROMISE AS ONE!
AHDRI...?
SAVAH'S HANDMAIDEN! ONLY...NO ONE KNOWS WHAT BECAME OF HER.
HEY! WE'RE WASTING TIME! I'LL FLY US TO THE NEW LAND IN THE PALACE! WE'LL KIDNAP A TROLL AND THAT'LL BE THAT!

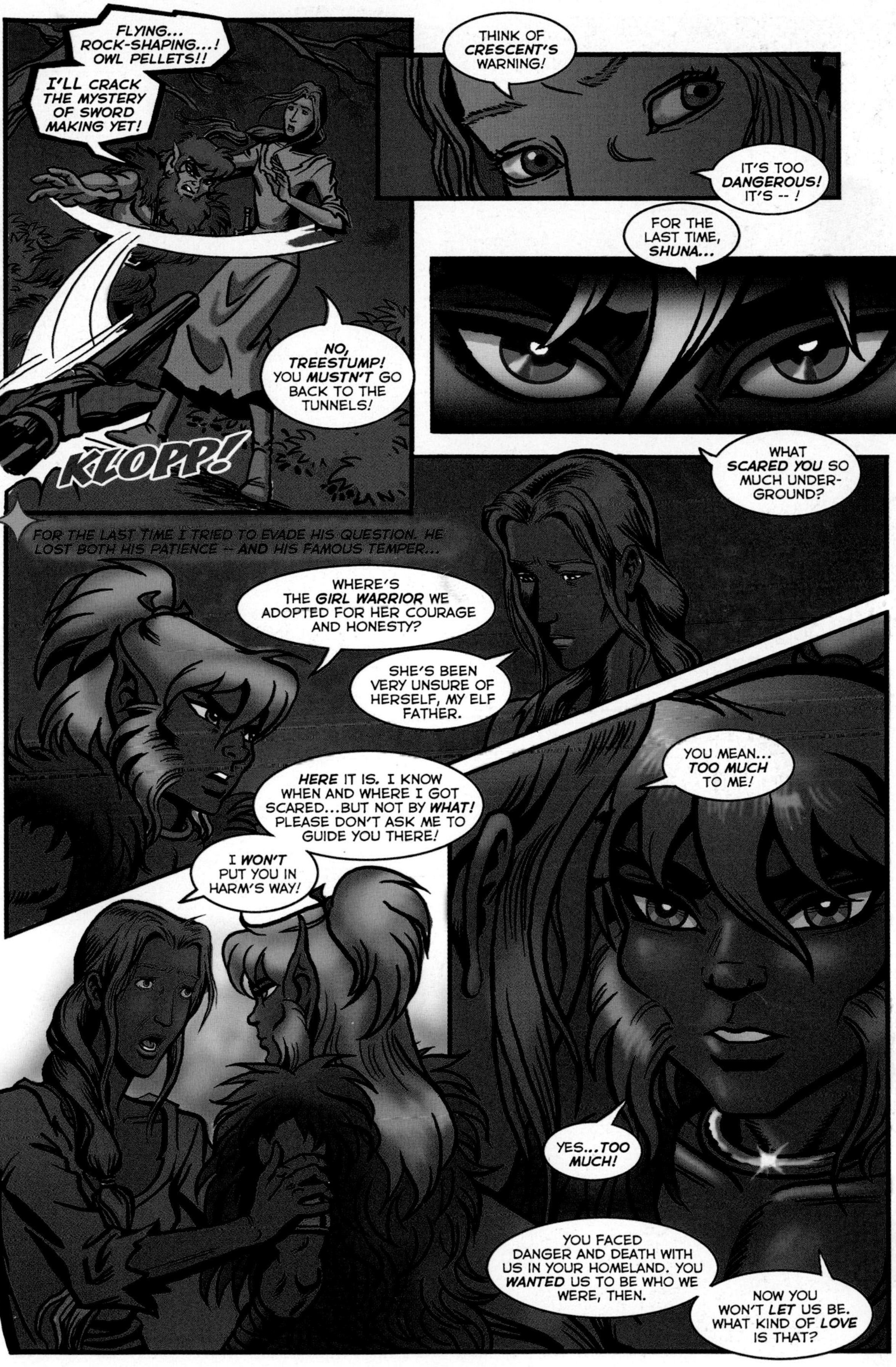
FLYING... ROCK-SHAPING...! OWL PELLETS!!
I'LL CRACK THE MYSTERY OF SWORD MAKING YET!
NO, TREESTUMP! YOU MUSTN'T GO BACK TO THE TUNNELS!
KLOPP!
THINK OF CRESCENT'S WARNING!
IT'S TOO DANGEROUS! IT'S -- !
FOR THE LAST TIME, SHUNA...
WHAT SCARED YOU SO MUCH UNDER-GROUND?
FOR THE LAST TIME I TRIED TO EVADE HIS QUESTION. HE LOST BOTH HIS PATIENCE -- AND HIS FAMOUS TEMPER...
WHERE'S THE GIRL WARRIOR WE ADOPTED FOR HER COURAGE AND HONESTY?
SHE'S BEEN VERY UNSURE OF HERSELF, MY ELF FATHER.
HERE IT IS. I KNOW WHEN AND WHERE I GOT SCARED...BUT NOT BY WHAT! PLEASE DON'T ASK ME TO GUIDE YOU THERE!
I WON'T PUT YOU IN HARM'S WAY!
YOU MEAN... TOO MUCH TO ME!
YES...TOO MUCH!
YOU FACED DANGER AND DEATH WITH US IN YOUR HOMELAND. YOU WANTED US TO BE WHO WE WERE, THEN.
NOW YOU WON'T LET US BE. WHAT KIND OF LOVE IS THAT?

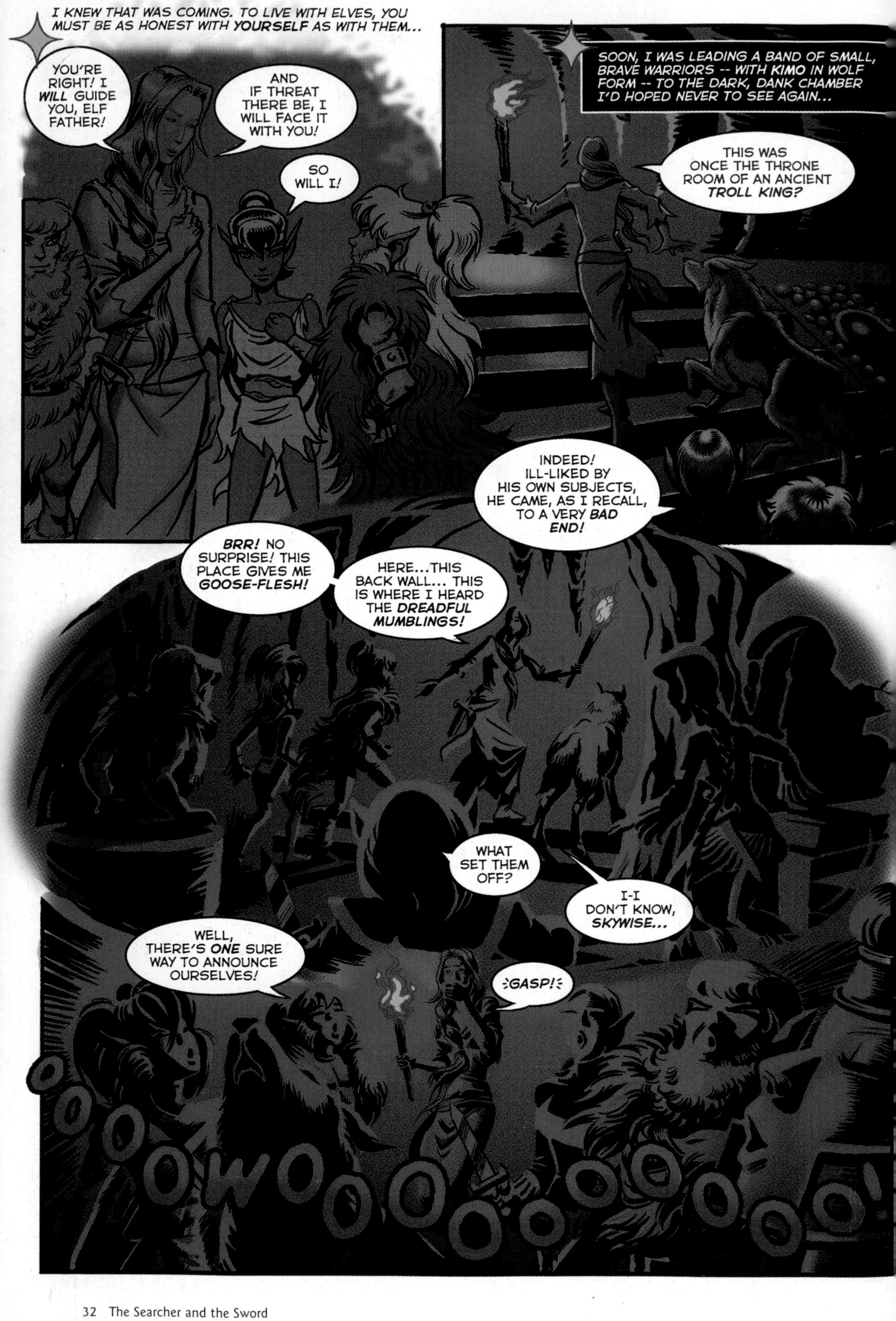

I KNEW THAT WAS COMING. TO LIVE WITH ELVES, YOU MUST BE AS HONEST WITH YOURSELF AS WITH THEM...
YOU'RE RIGHT! I WILL GUIDE YOU, ELF FATHER!
AND IF THREAT THERE BE, I WILL FACE IT WITH YOU!
SO WILL I!
SOON, I WAS LEADING A BAND OF SMALL, BRAVE WARRIORS -- WITH KIMO IN WOLF FORM -- TO THE DARK, DANK CHAMBER I'D HOPED NEVER TO SEE AGAIN...
THIS WAS ONCE THE THRONE ROOM OF AN ANCIENT TROLL KING?
INDEED! ILL-LIKED BY HIS OWN SUBJECTS, HE CAME, AS I RECALL, TO A VERY BAD END!
BRR! NO SURPRISE! THIS PLACE GIVES ME GOOSE-FLESH!
HERE...THIS BACK WALL... THIS IS WHERE I HEARD THE DREADFUL MUMBLINGS!
WHAT SET THEM OFF?
I-I DON'T KNOW, SKYWISE...
WELL, THERE'S ONE SURE WAY TO ANNOUNCE OURSELVES!
GASP!
OOOOOWOOOOOOOOOOOOOOO!

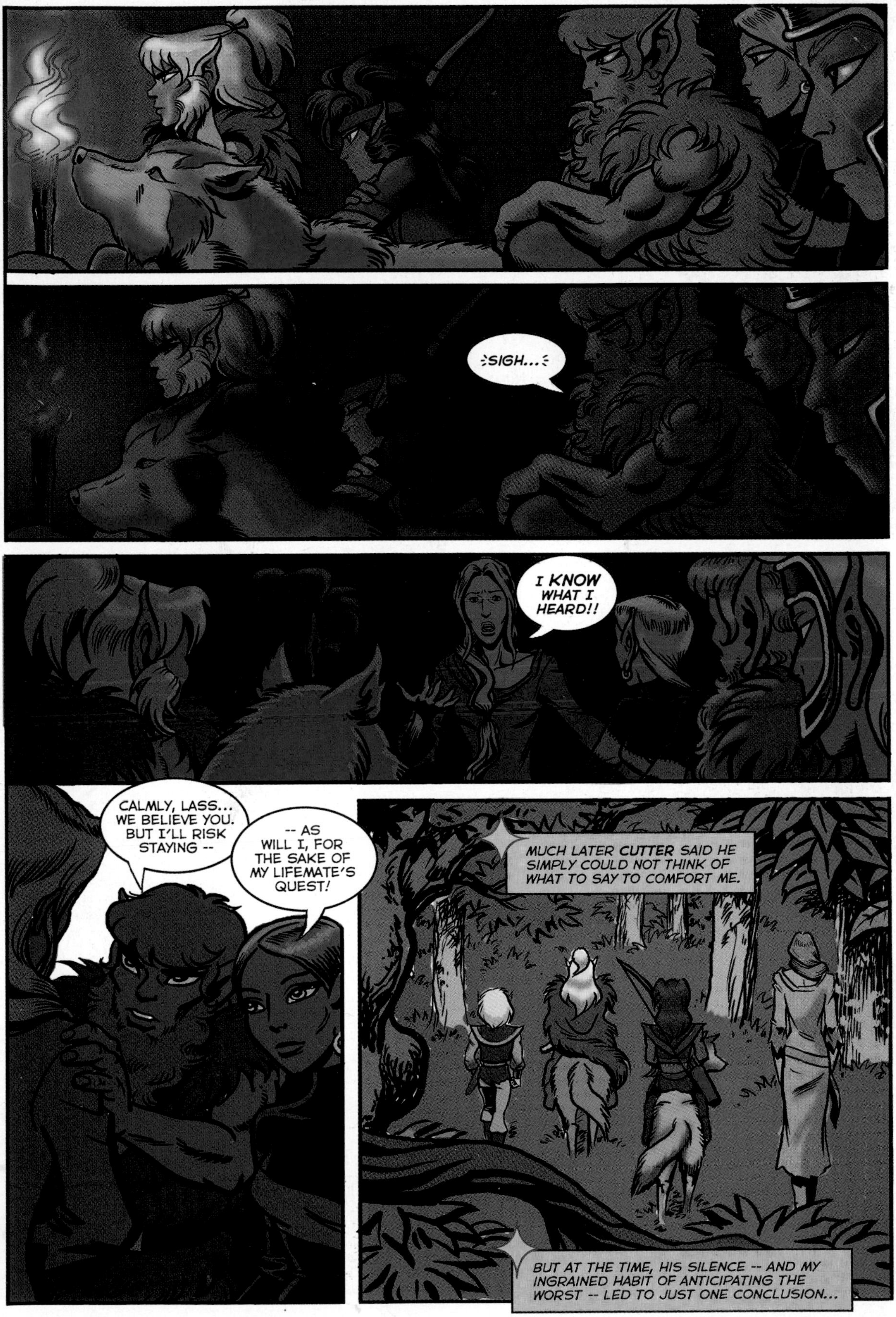
SIGH...
I KNOW WHAT I HEARD!!
CALMLY, LASS... WE BELIEVE YOU. BUT I'LL RISK STAYING --
-- AS WILL I, FOR THE SAKE OF MY LIFEMATE'S QUEST!
MUCH LATER CUTTER SAID HE SIMPLY COULD NOT THINK OF WHAT TO SAY TO COMFORT ME.
BUT AT THE TIME, HIS SILENCE -- AND MY INGRAINED HABIT OF ANTICIPATING THE WORST -- LED TO JUST ONE CONCLUSION...

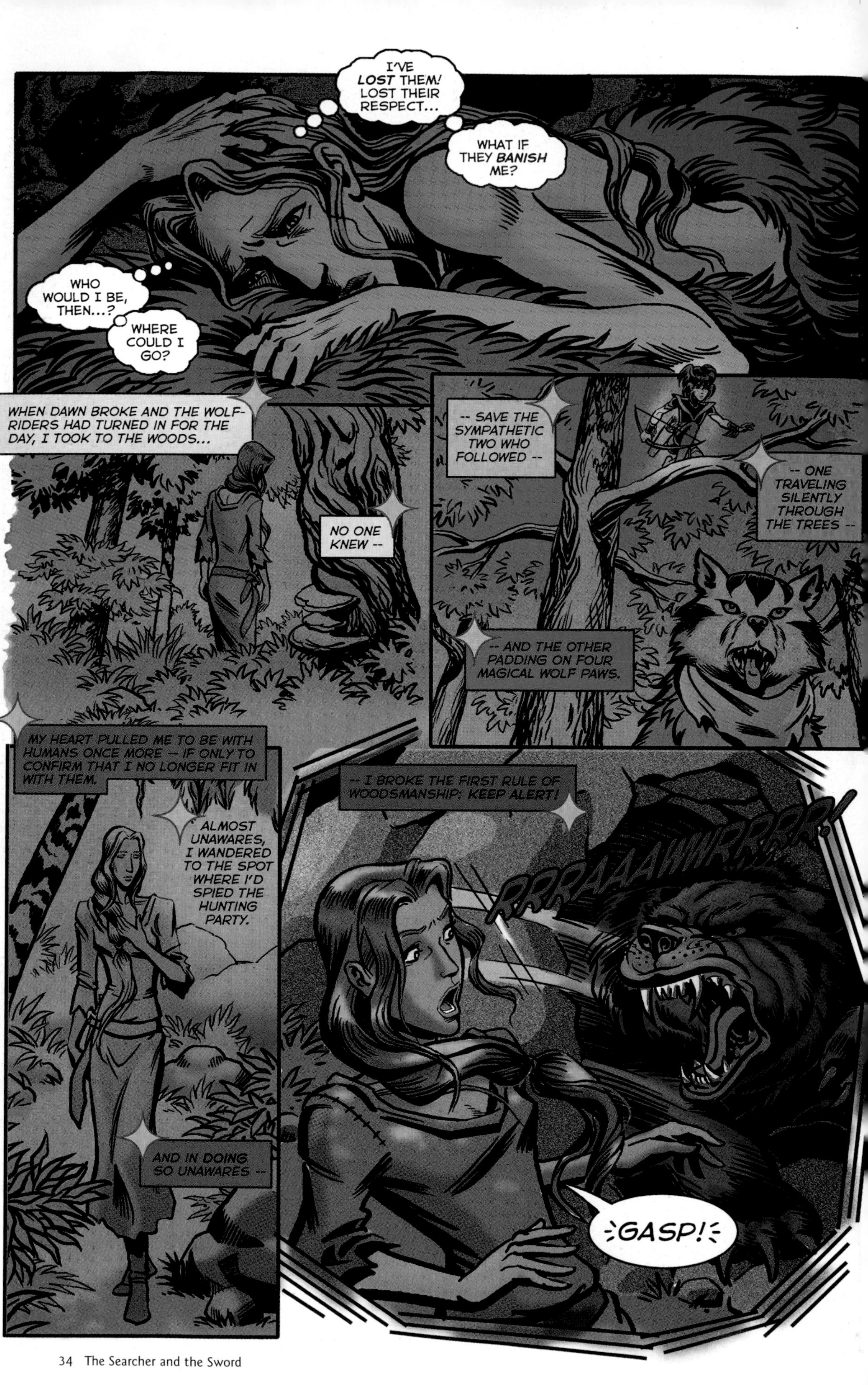
I'VE LOST THEM! LOST THEIR RESPECT...
WHAT IF THEY BANISH ME?
WHO WOULD I BE, THEN...?
WHERE COULD I GO?
WHEN DAWN BROKE AND THE WOLF-RIDERS HAD TURNED IN FOR THE DAY, I TOOK TO THE WOODS...
NO ONE KNEW --
-- SAVE THE SYMPATHETIC TWO WHO FOLLOWED --
-- ONE TRAVELING SILENTLY THROUGH THE TREES --
-- AND THE OTHER PADDING ON FOUR MAGICAL WOLF PAWS.
MY HEART PULLED ME TO BE WITH HUMANS ONCE MORE -- IF ONLY TO CONFIRM THAT I NO LONGER FIT IN WITH THEM.
ALMOST UNAWARES, I WANDERED TO THE SPOT WHERE I'D SPIED THE HUNTING PARTY.
AND IN DOING SO UNAWARES --
-- I BROKE THE FIRST RULE OF WOODSMANSHIP: KEEP ALERT!
RRRAAAAWWRRRRR!
GASP!

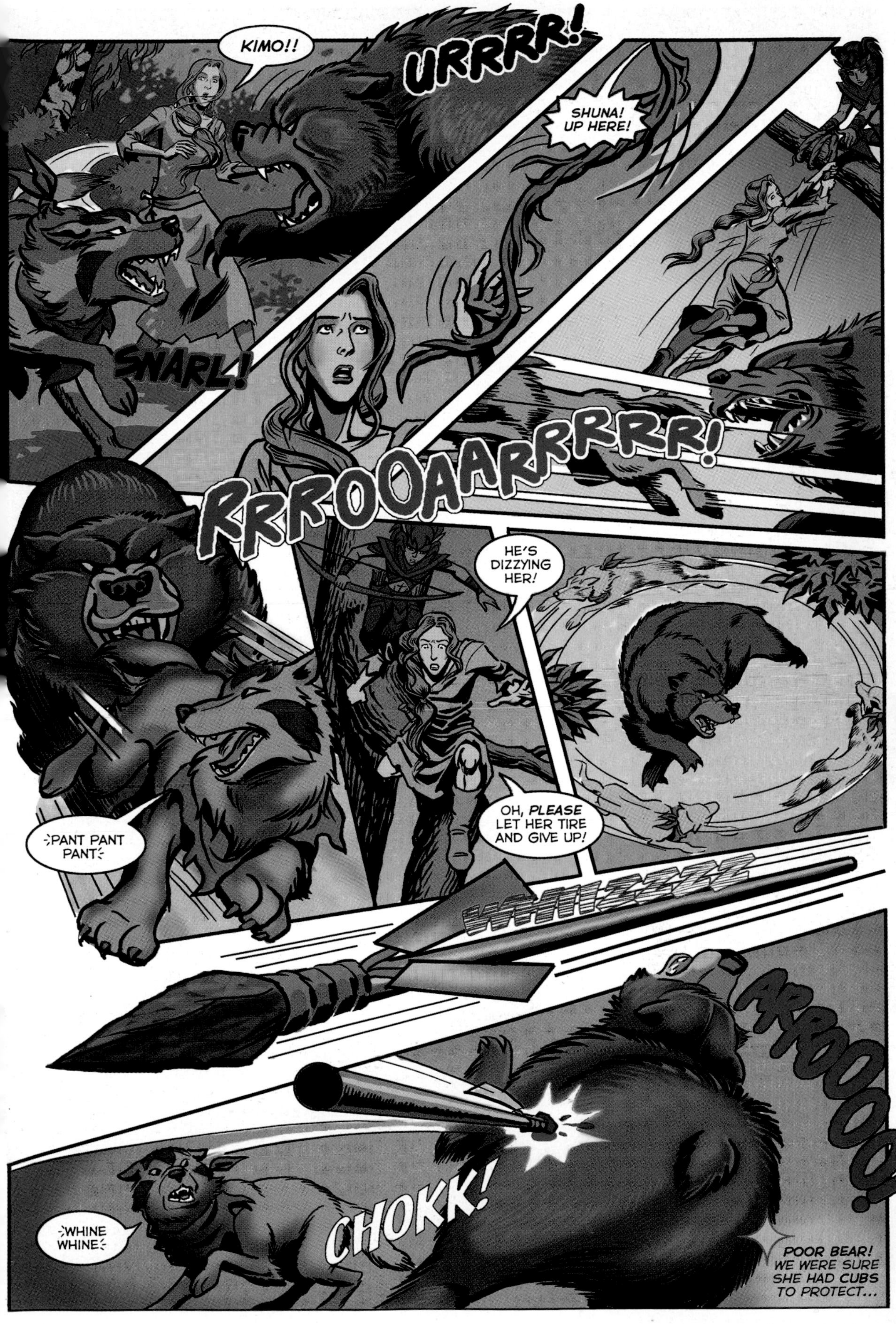
KIMO!!
URRRR!
SNARL!
SHUNA! UP HERE!
RRROOAARRRRR!
HE'S DIZZYING HER!
PANT PANT PANT
OH, PLEASE LET HER TIRE AND GIVE UP!
WHIZZZZ
ARROOOOO!
CHOKK!
WHINE WHINE
POOR BEAR! WE WERE SURE SHE HAD CUBS TO PROTECT...

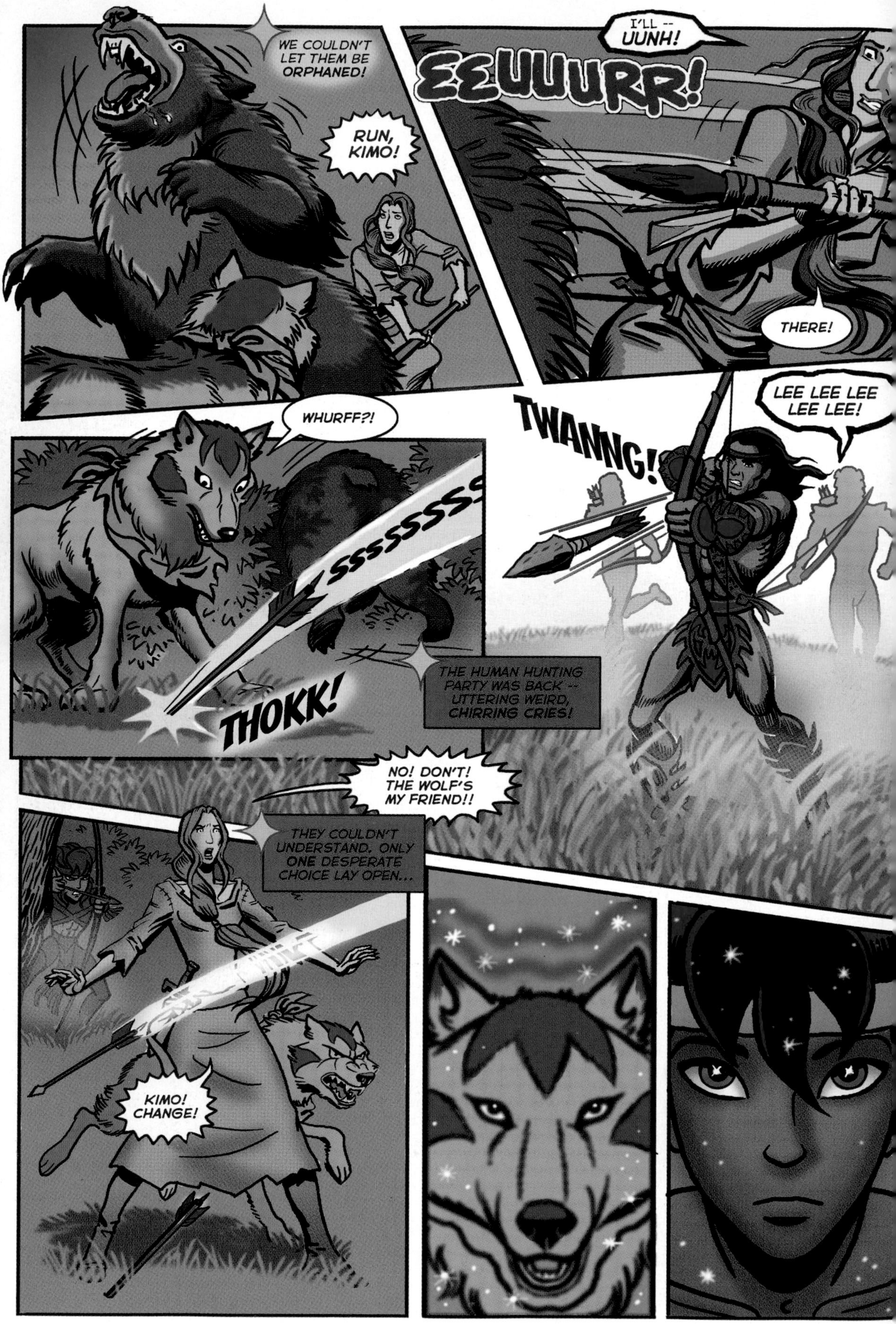
WE COULDN'T LET THEM BE ORPHANED!
RUN, KIMO!
I'LL -- UUNH!
EEUUURR!
THERE!
WHURFF?!
SSSSSSSSS
THOKK!
THE HUMAN HUNTING PARTY WAS BACK -- UTTERING WEIRD, CHIRRING CRIES!
TWANNG!
LEE LEE LEE LEE LEE!
NO! DON'T! THE WOLF'S MY FRIEND!!
THEY COULDN'T UNDERSTAND. ONLY ONE DESPERATE CHOICE LAY OPEN...
KIMO! CHANGE!

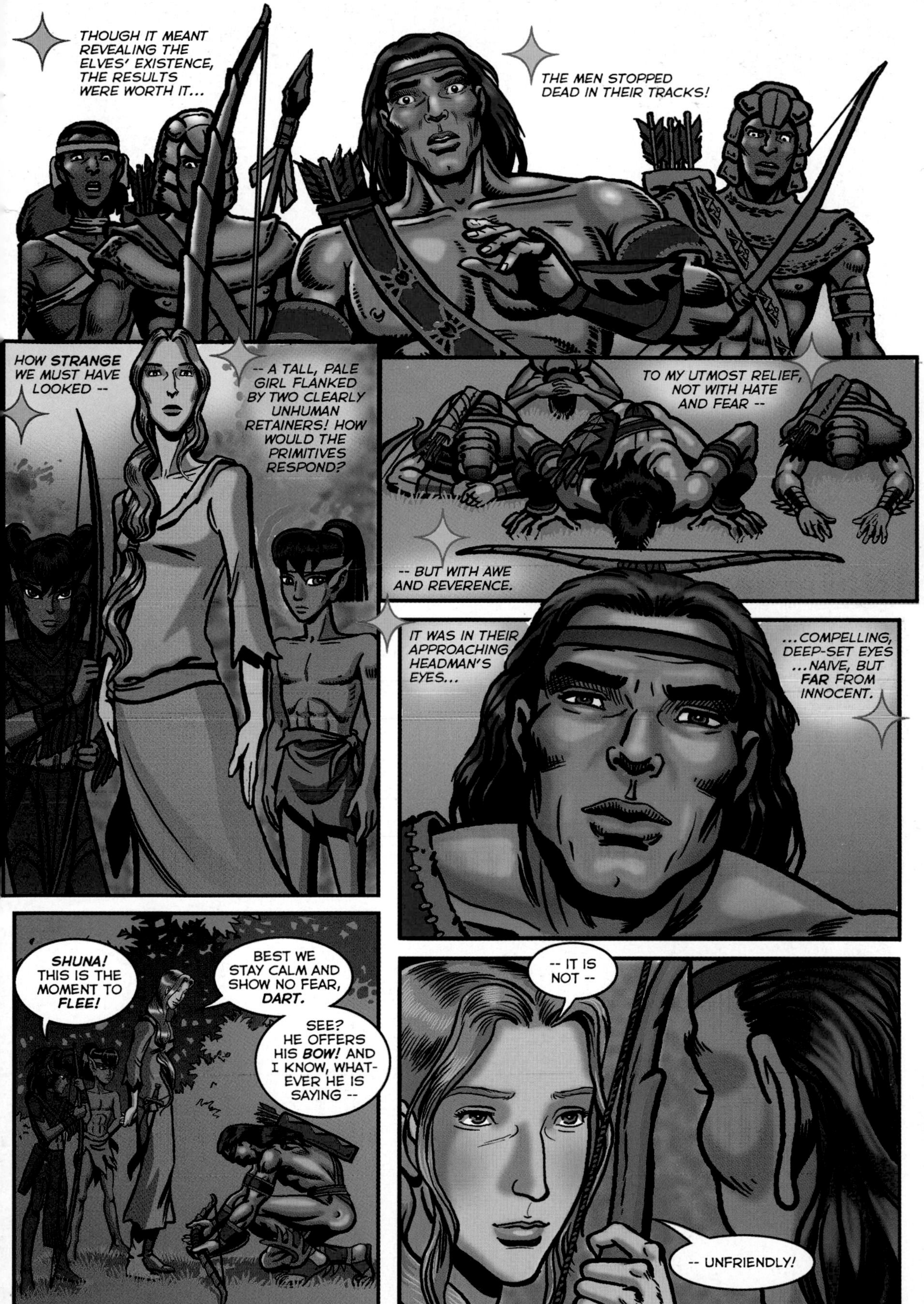
THOUGH IT MEANT REVEALING THE ELVES' EXISTENCE, THE RESULTS WERE WORTH IT...
THE MEN STOPPED DEAD IN THEIR TRACKS!
HOW STRANGE WE MUST HAVE LOOKED --
-- A TALL, PALE GIRL FLANKED BY TWO CLEARLY UNHUMAN RETAINERS! HOW WOULD THE PRIMITIVES RESPOND?
TO MY UTMOST RELIEF, NOT WITH HATE AND FEAR --
-- BUT WITH AWE AND REVERENCE.
IT WAS IN THEIR APPROACHING HEADMAN'S EYES...
...COMPELLING, DEEP-SET EYES ...NAIVE, BUT FAR FROM INNOCENT.
SHUNA! THIS IS THE MOMENT TO FLEE!
BEST WE STAY CALM AND SHOW NO FEAR, DART.
SEE? HE OFFERS HIS BOW! AND I KNOW, WHATEVER HE IS SAYING --
-- IT IS NOT --
-- UNFRIENDLY!

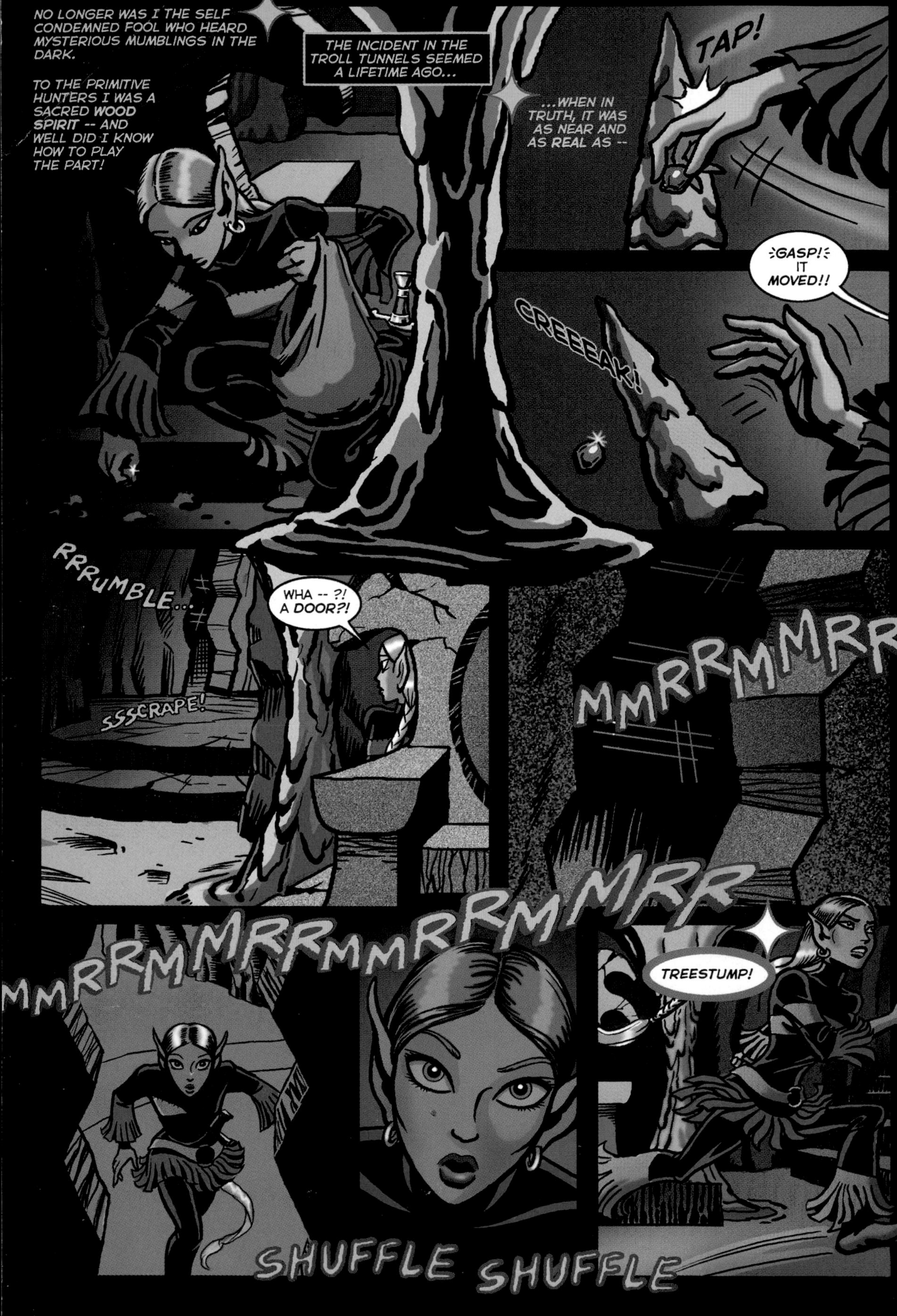
NO LONGER WAS I THE SELF CONDEMNED FOOL WHO HEARD MYSTERIOUS MUMBLINGS IN THE DARK.
TO THE PRIMITIVE HUNTERS I WAS A SACRED WOOD SPIRIT -- AND WELL DID I KNOW HOW TO PLAY THE PART!
THE INCIDENT IN THE TROLL TUNNELS SEEMED A LIFETIME AGO...
...WHEN IN TRUTH, IT WAS AS NEAR AND AS REAL AS --
TAP!
GASP! IT MOVED!!
CREEEEAK!
RRRUMBLE...
WHA -- ?! A DOOR?!
SSSCRAPE!
MMRRRMMMRR
MMRRMMMRRMMMRRRMMMRR
TREESTUMP!
SHUFFLE SHUFFLE

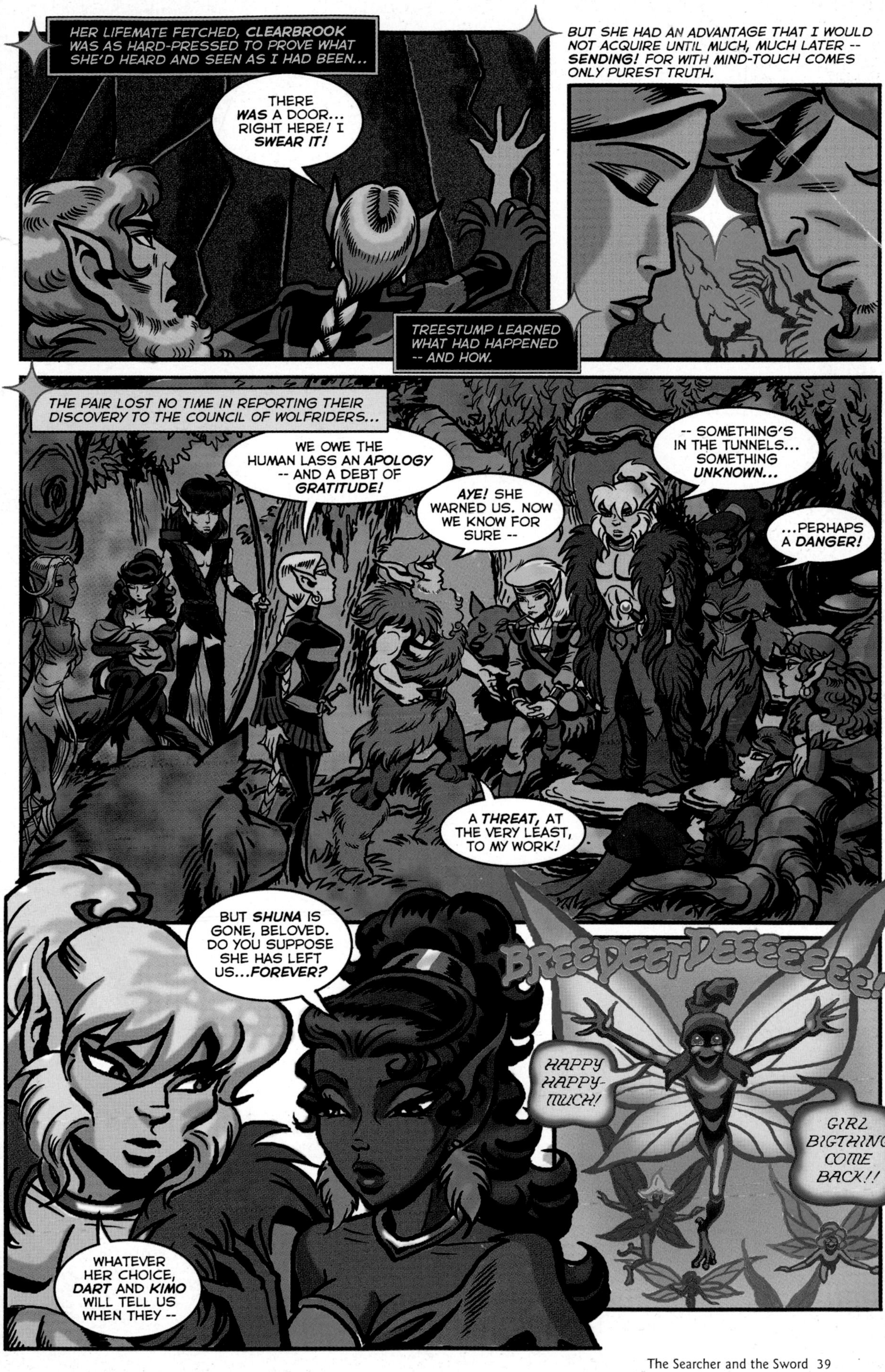
HER LIFEMATE FETCHED, CLEARBROOK WAS AS HARD-PRESSED TO PROVE WHAT SHE'D HEARD AND SEEN AS I HAD BEEN...
THERE WAS A DOOR... RIGHT HERE! I SWEAR IT!
BUT SHE HAD AN ADVANTAGE THAT I WOULD NOT ACQUIRE UNTIL MUCH, MUCH LATER -- SENDING! FOR WITH MIND-TOUCH COMES ONLY PUREST TRUTH.
TREESTUMP LEARNED WHAT HAD HAPPENED -- AND HOW.
THE PAIR LOST NO TIME IN REPORTING THEIR DISCOVERY TO THE COUNCIL OF WOLFRIDERS...
WE OWE THE HUMAN LASS AN APOLOGY -- AND A DEBT OF GRATITUDE!
AYE! SHE WARNED US. NOW WE KNOW FOR SURE --
-- SOMETHING'S IN THE TUNNELS... SOMETHING UNKNOWN...
...PERHAPS A DANGER!
A THREAT, AT THE VERY LEAST, TO MY WORK!
BUT SHUNA IS GONE, BELOVED. DO YOU SUPPOSE SHE HAS LEFT US...FOREVER?
WHATEVER HER CHOICE, DART AND KIMO WILL TELL US WHEN THEY --
BREEDEETDEEEEEEEE!
HAPPY HAPPY-MUCH!
GIRL BIGTHING COME BACK!!

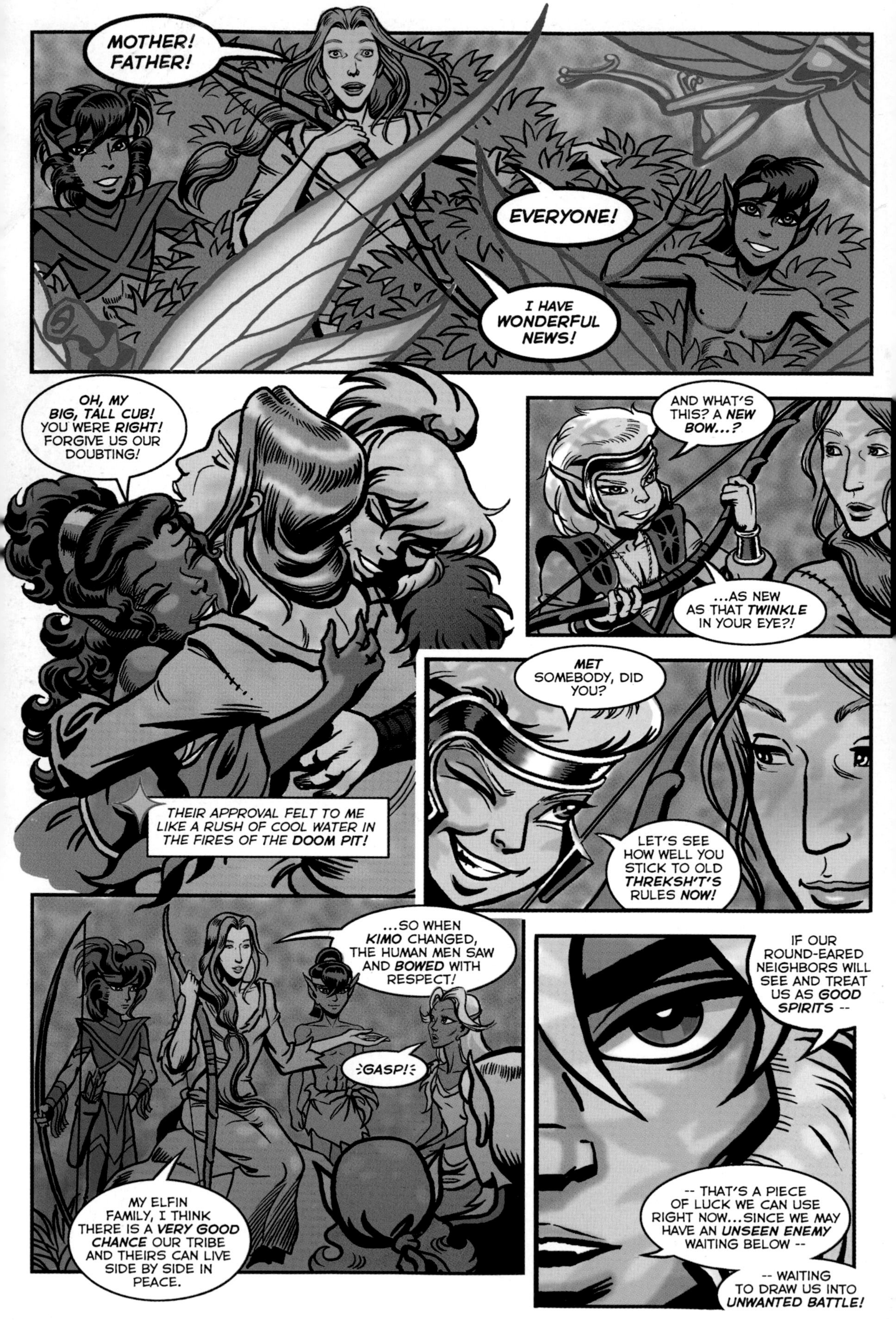
MOTHER! FATHER!
EVERYONE!
I HAVE WONDERFUL NEWS!
OH, MY BIG, TALL CUB! YOU WERE RIGHT! FORGIVE US OUR DOUBTING!
THEIR APPROVAL FELT TO ME LIKE A RUSH OF COOL WATER IN THE FIRES OF THE DOOM PIT!
AND WHAT'S THIS? A NEW BOW...?
...AS NEW AS THAT TWINKLE IN YOUR EYE?!
MET SOMEBODY, DID YOU?
LET'S SEE HOW WELL YOU STICK TO OLD THREKSH'T'S RULES NOW!
...SO WHEN KIMO CHANGED, THE HUMAN MEN SAW AND BOWED WITH RESPECT!
GASP!
MY ELFIN FAMILY, I THINK THERE IS A VERY GOOD CHANCE OUR TRIBE AND THEIRS CAN LIVE SIDE BY SIDE IN PEACE.
IF OUR ROUND-EARED NEIGHBORS WILL SEE AND TREAT US AS GOOD SPIRITS --
-- THAT'S A PIECE OF LUCK WE CAN USE RIGHT NOW...SINCE WE MAY HAVE AN UNSEEN ENEMY WAITING BELOW --
-- WAITING TO DRAW US INTO UNWANTED BATTLE!

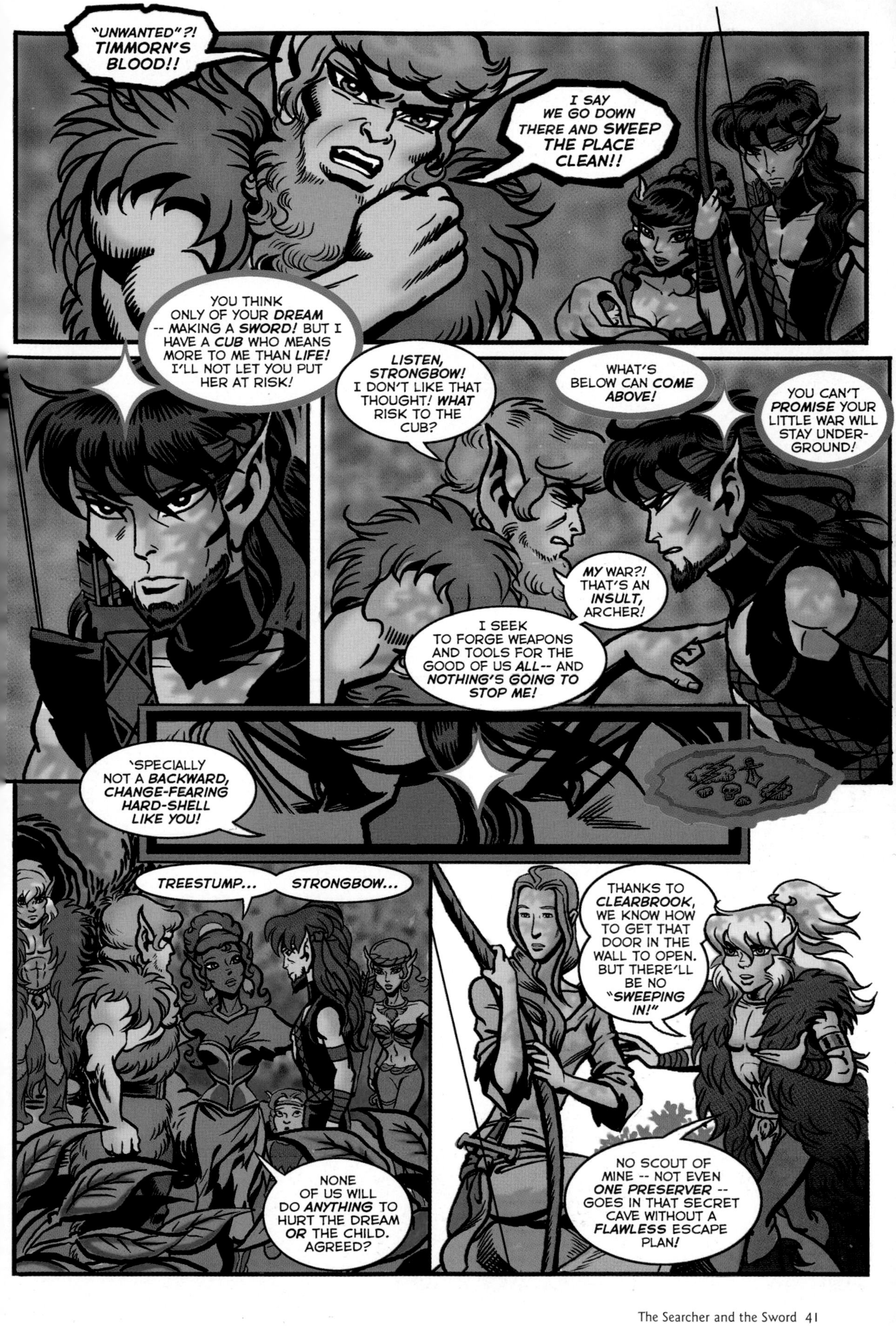
"UNWANTED"?! TIMMORN'S BLOOD!!
I SAY WE GO DOWN THERE AND SWEEP THE PLACE CLEAN!!
YOU THINK ONLY OF YOUR DREAM -- MAKING A SWORD! BUT I HAVE A CUB WHO MEANS MORE TO ME THAN LIFE! I'LL NOT LET YOU PUT HER AT RISK!
LISTEN, STRONGBOW! I DON'T LIKE THAT THOUGHT! WHAT RISK TO THE CUB?
WHAT'S BELOW CAN COME ABOVE!
YOU CAN'T PROMISE YOUR LITTLE WAR WILL STAY UNDER-GROUND!
MY WAR?! THAT'S AN INSULT, ARCHER!
I SEEK TO FORGE WEAPONS AND TOOLS FOR THE GOOD OF US ALL-- AND NOTHING'S GOING TO STOP ME!
'SPECIALLY NOT A BACKWARD, CHANGE-FEARING HARD-SHELL LIKE YOU!
TREESTUMP...
STRONGBOW...
NONE OF US WILL DO ANYTHING TO HURT THE DREAM OR THE CHILD. AGREED?
THANKS TO CLEARBROOK, WE KNOW HOW TO GET THAT DOOR IN THE WALL TO OPEN. BUT THERE'LL BE NO "SWEEPING IN!"
NO SCOUT OF MINE -- NOT EVEN ONE PRESERVER -- GOES IN THAT SECRET CAVE WITHOUT A FLAWLESS ESCAPE PLAN!

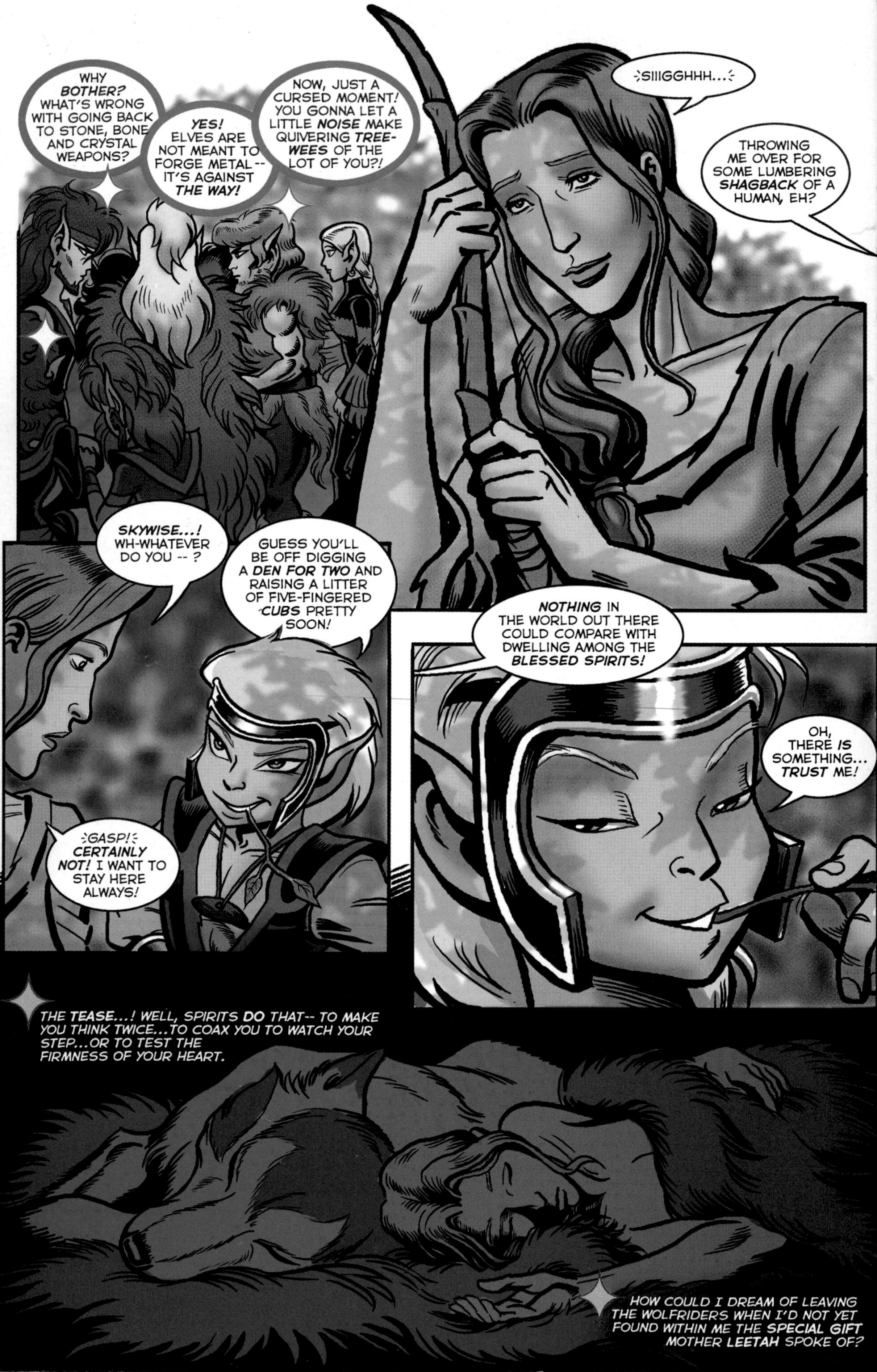
WHY BOTHER? WHAT'S WRONG WITH GOING BACK TO STONE, BONE AND CRYSTAL WEAPONS?
YES! ELVES ARE NOT MEANT TO FORGE METAL -- IT'S AGAINST THE WAY!
NOW, JUST A CURSED MOMENT! YOU GONNA LET A LITTLE NOISE MAKE QUIVERING TREE-WEES OF THE LOT OF YOU?!
SIIIGGHHH...
THROWING ME OVER FOR SOME LUMBERING SHAGBACK OF A HUMAN, EH?
SKYWISE...! WH-WHATEVER DO YOU -- ?
GUESS YOU'LL BE OFF DIGGING A DEN FOR TWO AND RAISING A LITTER OF FIVE-FINGERED CUBS PRETTY SOON!
GASP! CERTAINLY NOT! I WANT TO STAY HERE ALWAYS!
NOTHING IN THE WORLD OUT THERE COULD COMPARE WITH DWELLING AMONG THE BLESSED SPIRITS!
OH, THERE IS SOMETHING... TRUST ME!
THE TEASE...! WELL, SPIRITS DO THAT-- TO MAKE YOU THINK TWICE...TO COAX YOU TO WATCH YOUR STEP...OR TO TEST THE FIRMNESS OF YOUR HEART.
HOW COULD I DREAM OF LEAVING THE WOLFRIDERS WHEN I'D NOT YET FOUND WITHIN ME THE SPECIAL GIFT MOTHER LEETAH SPOKE OF?

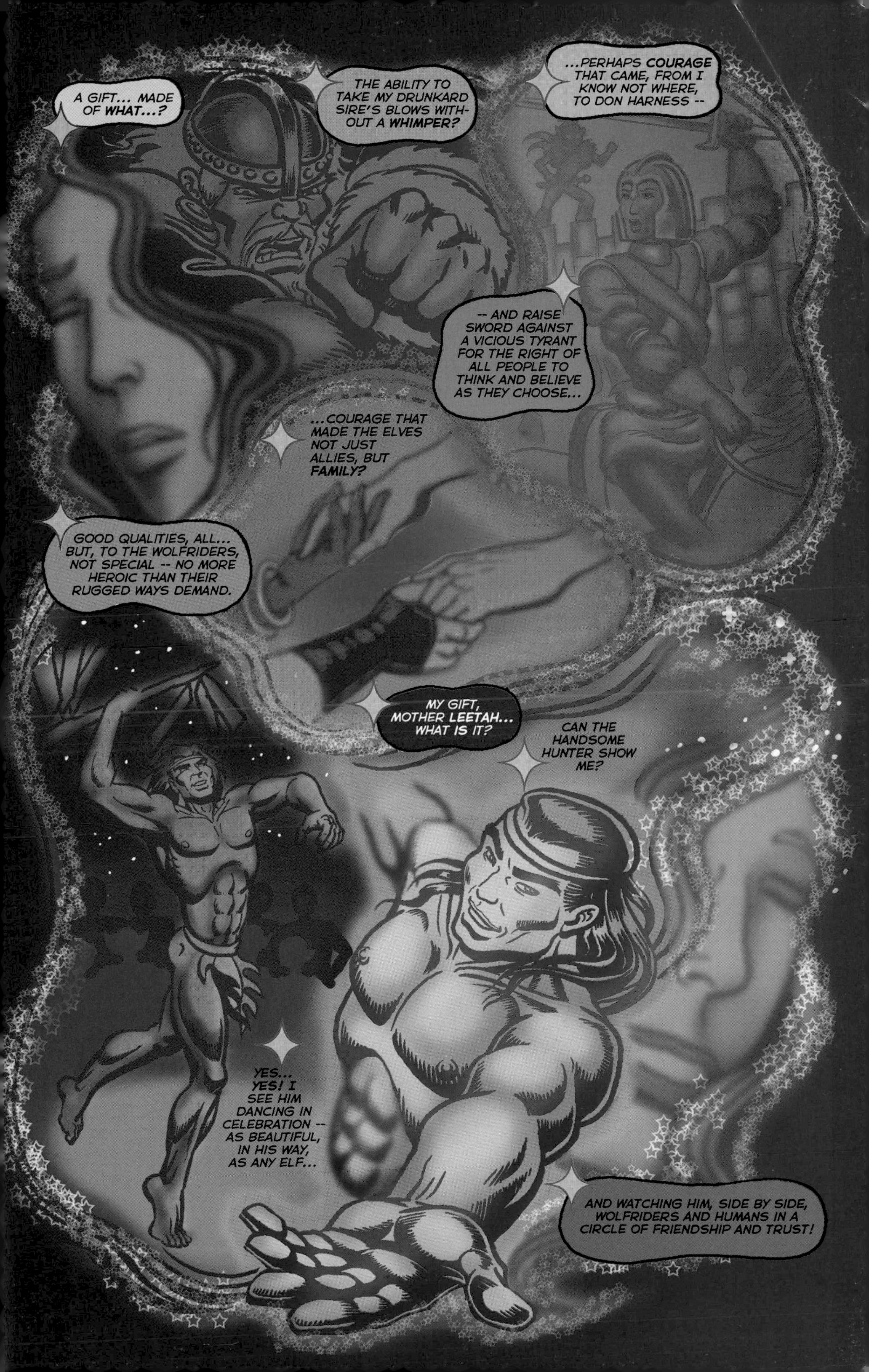
A GIFT... MADE OF WHAT...?
THE ABILITY TO TAKE MY DRUNKARD SIRE'S BLOWS WITH-OUT A WHIMPER?
...PERHAPS COURAGE THAT CAME, FROM I KNOW NOT WHERE, TO DON HARNESS --
-- AND RAISE SWORD AGAINST A VICIOUS TYRANT FOR THE RIGHT OF ALL PEOPLE TO THINK AND BELIEVE AS THEY CHOOSE...
...COURAGE THAT MADE THE ELVES NOT JUST ALLIES, BUT FAMILY?
GOOD QUALITIES, ALL... BUT, TO THE WOLFRIDERS, NOT SPECIAL -- NO MORE HEROIC THAN THEIR RUGGED WAYS DEMAND.
MY GIFT, MOTHER LEETAH... WHAT IS IT?
CAN THE HANDSOME HUNTER SHOW ME?
YES... YES! I SEE HIM DANCING IN CELEBRATION -- AS BEAUTIFUL, IN HIS WAY, AS ANY ELF...
AND WATCHING HIM, SIDE BY SIDE, WOLFRIDERS AND HUMANS IN A CIRCLE OF FRIENDSHIP AND TRUST!

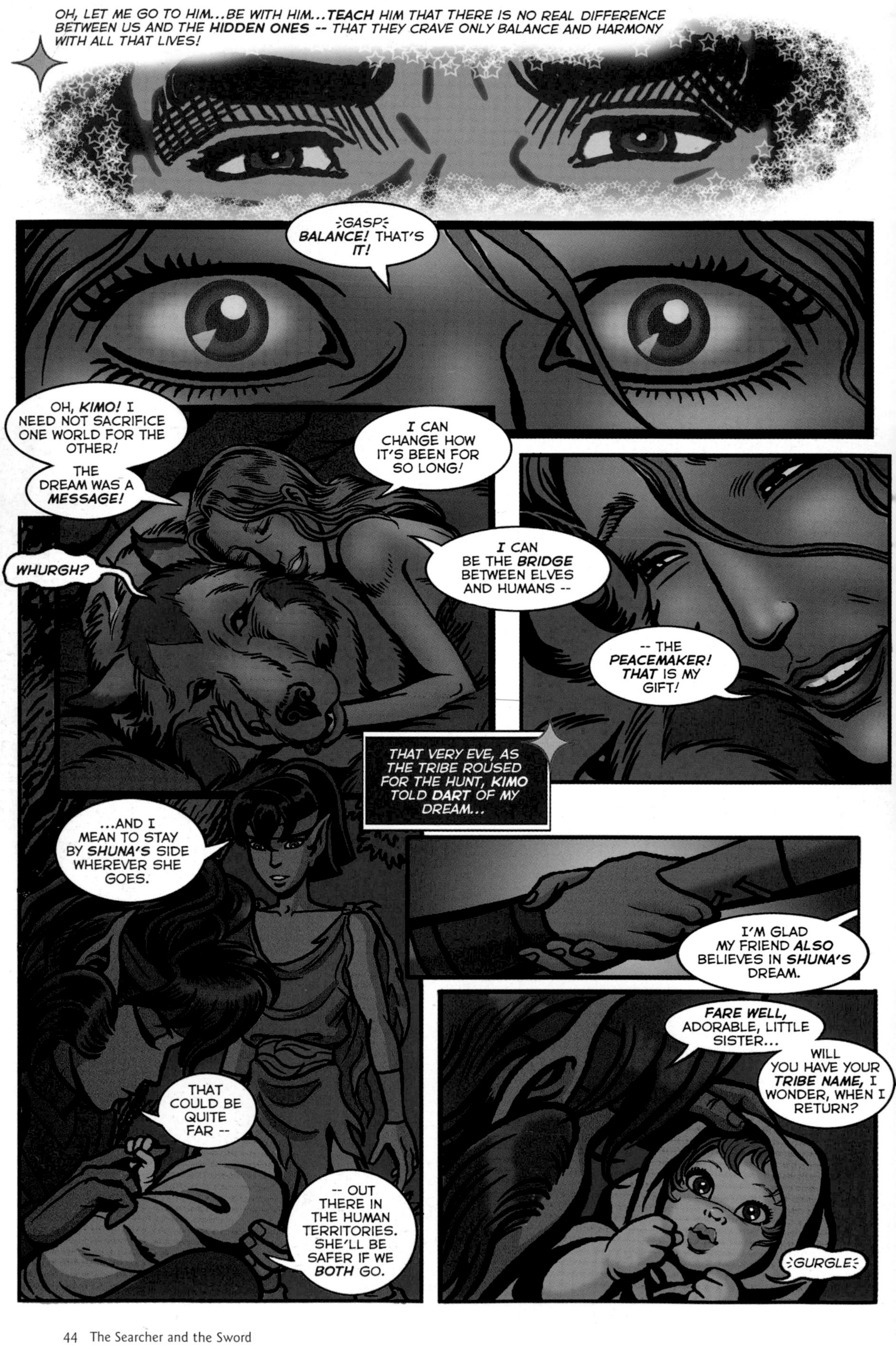
OH, LET ME GO TO HIM...BE WITH HIM...TEACH HIM THAT THERE IS NO REAL DIFFERENCE BETWEEN US AND THE HIDDEN ONES -- THAT THEY CRAVE ONLY BALANCE AND HARMONY WITH ALL THAT LIVES!
GASP BALANCE! THAT'S IT!
OH, KIMO! I NEED NOT SACRIFICE ONE WORLD FOR THE OTHER!
THE DREAM WAS A MESSAGE!
I CAN CHANGE HOW IT'S BEEN FOR SO LONG!
WHURGH?
I CAN BE THE BRIDGE BETWEEN ELVES AND HUMANS --
-- THE PEACEMAKER! THAT IS MY GIFT!
THAT VERY EVE, AS THE TRIBE ROUSED FOR THE HUNT, KIMO TOLD DART OF MY DREAM...
...AND I MEAN TO STAY BY SHUNA'S SIDE WHEREVER SHE GOES.
THAT COULD BE QUITE FAR --
-- OUT THERE IN THE HUMAN TERRITORIES. SHE'LL BE SAFER IF WE BOTH GO.
I'M GLAD MY FRIEND ALSO BELIEVES IN SHUNA'S DREAM.
FARE WELL, ADORABLE, LITTLE SISTER...
WILL YOU HAVE YOUR TRIBE NAME, I WONDER, WHEN I RETURN?
GURGLE

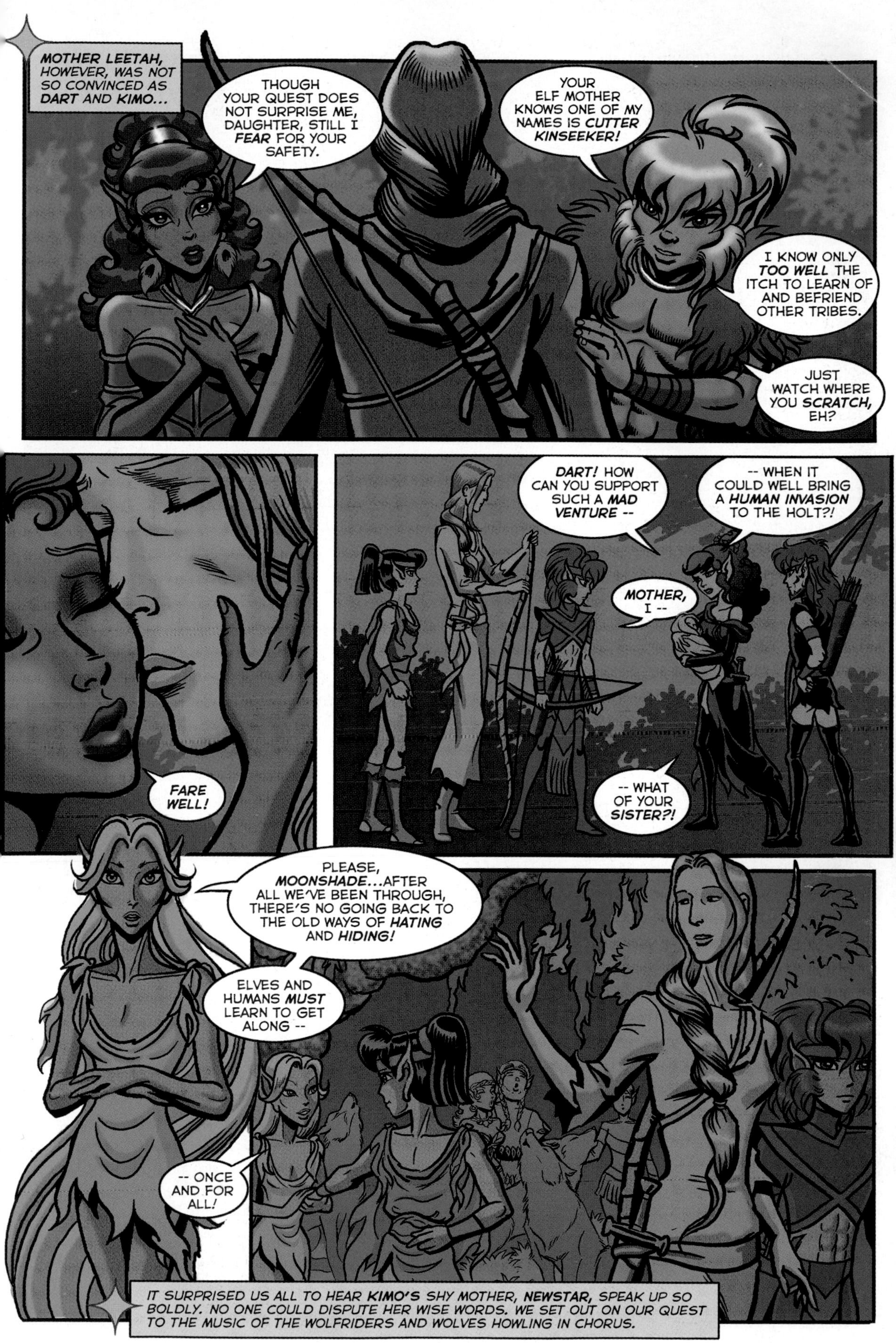
MOTHER LEETAH, HOWEVER, WAS NOT SO CONVINCED AS DART AND KIMO...
THOUGH YOUR QUEST DOES NOT SURPRISE ME, DAUGHTER, STILL I FEAR FOR YOUR SAFETY.
YOUR ELF MOTHER KNOWS ONE OF MY NAMES IS CUTTER KINSEEKER!
I KNOW ONLY TOO WELL THE ITCH TO LEARN OF AND BEFRIEND OTHER TRIBES.
JUST WATCH WHERE YOU SCRATCH, EH?
FARE WELL!
DART! HOW CAN YOU SUPPORT SUCH A MAD VENTURE --
-- WHEN IT COULD WELL BRING A HUMAN INVASION TO THE HOLT?!
MOTHER, I --
-- WHAT OF YOUR SISTER?!
PLEASE, MOONSHADE...AFTER ALL WE'VE BEEN THROUGH, THERE'S NO GOING BACK TO THE OLD WAYS OF HATING AND HIDING!
ELVES AND HUMANS MUST LEARN TO GET ALONG --
-- ONCE AND FOR ALL!
IT SURPRISED US ALL TO HEAR KIMO'S SHY MOTHER, NEWSTAR, SPEAK UP SO BOLDLY. NO ONE COULD DISPUTE HER WISE WORDS. WE SET OUT ON OUR QUEST TO THE MUSIC OF THE WOLFRIDERS AND WOLVES HOWLING IN CHORUS.

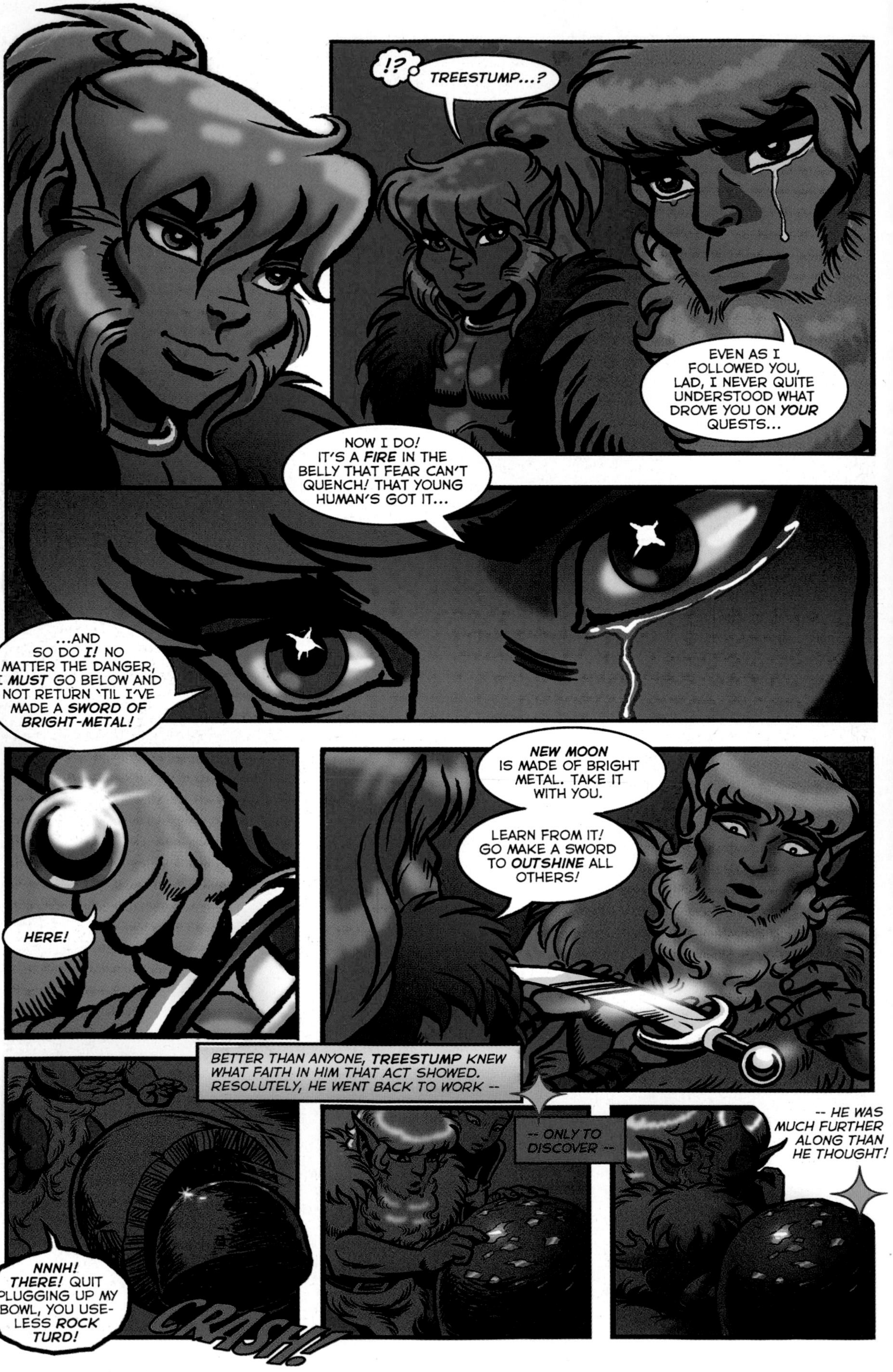
!?
TREESTUMP...?
EVEN AS I FOLLOWED YOU, LAD, I NEVER QUITE UNDERSTOOD WHAT DROVE YOU ON YOUR QUESTS...
NOW I DO! IT'S A FIRE IN THE BELLY THAT FEAR CAN'T QUENCH! THAT YOUNG HUMAN'S GOT IT...
...AND SO DO I! NO MATTER THE DANGER, I MUST GO BELOW AND NOT RETURN 'TIL I'VE MADE A SWORD OF BRIGHT-METAL!
HERE!
NEW MOON IS MADE OF BRIGHT METAL. TAKE IT WITH YOU.
LEARN FROM IT! GO MAKE A SWORD TO OUTSHINE ALL OTHERS!
BETTER THAN ANYONE, TREESTUMP KNEW WHAT FAITH IN HIM THAT ACT SHOWED. RESOLUTELY, HE WENT BACK TO WORK --
NNNH! THERE! QUIT PLUGGING UP MY BOWL, YOU USE-LESS ROCK TURD!
CRASH!
-- ONLY TO DISCOVER --
-- HE WAS MUCH FURTHER ALONG THAN HE THOUGHT!

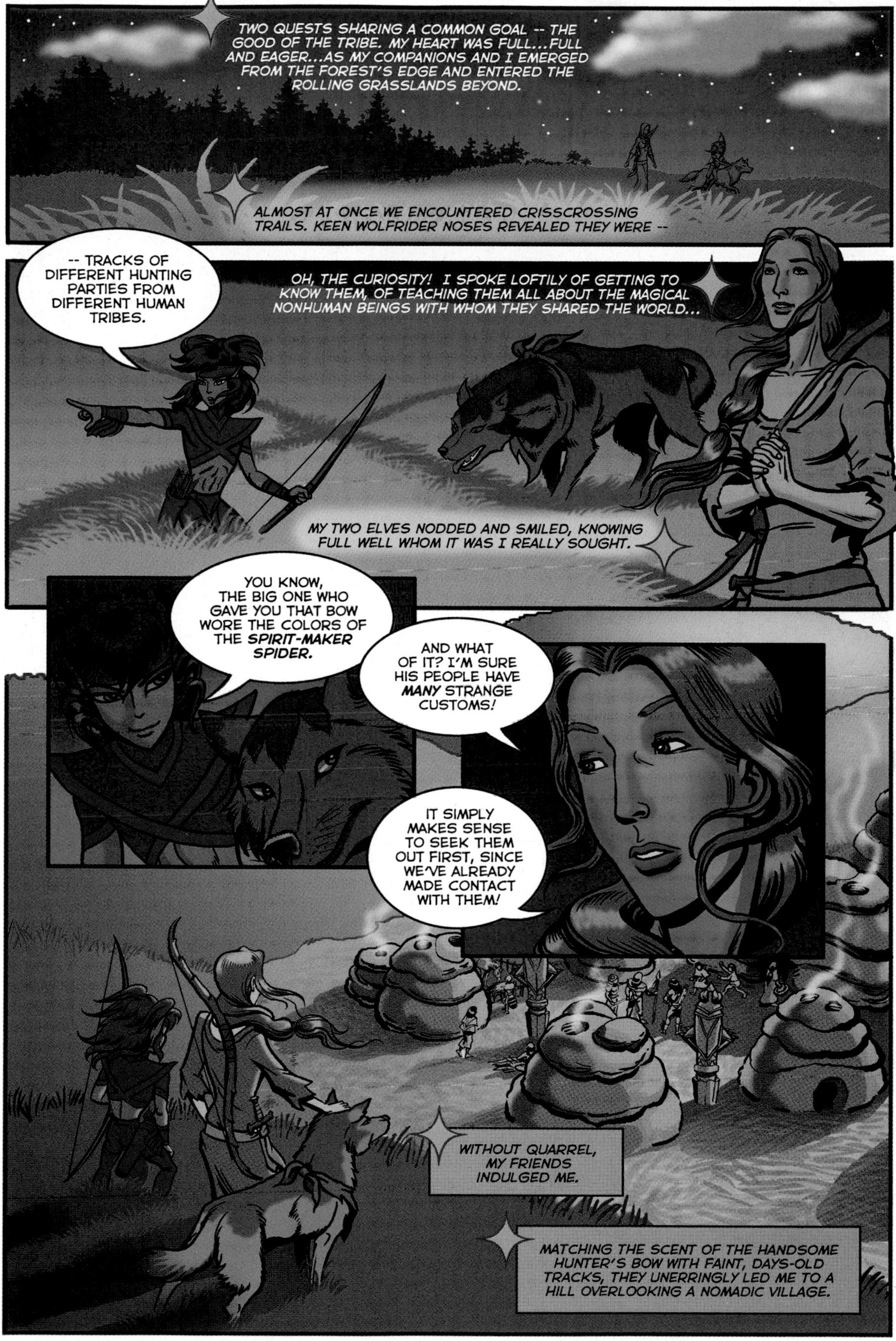
TWO QUESTS SHARING A COMMON GOAL -- THE GOOD OF THE TRIBE. MY HEART WAS FULL...FULL AND EAGER...AS MY COMPANIONS AND I EMERGED FROM THE FOREST'S EDGE AND ENTERED THE ROLLING GRASSLANDS BEYOND.
ALMOST AT ONCE WE ENCOUNTERED CRISSCROSSING TRAILS. KEEN WOLFRIDER NOSES REVEALED THEY WERE --
-- TRACKS OF DIFFERENT HUNTING PARTIES FROM DIFFERENT HUMAN TRIBES.
OH, THE CURIOSITY! I SPOKE LOFTILY OF GETTING TO KNOW THEM, OF TEACHING THEM ALL ABOUT THE MAGICAL NONHUMAN BEINGS WITH WHOM THEY SHARED THE WORLD...
MY TWO ELVES NODDED AND SMILED, KNOWING FULL WELL WHOM IT WAS I REALLY SOUGHT.
YOU KNOW, THE BIG ONE WHO GAVE YOU THAT BOW WORE THE COLORS OF THE SPIRIT-MAKER SPIDER.
AND WHAT OF IT? I'M SURE HIS PEOPLE HAVE MANY STRANGE CUSTOMS!
IT SIMPLY MAKES SENSE TO SEEK THEM OUT FIRST, SINCE WE'VE ALREADY MADE CONTACT WITH THEM!
WITHOUT QUARREL, MY FRIENDS INDULGED ME.
MATCHING THE SCENT OF THE HANDSOME HUNTER'S BOW WITH FAINT, DAYS-OLD TRACKS, THEY UNERRINGLY LED ME TO A HILL OVERLOOKING A NOMADIC VILLAGE.

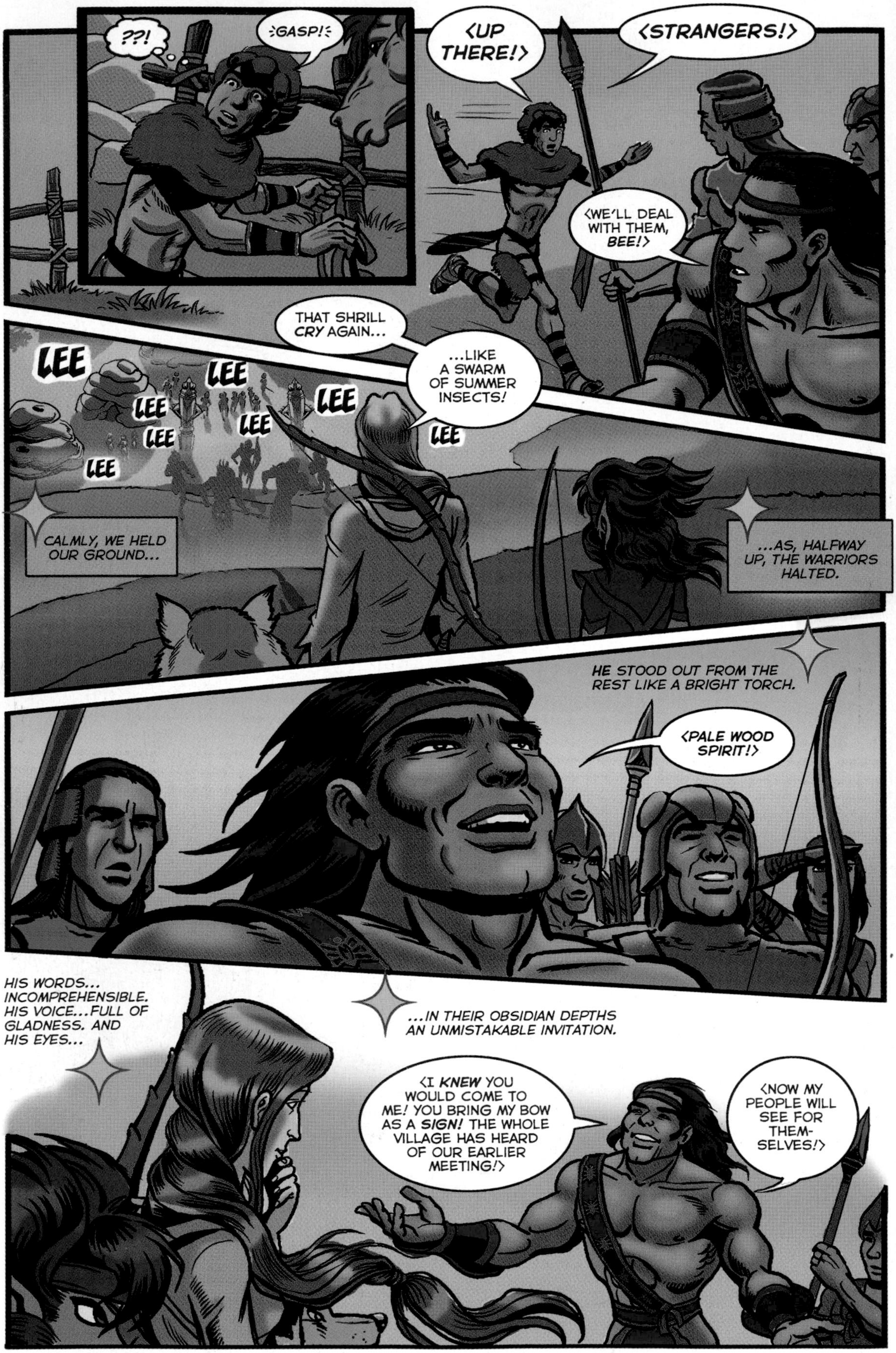

??!
:GASP!:
<UP THERE!>
<STRANGERS!>
<WE'LL DEAL WITH THEM, BEE!>
THAT SHRILL CRY AGAIN...
...LIKE A SWARM OF SUMMER INSECTS!
LEE LEE LEE LEE LEE LEE LEE LEE
CALMLY, WE HELD OUR GROUND...
...AS, HALFWAY UP, THE WARRIORS HALTED.
HE STOOD OUT FROM THE REST LIKE A BRIGHT TORCH.
<PALE WOOD SPIRIT!>
HIS WORDS... INCOMPREHENSIBLE. HIS VOICE...FULL OF GLADNESS. AND HIS EYES...
...IN THEIR OBSIDIAN DEPTHS AN UNMISTAKABLE INVITATION.
<I KNEW YOU WOULD COME TO ME! YOU BRING MY BOW AS A SIGN! THE WHOLE VILLAGE HAS HEARD OF OUR EARLIER MEETING!>
<NOW MY PEOPLE WILL SEE FOR THEM-SELVES!>

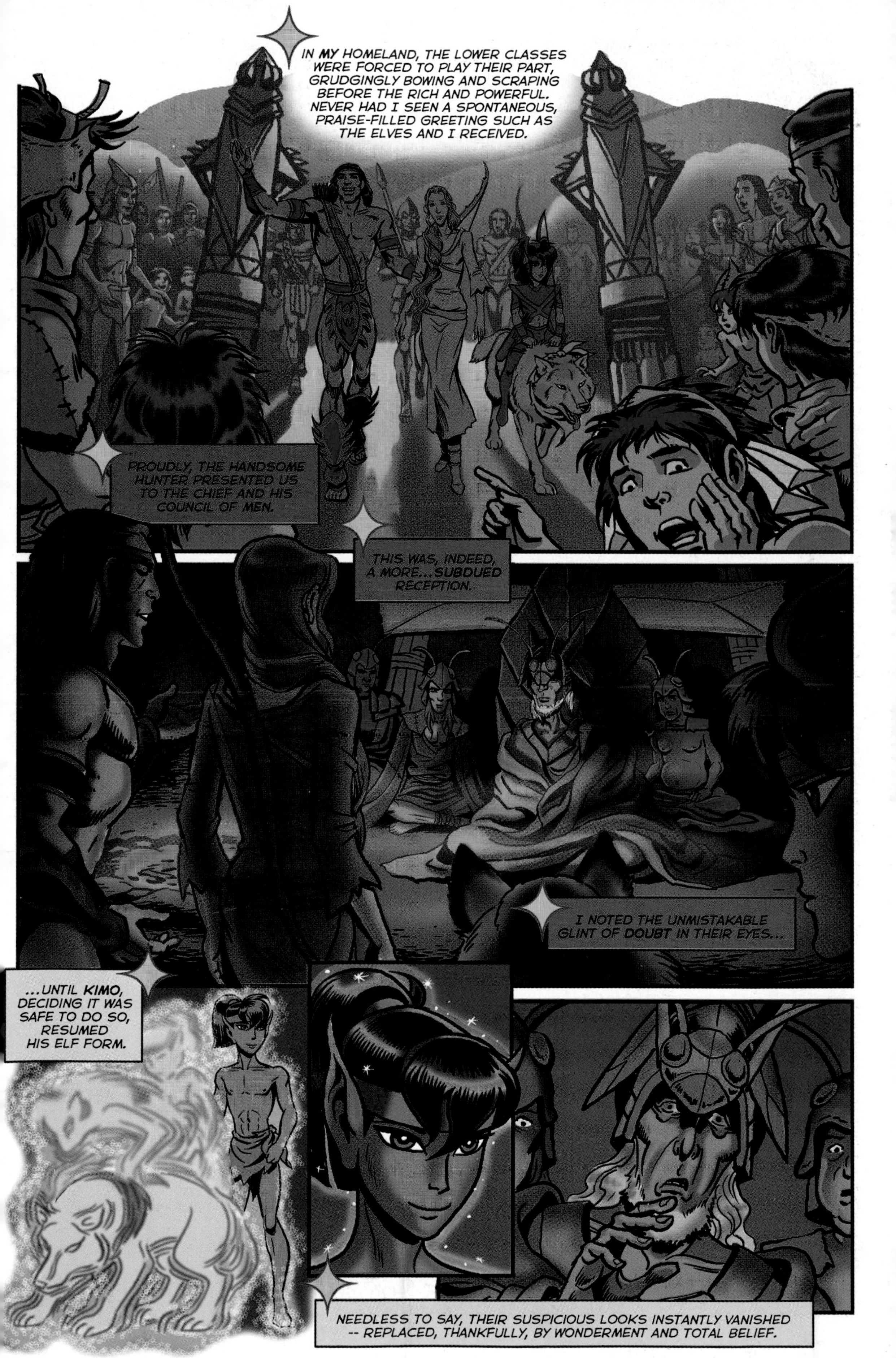
IN MY HOMELAND, THE LOWER CLASSES WERE FORCED TO PLAY THEIR PART, GRUDGINGLY BOWING AND SCRAPING BEFORE THE RICH AND POWERFUL. NEVER HAD I SEEN A SPONTANEOUS, PRAISE-FILLED GREETING SUCH AS THE ELVES AND I RECEIVED.
PROUDLY, THE HANDSOME HUNTER PRESENTED US TO THE CHIEF AND HIS COUNCIL OF MEN.
THIS WAS, INDEED, A MORE...SUBDUED RECEPTION.
I NOTED THE UNMISTAKABLE GLINT OF DOUBT IN THEIR EYES...
...UNTIL KIMO, DECIDING IT WAS SAFE TO DO SO, RESUMED HIS ELF FORM.
NEEDLESS TO SAY, THEIR SUSPICIOUS LOOKS INSTANTLY VANISHED -- REPLACED, THANKFULLY, BY WONDERMENT AND TOTAL BELIEF.

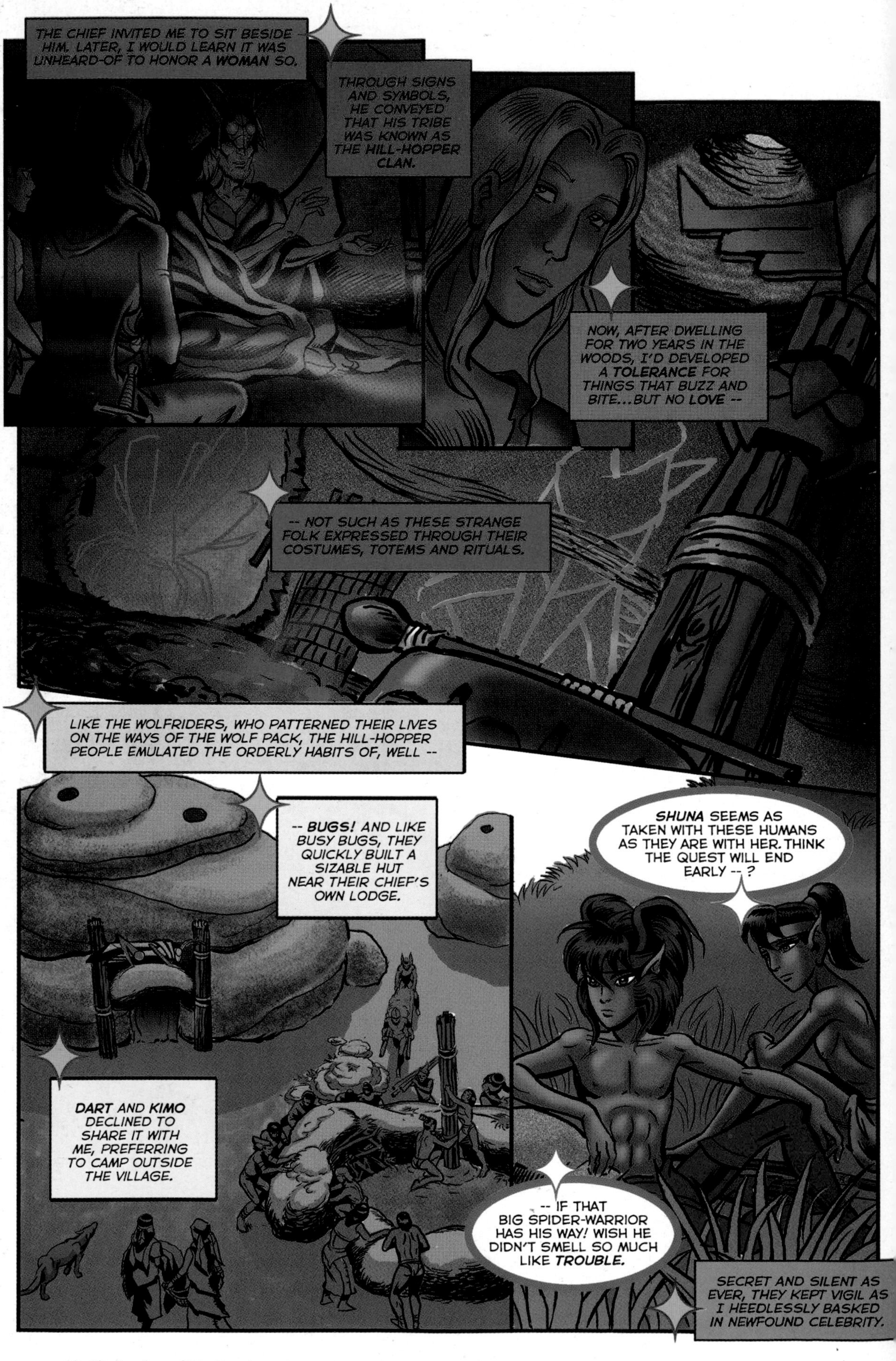
THE CHIEF INVITED ME TO SIT BESIDE HIM. LATER, I WOULD LEARN IT WAS UNHEARD-OF TO HONOR A WOMAN SO.
THROUGH SIGNS AND SYMBOLS, HE CONVEYED THAT HIS TRIBE WAS KNOWN AS THE HILL-HOPPER CLAN.
NOW, AFTER DWELLING FOR TWO YEARS IN THE WOODS, I'D DEVELOPED A TOLERANCE FOR THINGS THAT BUZZ AND BITE...BUT NO LOVE --
-- NOT SUCH AS THESE STRANGE FOLK EXPRESSED THROUGH THEIR COSTUMES, TOTEMS AND RITUALS.
LIKE THE WOLFRIDERS, WHO PATTERNED THEIR LIVES ON THE WAYS OF THE WOLF PACK, THE HILL-HOPPER PEOPLE EMULATED THE ORDERLY HABITS OF, WELL --
-- BUGS! AND LIKE BUSY BUGS, THEY QUICKLY BUILT A SIZABLE HUT NEAR THEIR CHIEF'S OWN LODGE.
DART AND KIMO DECLINED TO SHARE IT WITH ME, PREFERRING TO CAMP OUTSIDE THE VILLAGE.
SHUNA SEEMS AS TAKEN WITH THESE HUMANS AS THEY ARE WITH HER. THINK THE QUEST WILL END EARLY -- ?
-- IF THAT BIG SPIDER-WARRIOR HAS HIS WAY! WISH HE DIDN'T SMELL SO MUCH LIKE TROUBLE.
SECRET AND SILENT AS EVER, THEY KEPT VIGIL AS I HEEDLESSLY BASKED IN NEWFOUND CELEBRITY.

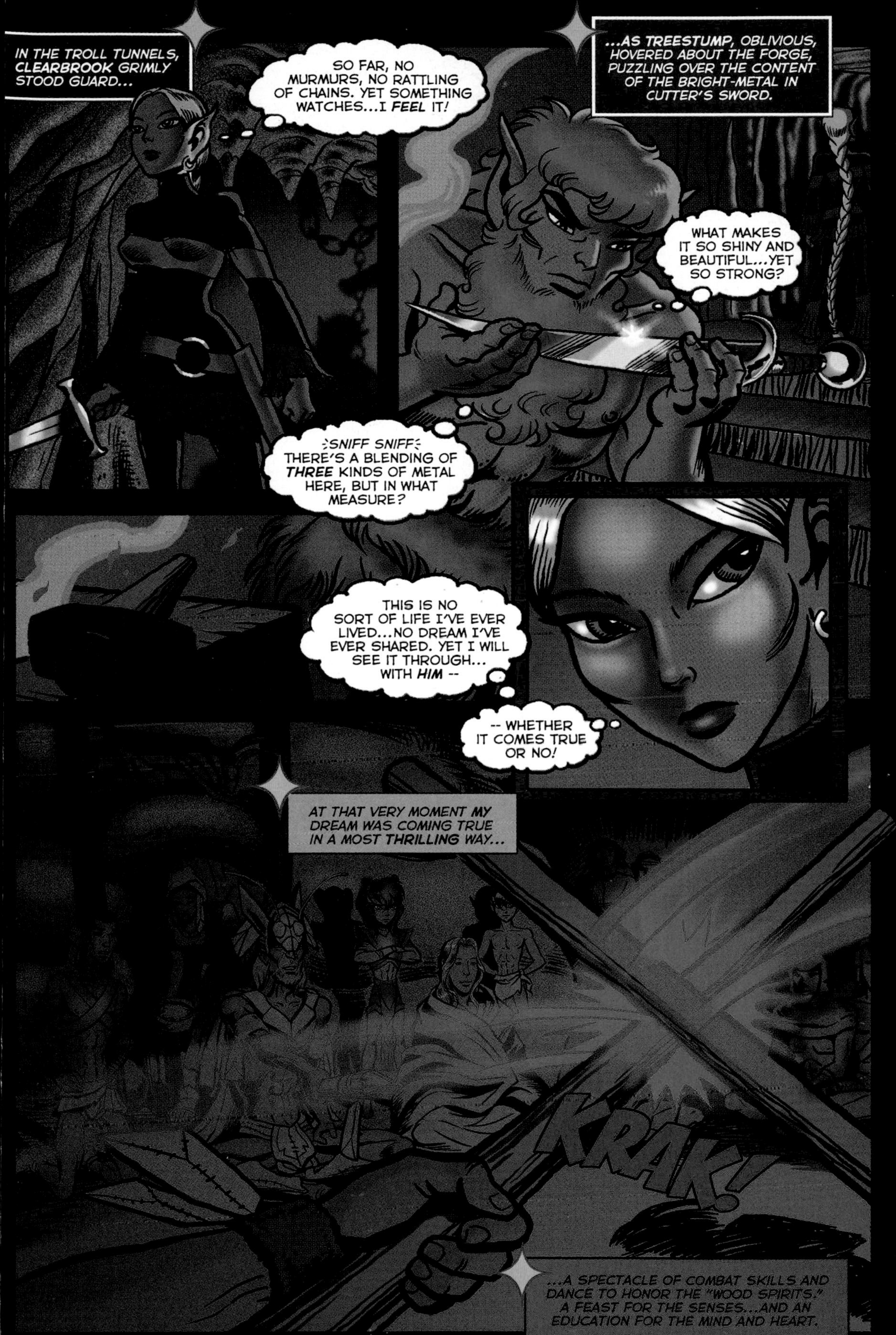
IN THE TROLL TUNNELS, CLEARBROOK GRIMLY STOOD GUARD...
SO FAR, NO MURMURS, NO RATTLING OF CHAINS. YET SOMETHING WATCHES...I FEEL IT!
...AS TREESTUMP, OBLIVIOUS, HOVERED ABOUT THE FORGE, PUZZLING OVER THE CONTENT OF THE BRIGHT-METAL IN CUTTER'S SWORD.
WHAT MAKES IT SO SHINY AND BEAUTIFUL...YET SO STRONG?
SNIFF SNIFF THERE'S A BLENDING OF THREE KINDS OF METAL HERE, BUT IN WHAT MEASURE?
THIS IS NO SORT OF LIFE I'VE EVER LIVED...NO DREAM I'VE EVER SHARED. YET I WILL SEE IT THROUGH... WITH HIM --
-- WHETHER IT COMES TRUE OR NO!
AT THAT VERY MOMENT MY DREAM WAS COMING TRUE IN A MOST THRILLING WAY...
KRAK!
...A SPECTACLE OF COMBAT SKILLS AND DANCE TO HONOR THE "WOOD SPIRITS." A FEAST FOR THE SENSES...AND AN EDUCATION FOR THE MIND AND HEART.

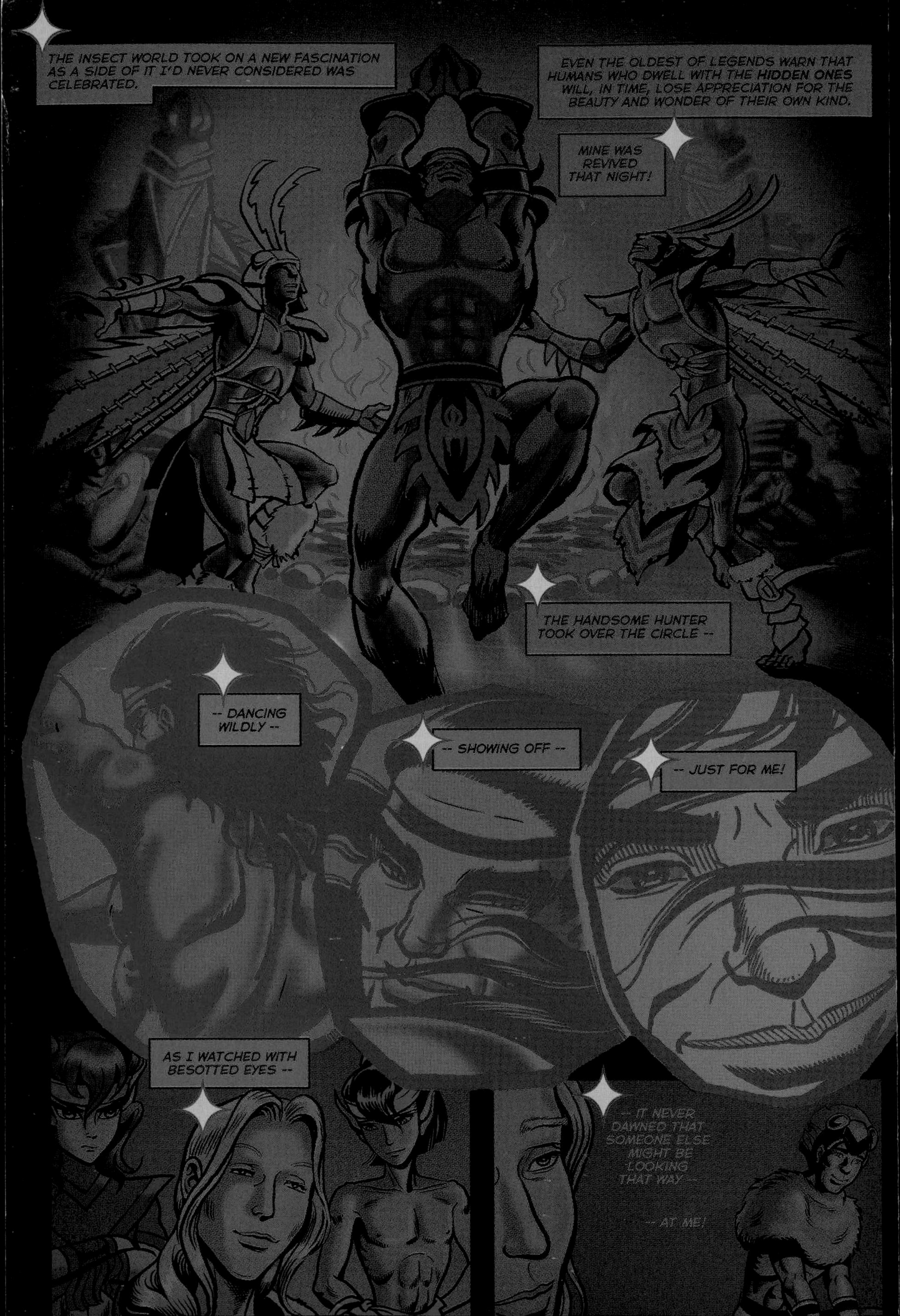
THE INSECT WORLD TOOK ON A NEW FASCINATION AS A SIDE OF IT I'D NEVER CONSIDERED WAS CELEBRATED.
EVEN THE OLDEST OF LEGENDS WARN THAT HUMANS WHO DWELL WITH THE HIDDEN ONES WILL, IN TIME, LOSE APPRECIATION FOR THE BEAUTY AND WONDER OF THEIR OWN KIND.
MINE WAS REVIVED THAT NIGHT!
THE HANDSOME HUNTER TOOK OVER THE CIRCLE --
-- DANCING WILDLY --
-- SHOWING OFF --
-- JUST FOR ME!
AS I WATCHED WITH BESOTTED EYES --
-- IT NEVER DAWNED THAT SOMEONE ELSE MIGHT BE LOOKING THAT WAY--
-- AT ME!

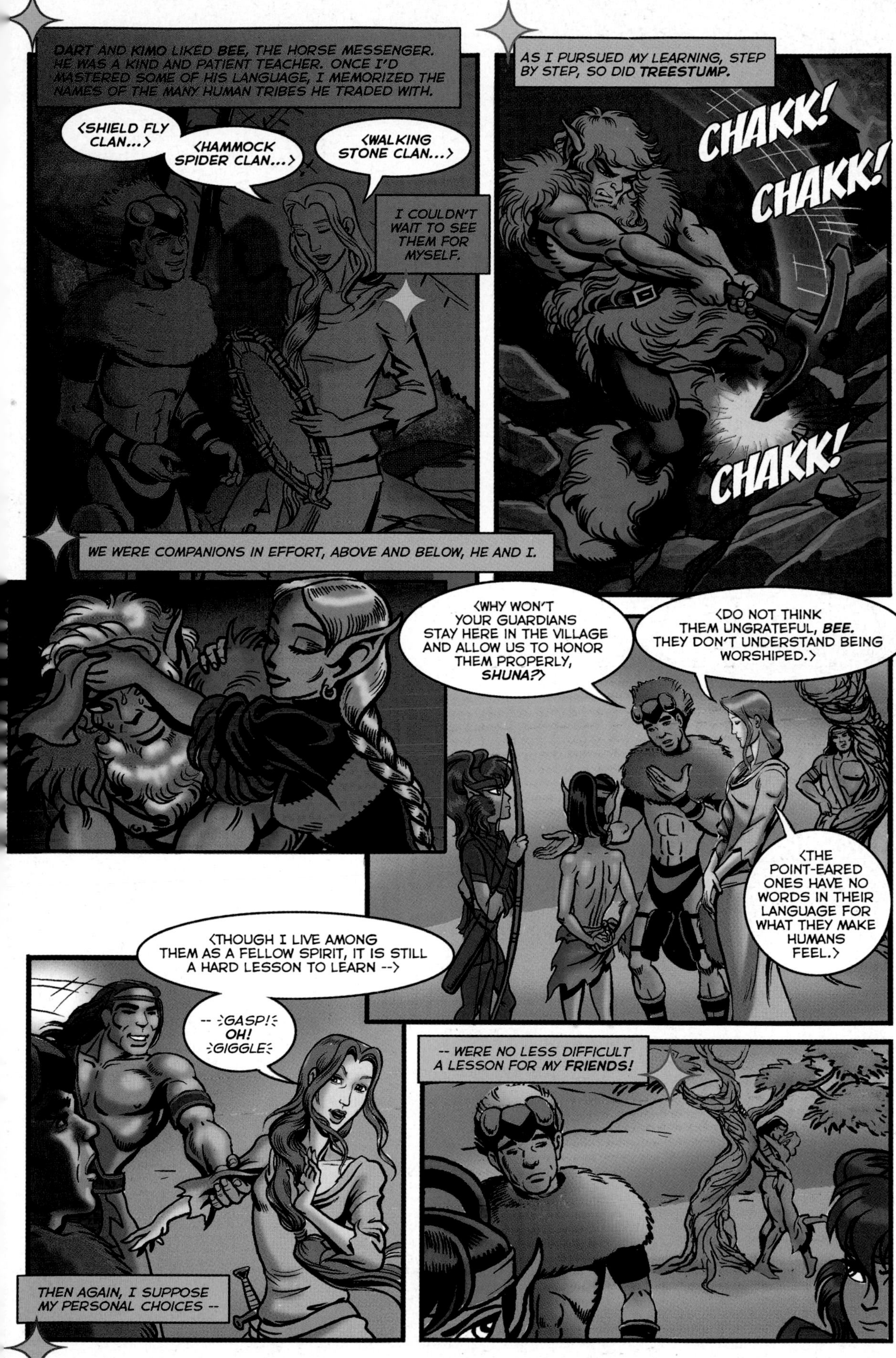
DART AND KIMO LIKED BEE, THE HORSE MESSENGER. HE WAS A KIND AND PATIENT TEACHER. ONCE I'D MASTERED SOME OF HIS LANGUAGE, I MEMORIZED THE NAMES OF THE MANY HUMAN TRIBES HE TRADED WITH.
<SHIELD FLY CLAN...>
<HAMMOCK SPIDER CLAN...>
<WALKING STONE CLAN...>
I COULDN'T WAIT TO SEE THEM FOR MYSELF.
AS I PURSUED MY LEARNING, STEP BY STEP, SO DID TREESTUMP.
CHAKK!
CHAKK!
CHAKK!
WE WERE COMPANIONS IN EFFORT, ABOVE AND BELOW, HE AND I.
<WHY WON'T YOUR GUARDIANS STAY HERE IN THE VILLAGE AND ALLOW US TO HONOR THEM PROPERLY, SHUNA?>
<DO NOT THINK THEM UNGRATEFUL, BEE. THEY DON'T UNDERSTAND BEING WORSHIPED.>
<THE POINT-EARED ONES HAVE NO WORDS IN THEIR LANGUAGE FOR WHAT THEY MAKE HUMANS FEEL.>
<THOUGH I LIVE AMONG THEM AS A FELLOW SPIRIT, IT IS STILL A HARD LESSON TO LEARN -->
-- GASP! OH! GIGGLE
THEN AGAIN, I SUPPOSE MY PERSONAL CHOICES --
-- WERE NO LESS DIFFICULT A LESSON FOR MY FRIENDS!

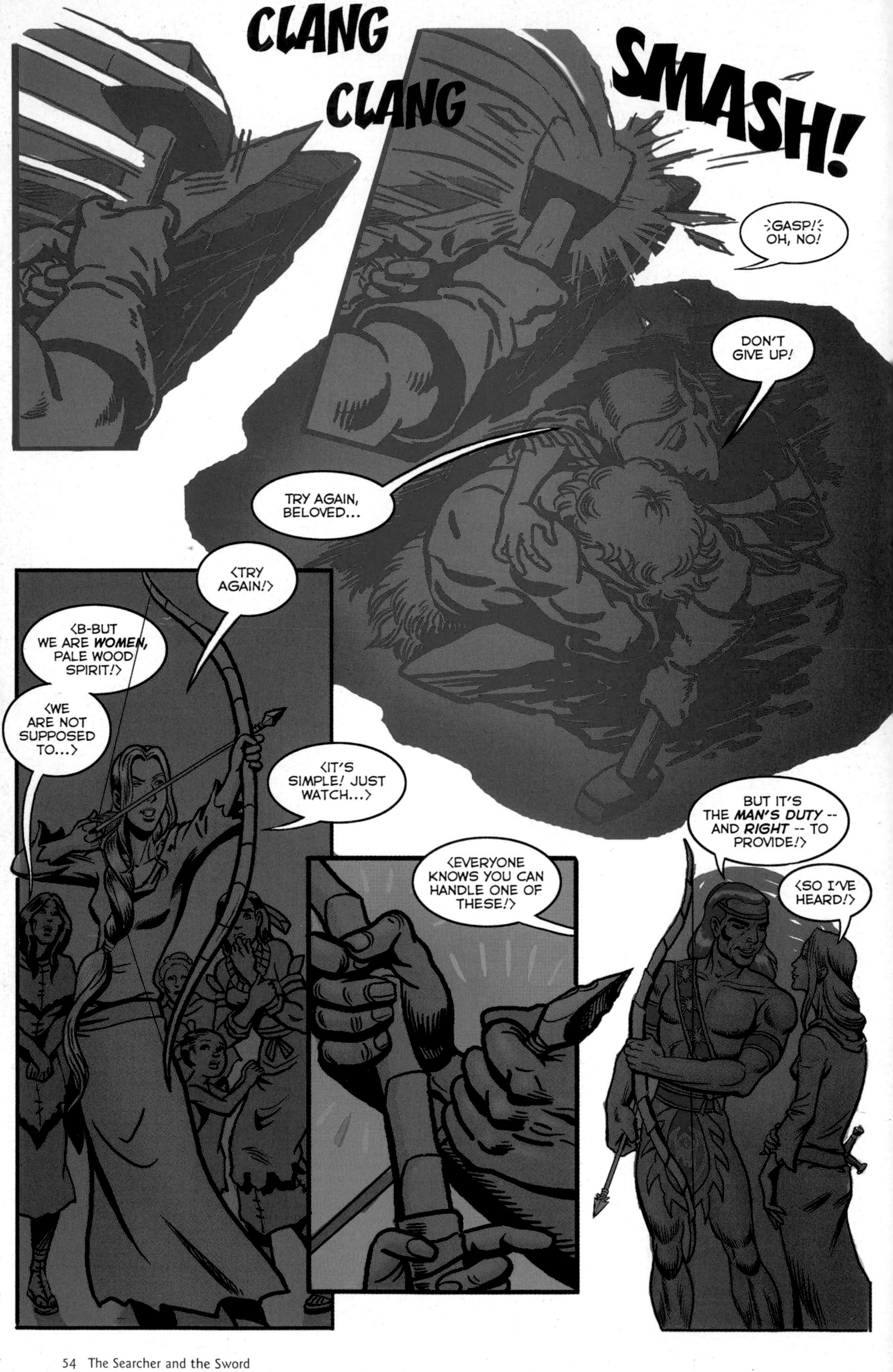
CLANG
CLANG
SMASH!
GASP! OH, NO!
DON'T GIVE UP!
TRY AGAIN, BELOVED...
<TRY AGAIN!>
<B-BUT WE ARE WOMEN, PALE WOOD SPIRIT!>
<WE ARE NOT SUPPOSED TO...>
<IT'S SIMPLE! JUST WATCH...>
<EVERYONE KNOWS YOU CAN HANDLE ONE OF THESE!>
BUT IT'S THE MAN'S DUTY -- AND RIGHT -- TO PROVIDE!>
<SO I'VE HEARD!>

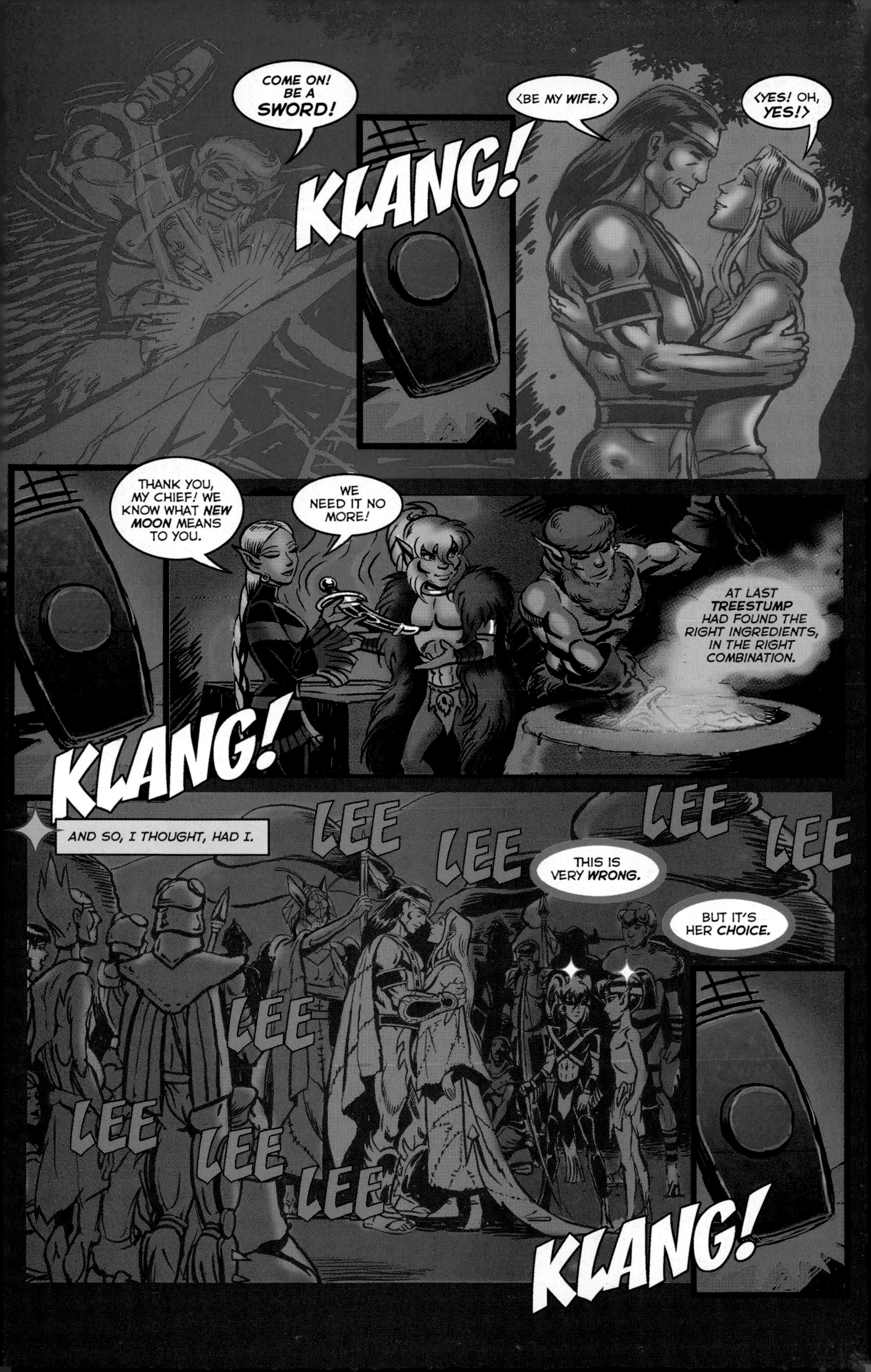
COME ON! BE A SWORD!
KLANG!
‹BE MY WIFE.›
‹YES! OH, YES!›
THANK YOU, MY CHIEF! WE KNOW WHAT NEW MOON MEANS TO YOU.
WE NEED IT NO MORE!
AT LAST TREESTUMP HAD FOUND THE RIGHT INGREDIENTS, IN THE RIGHT COMBINATION.
KLANG!
AND SO, I THOUGHT, HAD I.
LEE LEE LEE LEE
THIS IS VERY WRONG.
BUT IT'S HER CHOICE.
LEE LEE LEE LEE
KLANG!

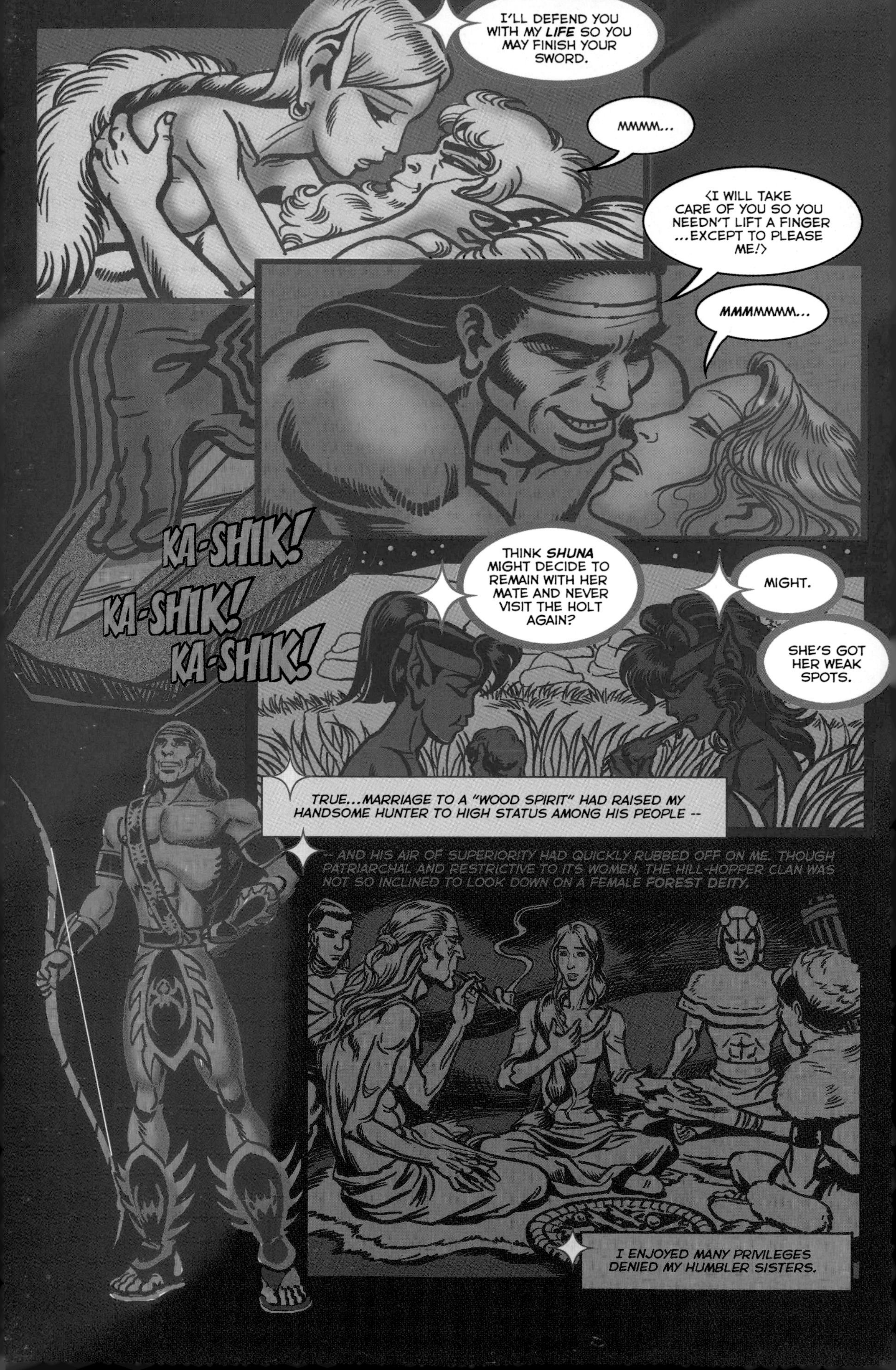
I'LL DEFEND YOU WITH MY *LIFE* SO YOU MAY FINISH YOUR SWORD.
MMMM...
<I WILL TAKE CARE OF YOU SO YOU NEEDN'T LIFT A FINGER ...EXCEPT TO PLEASE ME!>
MMMMMMM...
KA-SHIK! KA-SHIK! KA-SHIK!
THINK *SHUNA* MIGHT DECIDE TO REMAIN WITH HER MATE AND NEVER VISIT THE HOLT AGAIN?
MIGHT.
SHE'S GOT HER WEAK SPOTS.
TRUE...MARRIAGE TO A "WOOD SPIRIT" HAD RAISED MY HANDSOME HUNTER TO HIGH STATUS AMONG HIS PEOPLE --
-- AND HIS AIR OF SUPERIORITY HAD QUICKLY RUBBED OFF ON ME. THOUGH PATRIARCHAL AND RESTRICTIVE TO ITS WOMEN, THE HILL-HOPPER CLAN WAS NOT SO INCLINED TO LOOK DOWN ON A FEMALE *FOREST DEITY.*
I ENJOYED MANY PRIVILEGES DENIED MY HUMBLER SISTERS.

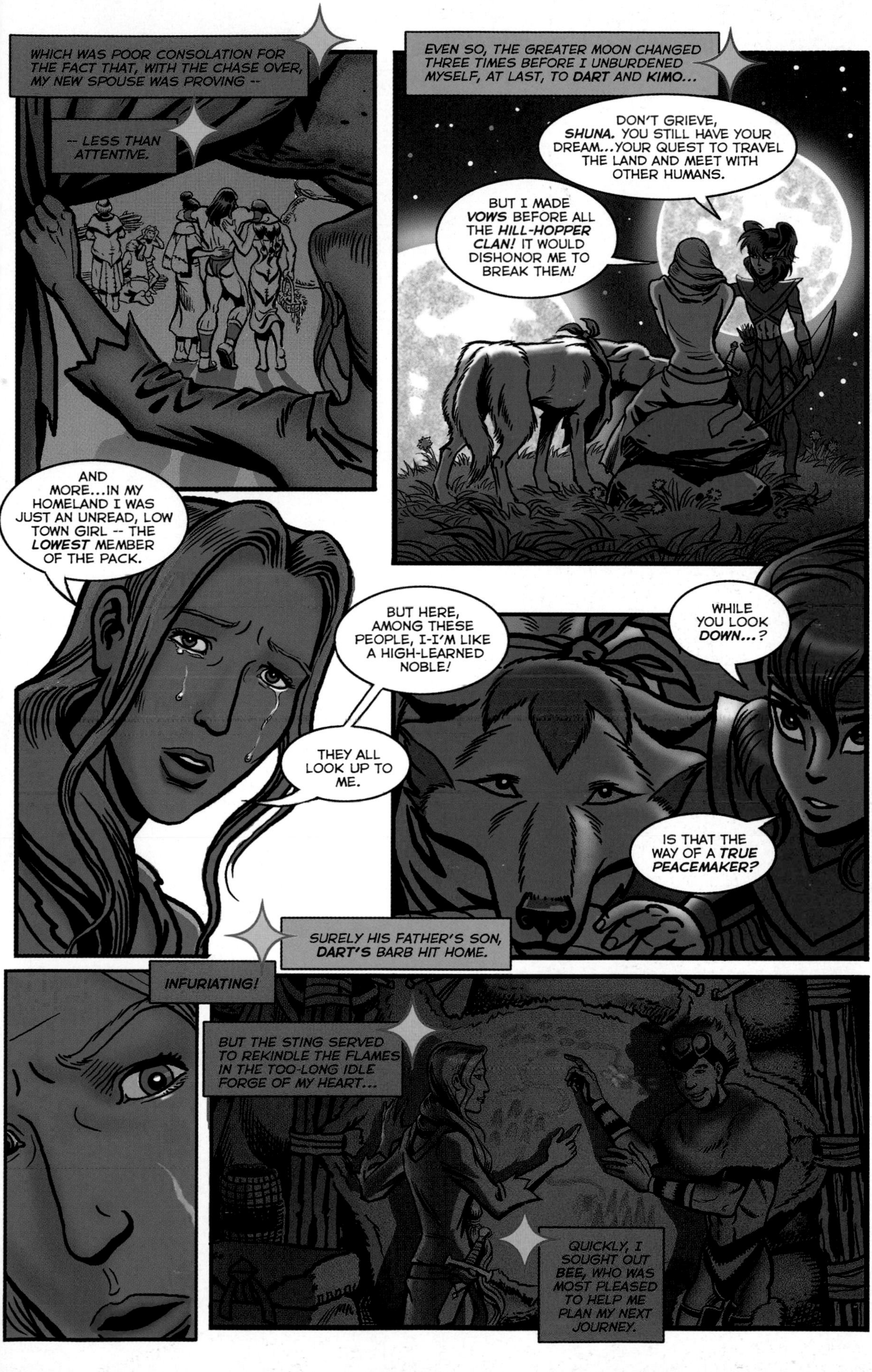
WHICH WAS POOR CONSOLATION FOR THE FACT THAT, WITH THE CHASE OVER, MY NEW SPOUSE WAS PROVING --
-- LESS THAN ATTENTIVE.
EVEN SO, THE GREATER MOON CHANGED THREE TIMES BEFORE I UNBURDENED MYSELF, AT LAST, TO DART AND KIMO...
DON'T GRIEVE, SHUNA. YOU STILL HAVE YOUR DREAM...YOUR QUEST TO TRAVEL THE LAND AND MEET WITH OTHER HUMANS.
BUT I MADE VOWS BEFORE ALL THE HILL-HOPPER CLAN! IT WOULD DISHONOR ME TO BREAK THEM!
AND MORE...IN MY HOMELAND I WAS JUST AN UNREAD, LOW TOWN GIRL -- THE LOWEST MEMBER OF THE PACK.
BUT HERE, AMONG THESE PEOPLE, I-I'M LIKE A HIGH-LEARNED NOBLE!
THEY ALL LOOK UP TO ME.
WHILE YOU LOOK DOWN...?
IS THAT THE WAY OF A TRUE PEACEMAKER?
SURELY HIS FATHER'S SON, DART'S BARB HIT HOME.
INFURIATING!
BUT THE STING SERVED TO REKINDLE THE FLAMES IN THE TOO-LONG IDLE FORGE OF MY HEART...
QUICKLY, I SOUGHT OUT BEE, WHO WAS MOST PLEASED TO HELP ME PLAN MY NEXT JOURNEY.

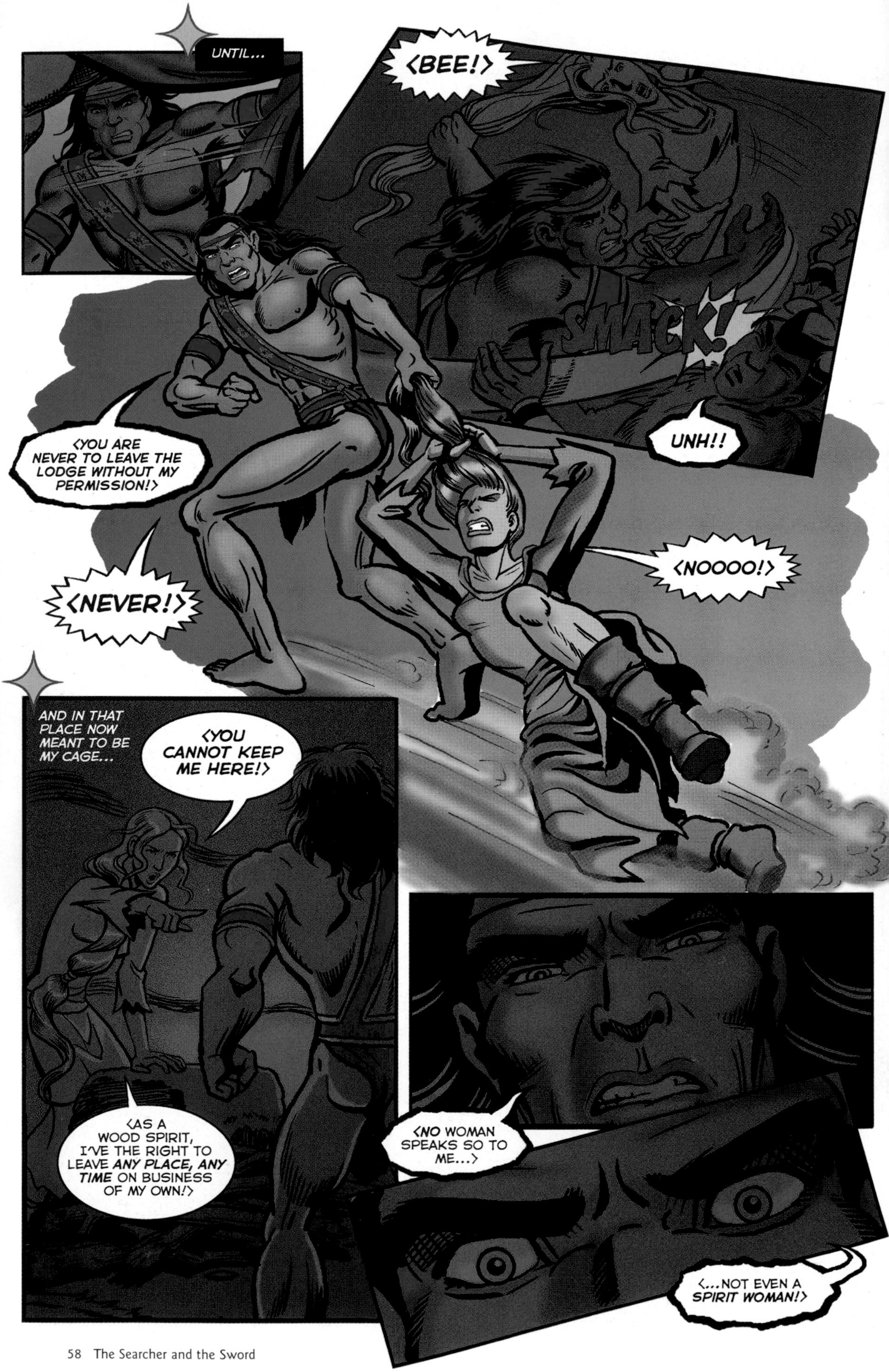
UNTIL...
<BEE!>
SMACK!
UNH!!
<YOU ARE NEVER TO LEAVE THE LODGE WITHOUT MY PERMISSION!>
<NEVER!>
<NOOOO!>
AND IN THAT PLACE NOW MEANT TO BE MY CAGE...
<YOU CANNOT KEEP ME HERE!>
<AS A WOOD SPIRIT, I'VE THE RIGHT TO LEAVE ANY PLACE, ANY TIME ON BUSINESS OF MY OWN!>
<NO WOMAN SPEAKS SO TO ME...>
<...NOT EVEN A SPIRIT WOMAN!>

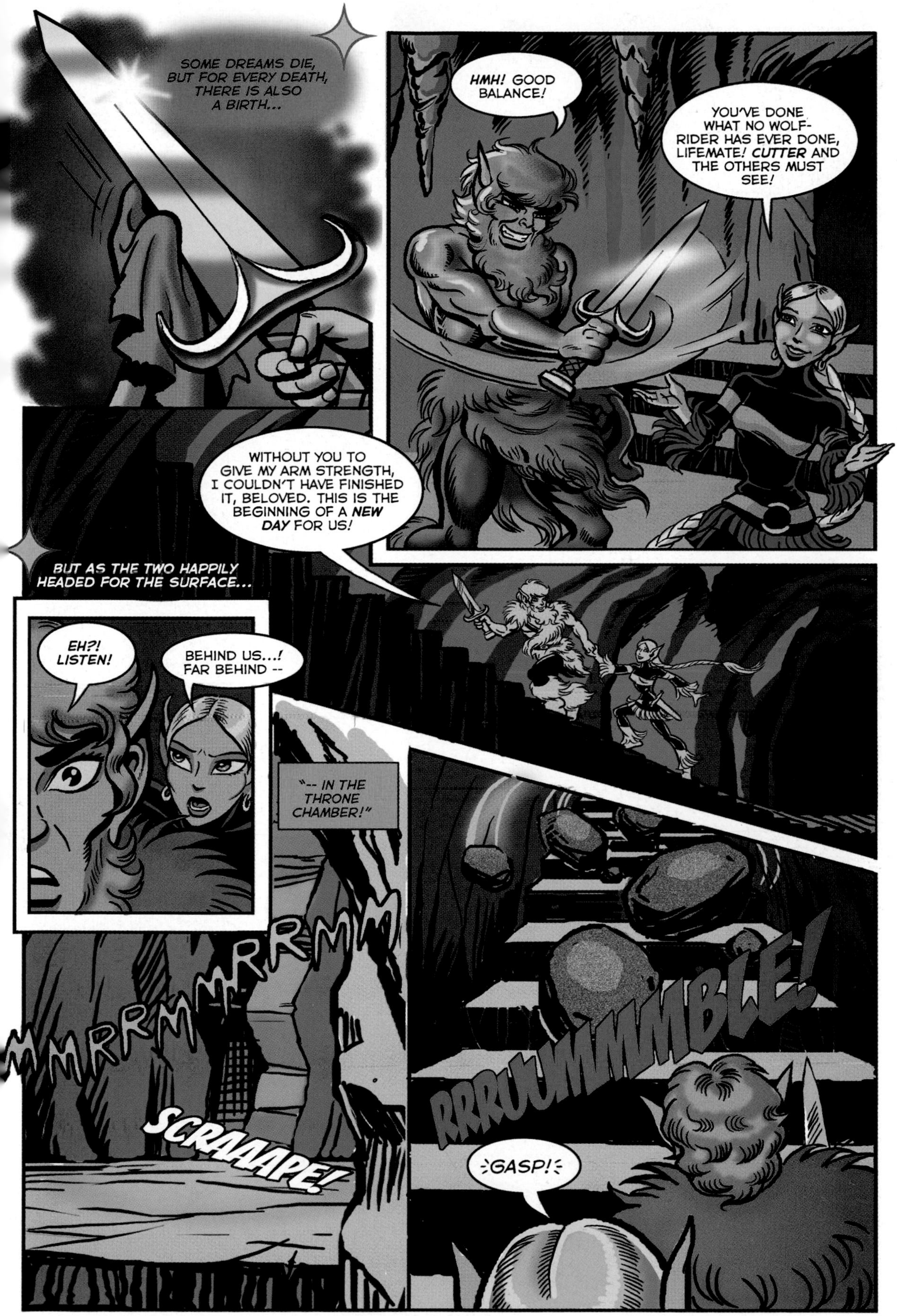
SOME DREAMS DIE, BUT FOR EVERY DEATH, THERE IS ALSO A BIRTH...
HMH! GOOD BALANCE!
YOU'VE DONE WHAT NO WOLF-RIDER HAS EVER DONE, LIFEMATE! CUTTER AND THE OTHERS MUST SEE!
WITHOUT YOU TO GIVE MY ARM STRENGTH, I COULDN'T HAVE FINISHED IT, BELOVED. THIS IS THE BEGINNING OF A NEW DAY FOR US!
BUT AS THE TWO HAPPILY HEADED FOR THE SURFACE...
EH?! LISTEN!
BEHIND US...! FAR BEHIND --
"-- IN THE THRONE CHAMBER!"
MMRRRMMRRRMMM
SCRAAAAPE!
RRRUUMMMMBLE!
GASP!

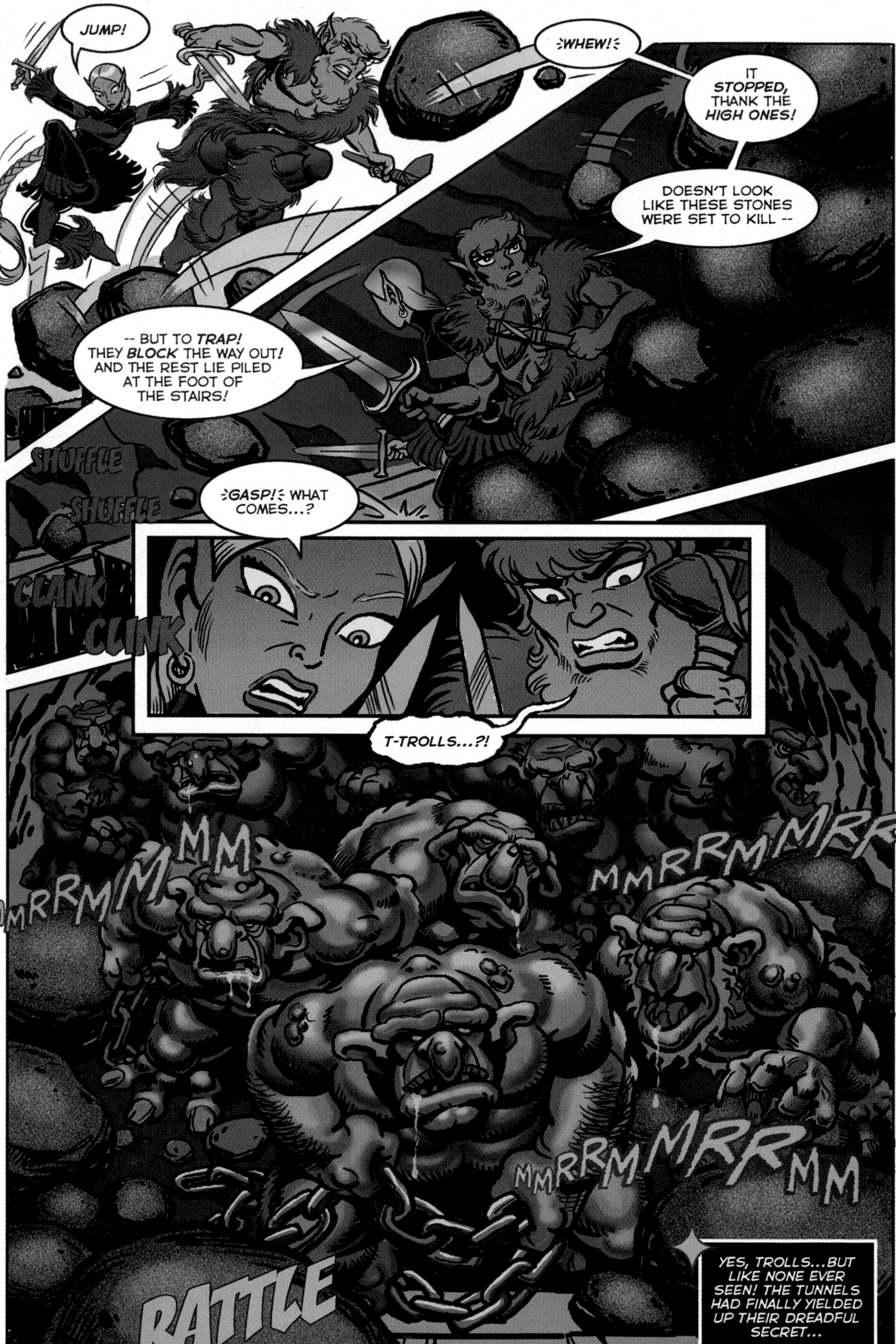
JUMP!
WHEW!
IT STOPPED, THANK THE HIGH ONES!
DOESN'T LOOK LIKE THESE STONES WERE SET TO KILL --
-- BUT TO TRAP! THEY BLOCK THE WAY OUT! AND THE REST LIE PILED AT THE FOOT OF THE STAIRS!
SHUFFLE
SHUFFLE
CLANK
CLINK
GASP! WHAT COMES...?
T-TROLLS...?!
MMRRMMMM
MMRRMMMRR
MMRRMMRRMM
RATTLE
YES, TROLLS...BUT LIKE NONE EVER SEEN! THE TUNNELS HAD FINALLY YIELDED UP THEIR DREADFUL SECRET...

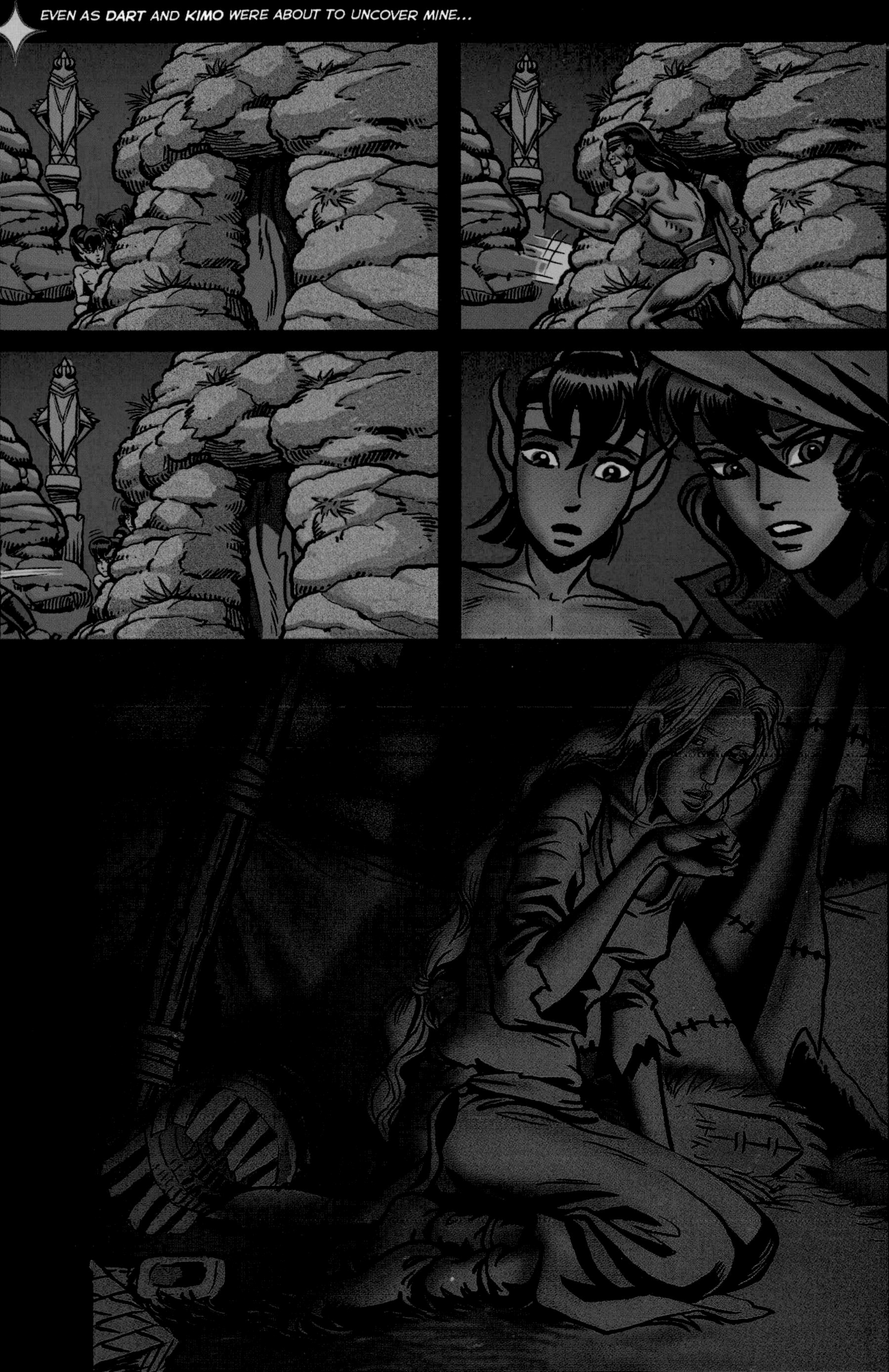
EVEN AS DART AND KIMO WERE ABOUT TO UNCOVER MINE...

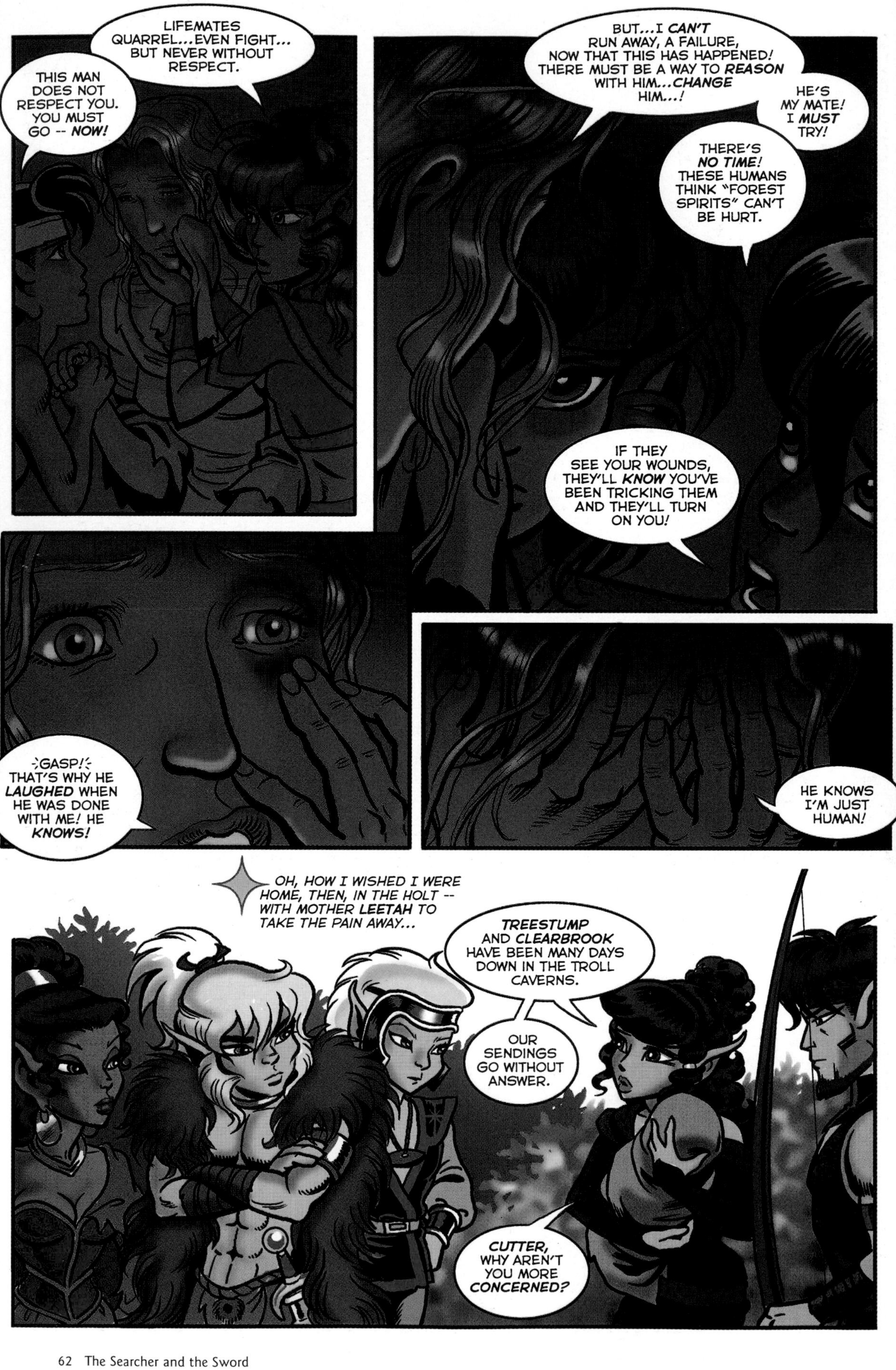
LIFEMATES QUARREL...EVEN FIGHT... BUT NEVER WITHOUT RESPECT.
THIS MAN DOES NOT RESPECT YOU. YOU MUST GO -- NOW!
BUT...I CAN'T RUN AWAY, A FAILURE, NOW THAT THIS HAS HAPPENED! THERE MUST BE A WAY TO REASON WITH HIM...CHANGE HIM...!
HE'S MY MATE! I MUST TRY!
THERE'S NO TIME! THESE HUMANS THINK "FOREST SPIRITS" CAN'T BE HURT.
IF THEY SEE YOUR WOUNDS, THEY'LL KNOW YOU'VE BEEN TRICKING THEM AND THEY'LL TURN ON YOU!
GASP! THAT'S WHY HE LAUGHED WHEN HE WAS DONE WITH ME! HE KNOWS!
HE KNOWS I'M JUST HUMAN!
OH, HOW I WISHED I WERE HOME, THEN, IN THE HOLT -- WITH MOTHER LEETAH TO TAKE THE PAIN AWAY...
TREESTUMP AND CLEARBROOK HAVE BEEN MANY DAYS DOWN IN THE TROLL CAVERNS.
OUR SENDINGS GO WITHOUT ANSWER.
CUTTER, WHY AREN'T YOU MORE CONCERNED?

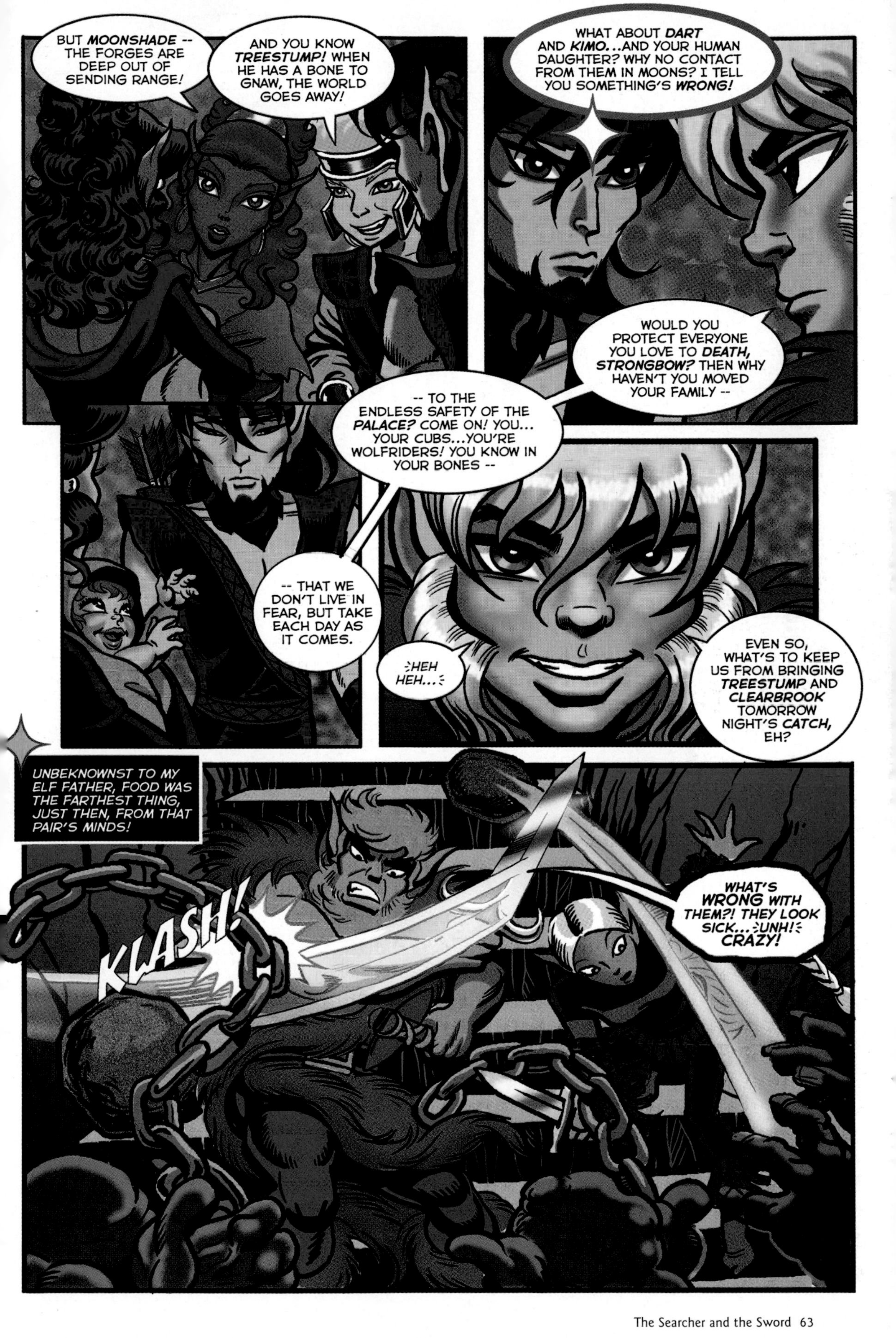
BUT MOONSHADE -- THE FORGES ARE DEEP OUT OF SENDING RANGE!
AND YOU KNOW TREESTUMP! WHEN HE HAS A BONE TO GNAW, THE WORLD GOES AWAY!
WHAT ABOUT DART AND KIMO...AND YOUR HUMAN DAUGHTER? WHY NO CONTACT FROM THEM IN MOONS? I TELL YOU SOMETHING'S WRONG!
WOULD YOU PROTECT EVERYONE YOU LOVE TO DEATH, STRONGBOW? THEN WHY HAVEN'T YOU MOVED YOUR FAMILY --
-- TO THE ENDLESS SAFETY OF THE PALACE? COME ON! YOU... YOUR CUBS...YOU'RE WOLFRIDERS! YOU KNOW IN YOUR BONES --
-- THAT WE DON'T LIVE IN FEAR, BUT TAKE EACH DAY AS IT COMES.
HEH HEH...
EVEN SO, WHAT'S TO KEEP US FROM BRINGING TREESTUMP AND CLEARBROOK TOMORROW NIGHT'S CATCH, EH?
UNBEKNOWNST TO MY ELF FATHER, FOOD WAS THE FARTHEST THING, JUST THEN, FROM THAT PAIR'S MINDS!
KLASH!
WHAT'S WRONG WITH THEM?! THEY LOOK SICK... UNH! CRAZY!

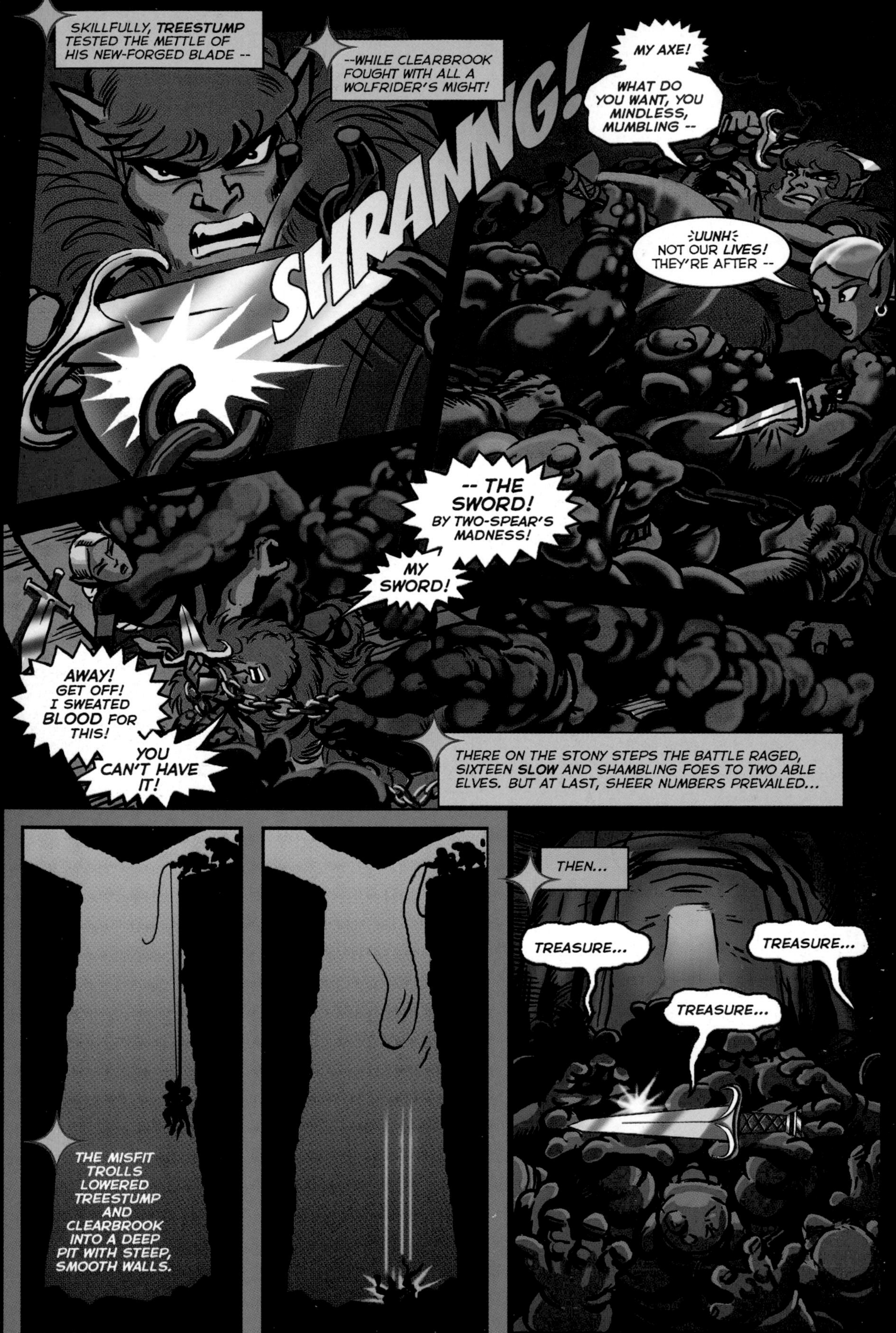
SKILLFULLY, TREESTUMP TESTED THE METTLE OF HIS NEW-FORGED BLADE --
--WHILE CLEARBROOK FOUGHT WITH ALL A WOLFRIDER'S MIGHT!
SHRANNG!
MY AXE!
WHAT DO YOU WANT, YOU MINDLESS, MUMBLING --
UUNH NOT OUR LIVES! THEY'RE AFTER --
-- THE SWORD! BY TWO-SPEAR'S MADNESS!
MY SWORD!
AWAY! GET OFF! I SWEATED BLOOD FOR THIS!
YOU CAN'T HAVE IT!
THERE ON THE STONY STEPS THE BATTLE RAGED, SIXTEEN SLOW AND SHAMBLING FOES TO TWO ABLE ELVES. BUT AT LAST, SHEER NUMBERS PREVAILED...
THE MISFIT TROLLS LOWERED TREESTUMP AND CLEARBROOK INTO A DEEP PIT WITH STEEP, SMOOTH WALLS.
THEN...
TREASURE...
TREASURE...
TREASURE...

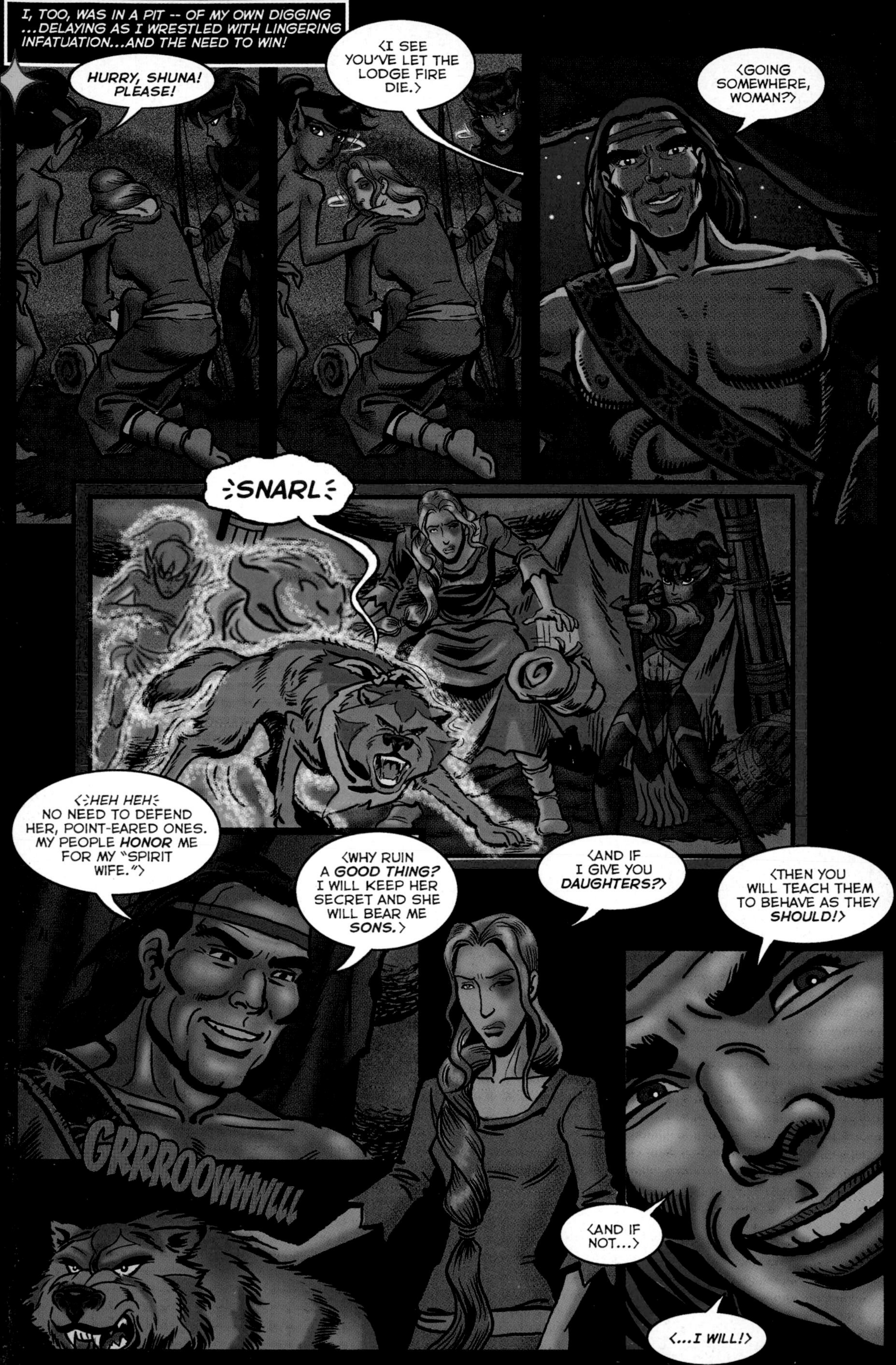

I, TOO, WAS IN A PIT -- OF MY OWN DIGGING ...DELAYING AS I WRESTLED WITH LINGERING INFATUATION...AND THE NEED TO WIN!
HURRY, SHUNA! PLEASE!
<I SEE YOU'VE LET THE LODGE FIRE DIE.>
<GOING SOMEWHERE, WOMAN?>
SNARL
<HEH HEH NO NEED TO DEFEND HER, POINT-EARED ONES. MY PEOPLE HONOR ME FOR MY "SPIRIT WIFE.">
<WHY RUIN A GOOD THING? I WILL KEEP HER SECRET AND SHE WILL BEAR ME SONS.>
<AND IF I GIVE YOU DAUGHTERS?>
<THEN YOU WILL TEACH THEM TO BEHAVE AS THEY SHOULD!>
GRRROOWWWLLL
<AND IF NOT...>
<...I WILL!>

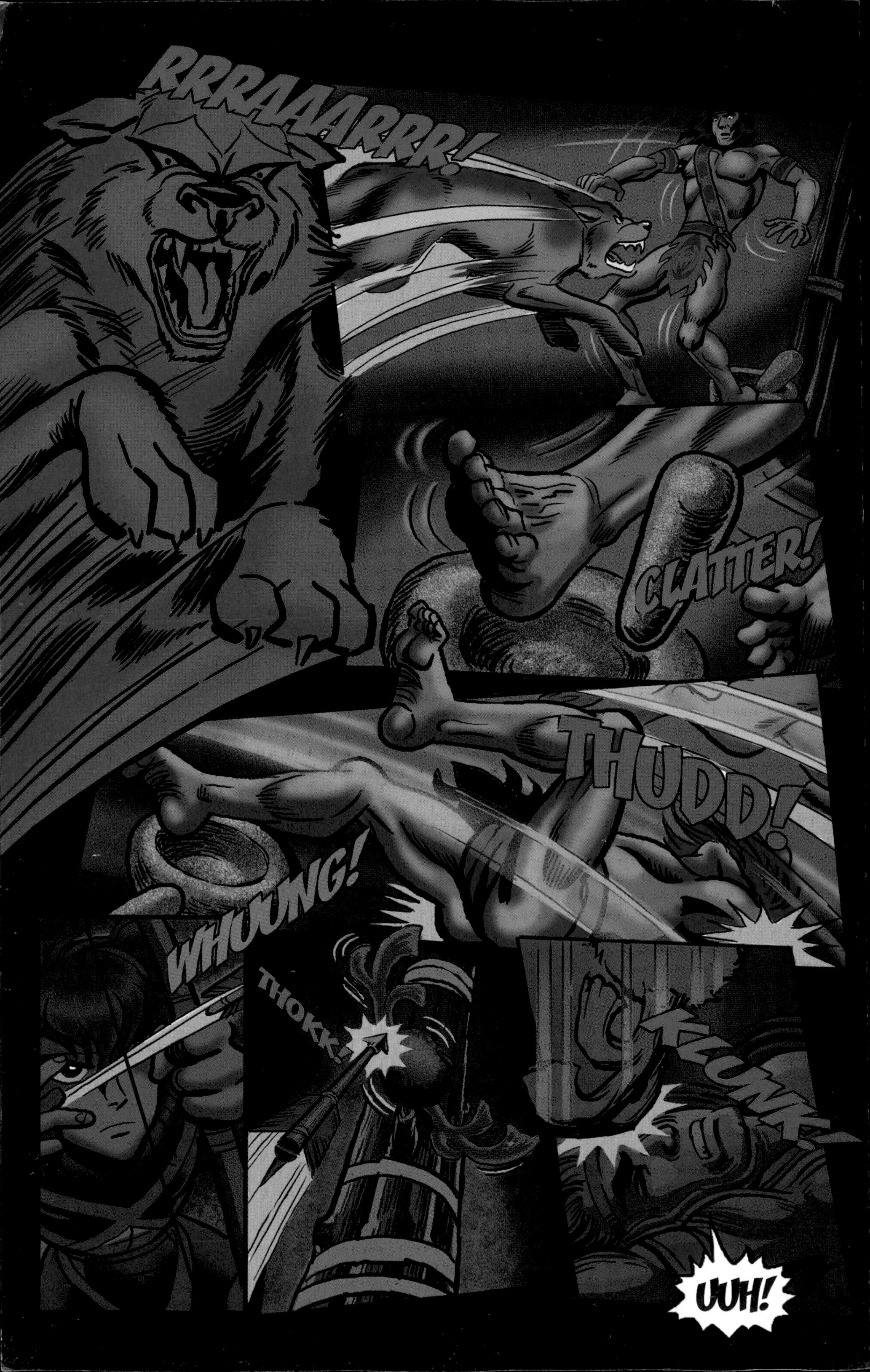
RRRAAAARRRR!
CLATTER!
THUDD!
WHOUNG!
THOKK!
KLUNK!
UUH!

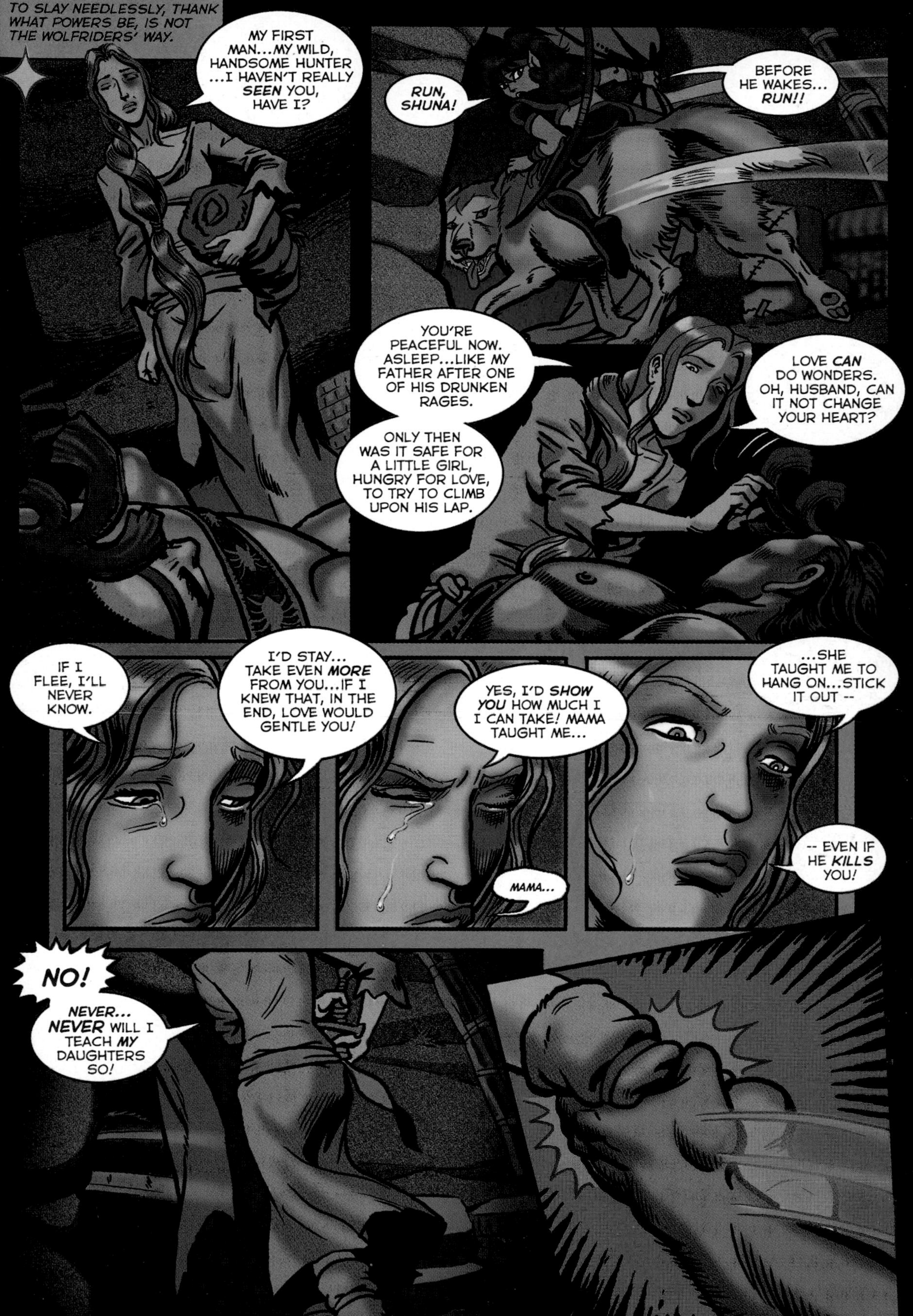
TO SLAY NEEDLESSLY, THANK WHAT POWERS BE, IS NOT THE WOLFRIDERS' WAY.
MY FIRST MAN...MY WILD, HANDSOME HUNTER ...I HAVEN'T REALLY SEEN YOU, HAVE I?
RUN, SHUNA!
BEFORE HE WAKES... RUN!!
YOU'RE PEACEFUL NOW. ASLEEP...LIKE MY FATHER AFTER ONE OF HIS DRUNKEN RAGES.
ONLY THEN WAS IT SAFE FOR A LITTLE GIRL, HUNGRY FOR LOVE, TO TRY TO CLIMB UPON HIS LAP.
LOVE CAN DO WONDERS. OH, HUSBAND, CAN IT NOT CHANGE YOUR HEART?
IF I FLEE, I'LL NEVER KNOW.
I'D STAY... TAKE EVEN MORE FROM YOU...IF I KNEW THAT, IN THE END, LOVE WOULD GENTLE YOU!
YES, I'D SHOW YOU HOW MUCH I I CAN TAKE! MAMA TAUGHT ME...
MAMA...
...SHE TAUGHT ME TO HANG ON...STICK IT OUT --
-- EVEN IF HE KILLS YOU!
NO!
NEVER... NEVER WILL I TEACH MY DAUGHTERS SO!

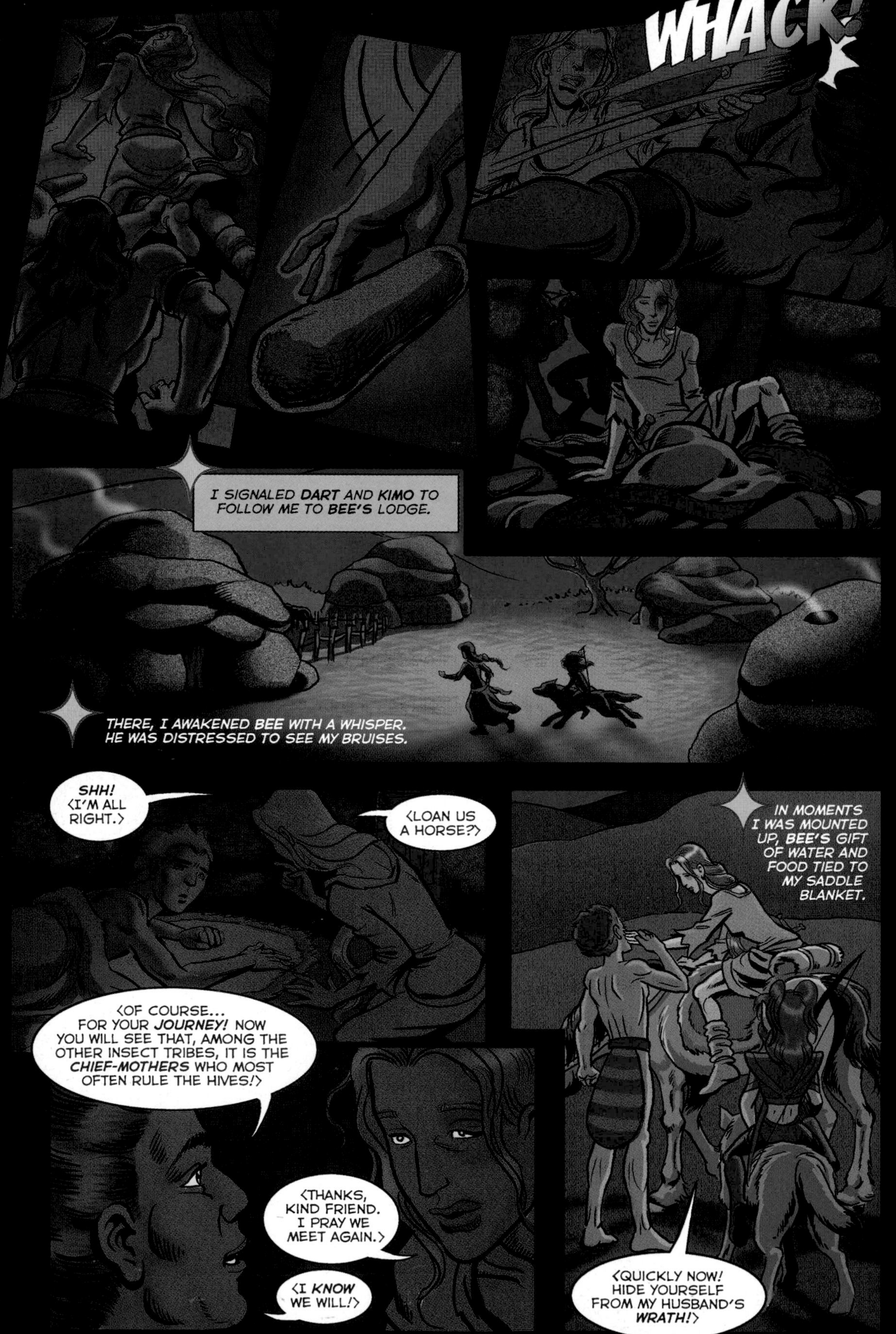
WHACK!
I SIGNALED DART AND KIMO TO FOLLOW ME TO BEE'S LODGE.
THERE, I AWAKENED BEE WITH A WHISPER. HE WAS DISTRESSED TO SEE MY BRUISES.
SHH! <I'M ALL RIGHT.>
<LOAN US A HORSE?>
<OF COURSE... FOR YOUR JOURNEY! NOW YOU WILL SEE THAT, AMONG THE OTHER INSECT TRIBES, IT IS THE CHIEF-MOTHERS WHO MOST OFTEN RULE THE HIVES!>
<THANKS, KIND FRIEND. I PRAY WE MEET AGAIN.>
<I KNOW WE WILL!>
IN MOMENTS I WAS MOUNTED UP, BEE'S GIFT OF WATER AND FOOD TIED TO MY SADDLE BLANKET.
<QUICKLY NOW! HIDE YOURSELF FROM MY HUSBAND'S WRATH!>

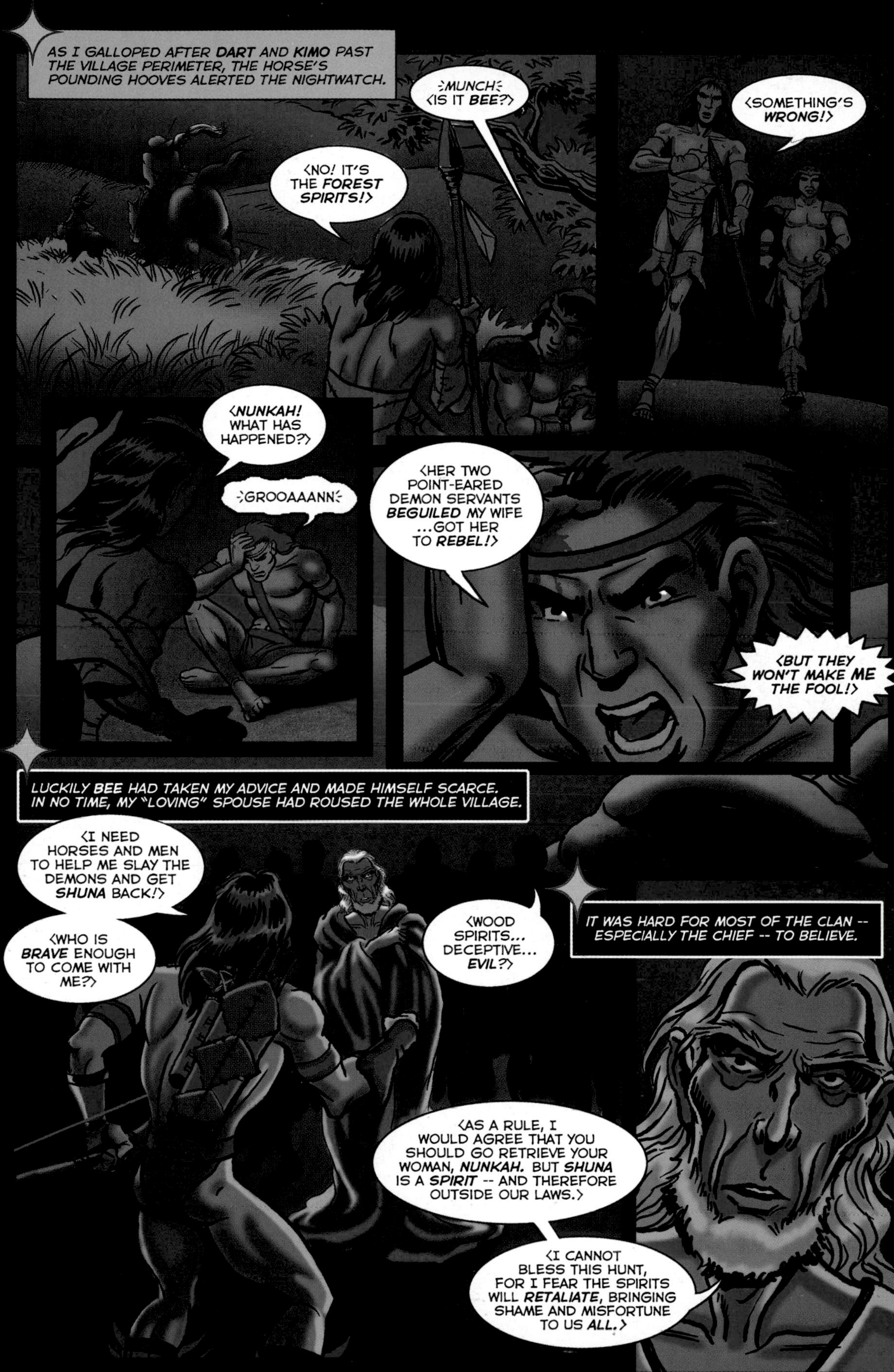
AS I GALLOPED AFTER DART AND KIMO PAST THE VILLAGE PERIMETER, THE HORSE'S POUNDING HOOVES ALERTED THE NIGHTWATCH.
MUNCH
<IS IT BEE?>
<NO! IT'S THE FOREST SPIRITS!>
<SOMETHING'S WRONG!>
<NUNKAH! WHAT HAS HAPPENED?>
GROOAAANN
<HER TWO POINT-EARED DEMON SERVANTS BEGUILED MY WIFE ...GOT HER TO REBEL!>
<BUT THEY WON'T MAKE ME THE FOOL!>
LUCKILY BEE HAD TAKEN MY ADVICE AND MADE HIMSELF SCARCE. IN NO TIME, MY "LOVING" SPOUSE HAD ROUSED THE WHOLE VILLAGE.
<I NEED HORSES AND MEN TO HELP ME SLAY THE DEMONS AND GET SHUNA BACK!>
<WHO IS BRAVE ENOUGH TO COME WITH ME?>
<WOOD SPIRITS... DECEPTIVE... EVIL?>
IT WAS HARD FOR MOST OF THE CLAN -- ESPECIALLY THE CHIEF -- TO BELIEVE.
<AS A RULE, I WOULD AGREE THAT YOU SHOULD GO RETRIEVE YOUR WOMAN, NUNKAH. BUT SHUNA IS A SPIRIT -- AND THEREFORE OUTSIDE OUR LAWS.>
<I CANNOT BLESS THIS HUNT, FOR I FEAR THE SPIRITS WILL RETALIATE, BRINGING SHAME AND MISFORTUNE TO US ALL.>

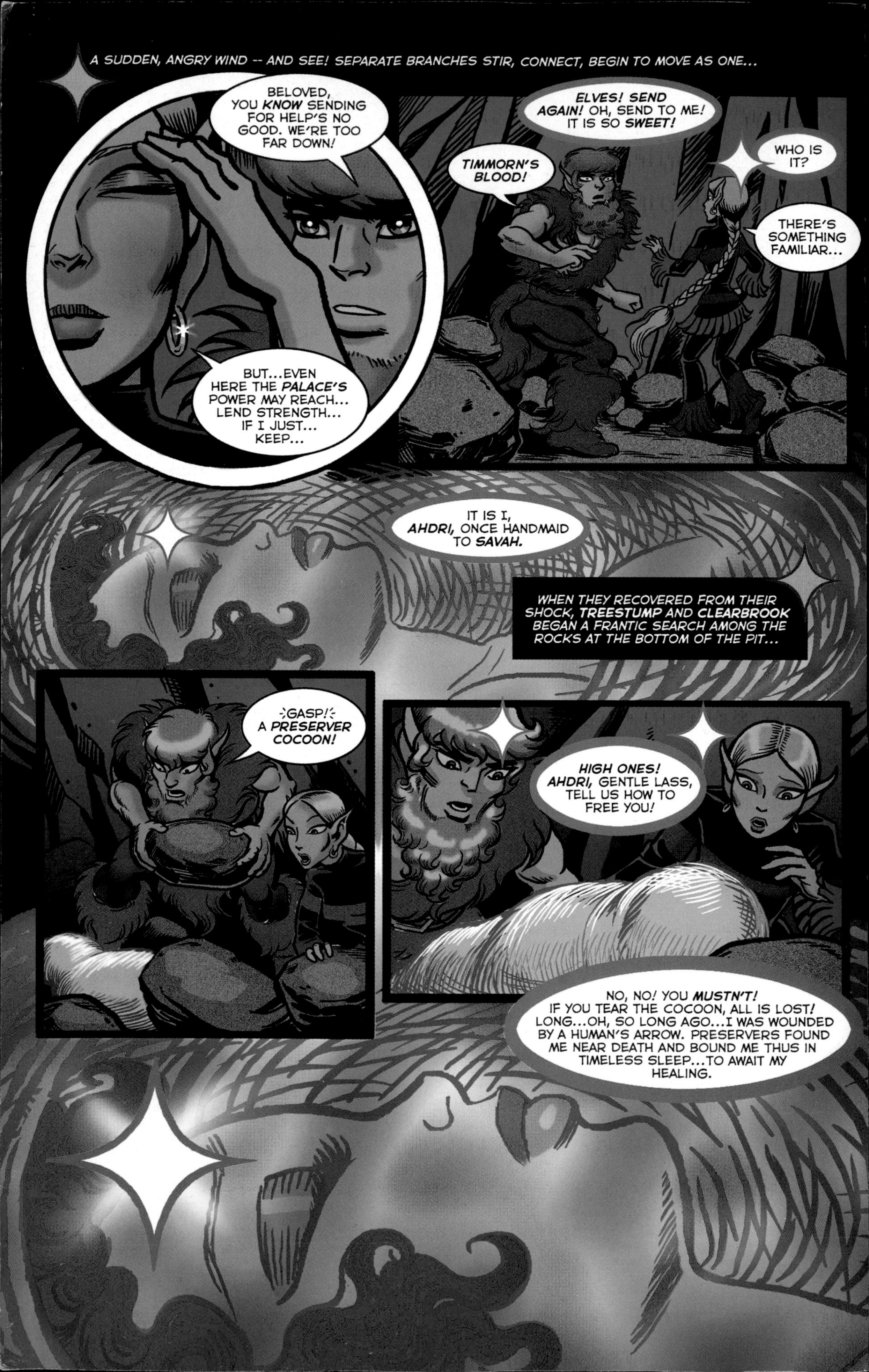
A SUDDEN, ANGRY WIND -- AND SEE! SEPARATE BRANCHES STIR, CONNECT, BEGIN TO MOVE AS ONE...
BELOVED, YOU KNOW SENDING FOR HELP'S NO GOOD. WE'RE TOO FAR DOWN!
BUT...EVEN HERE THE PALACE'S POWER MAY REACH... LEND STRENGTH... IF I JUST... KEEP...
ELVES! SEND AGAIN! OH, SEND TO ME! IT IS SO SWEET!
TIMMORN'S BLOOD!
WHO IS IT?
THERE'S SOMETHING FAMILIAR...
IT IS I, AHDRI, ONCE HANDMAID TO SAVAH.
WHEN THEY RECOVERED FROM THEIR SHOCK, TREESTUMP AND CLEARBROOK BEGAN A FRANTIC SEARCH AMONG THE ROCKS AT THE BOTTOM OF THE PIT...
GASP! A PRESERVER COCOON!
HIGH ONES! AHDRI, GENTLE LASS, TELL US HOW TO FREE YOU!
NO, NO! YOU MUSTN'T! IF YOU TEAR THE COCOON, ALL IS LOST! LONG...OH, SO LONG AGO...I WAS WOUNDED BY A HUMAN'S ARROW. PRESERVERS FOUND ME NEAR DEATH AND BOUND ME THUS IN TIMELESS SLEEP...TO AWAIT MY HEALING.

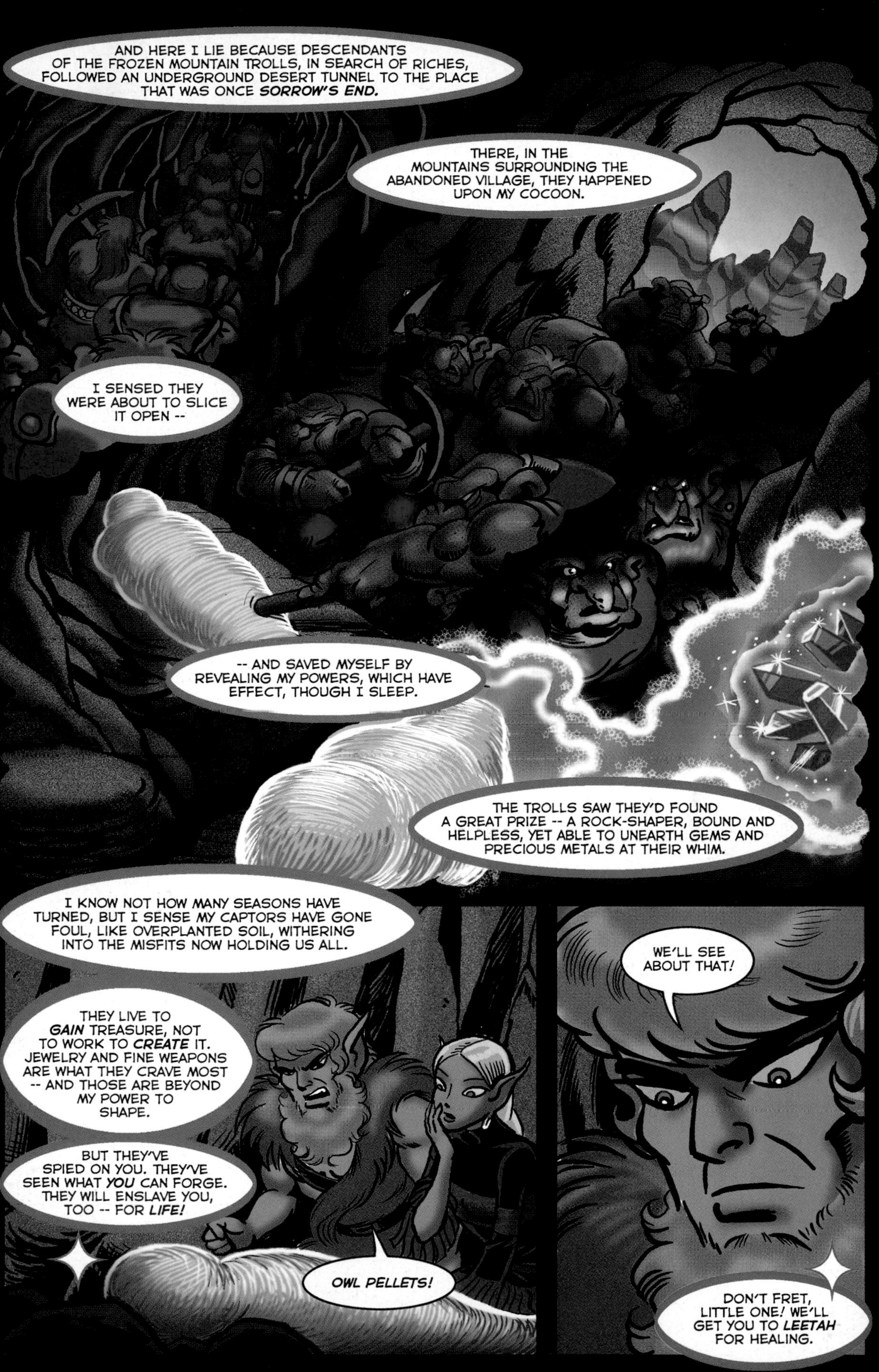
AND HERE I LIE BECAUSE DESCENDANTS OF THE FROZEN MOUNTAIN TROLLS, IN SEARCH OF RICHES, FOLLOWED AN UNDERGROUND DESERT TUNNEL TO THE PLACE THAT WAS ONCE SORROW'S END.
THERE, IN THE MOUNTAINS SURROUNDING THE ABANDONED VILLAGE, THEY HAPPENED UPON MY COCOON.
I SENSED THEY WERE ABOUT TO SLICE IT OPEN --
-- AND SAVED MYSELF BY REVEALING MY POWERS, WHICH HAVE EFFECT, THOUGH I SLEEP.
THE TROLLS SAW THEY'D FOUND A GREAT PRIZE -- A ROCK-SHAPER, BOUND AND HELPLESS, YET ABLE TO UNEARTH GEMS AND PRECIOUS METALS AT THEIR WHIM.
I KNOW NOT HOW MANY SEASONS HAVE TURNED, BUT I SENSE MY CAPTORS HAVE GONE FOUL, LIKE OVERPLANTED SOIL, WITHERING INTO THE MISFITS NOW HOLDING US ALL.
THEY LIVE TO GAIN TREASURE, NOT TO WORK TO CREATE IT. JEWELRY AND FINE WEAPONS ARE WHAT THEY CRAVE MOST -- AND THOSE ARE BEYOND MY POWER TO SHAPE.
BUT THEY'VE SPIED ON YOU. THEY'VE SEEN WHAT YOU CAN FORGE. THEY WILL ENSLAVE YOU, TOO -- FOR LIFE!
OWL PELLETS!
WE'LL SEE ABOUT THAT!
DON'T FRET, LITTLE ONE! WE'LL GET YOU TO LEETAH FOR HEALING.

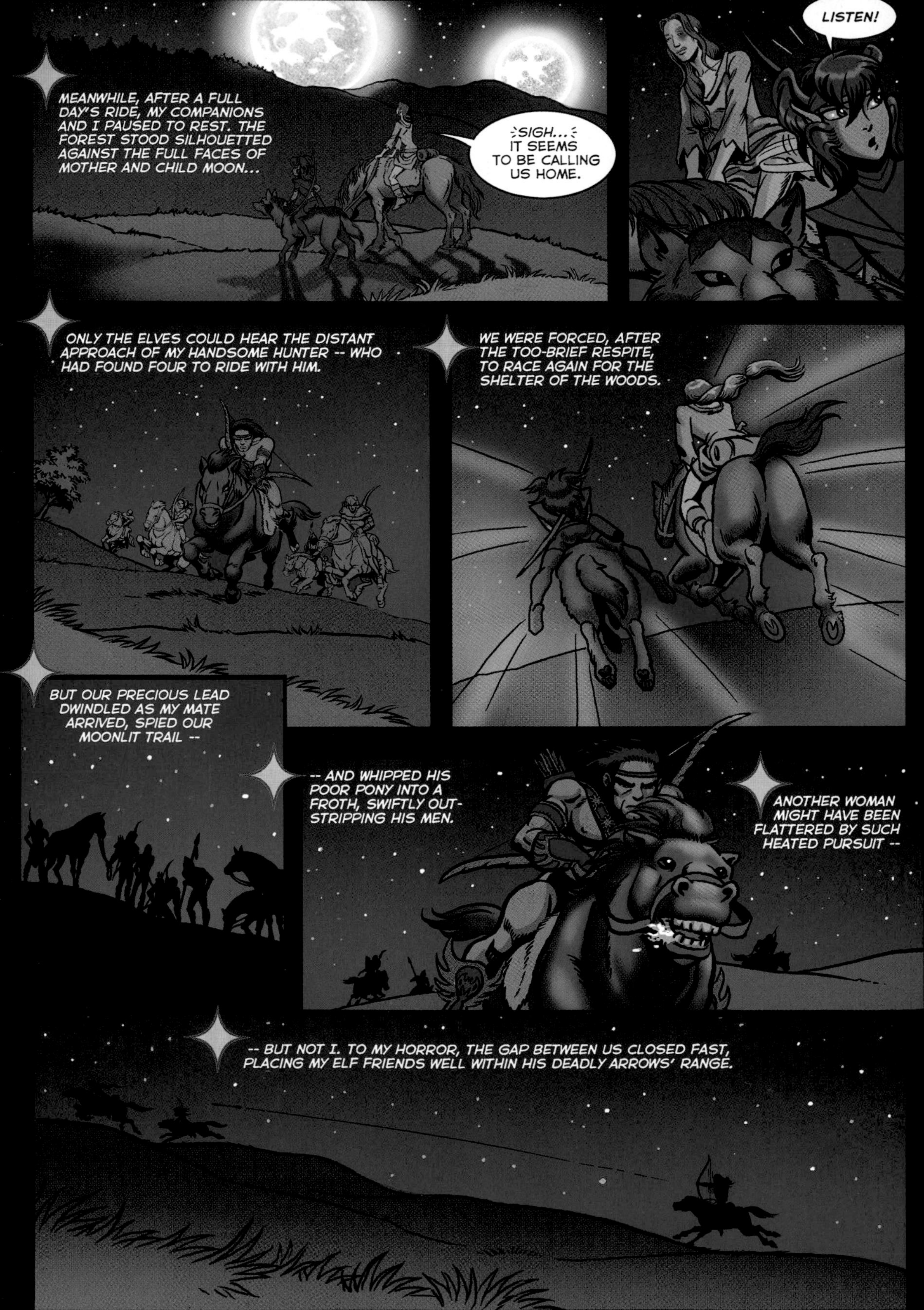
MEANWHILE, AFTER A FULL DAY'S RIDE, MY COMPANIONS AND I PAUSED TO REST. THE FOREST STOOD SILHOUETTED AGAINST THE FULL FACES OF MOTHER AND CHILD MOON...
SIGH... IT SEEMS TO BE CALLING US HOME.
LISTEN!
ONLY THE ELVES COULD HEAR THE DISTANT APPROACH OF MY HANDSOME HUNTER -- WHO HAD FOUND FOUR TO RIDE WITH HIM.
WE WERE FORCED, AFTER THE TOO-BRIEF RESPITE, TO RACE AGAIN FOR THE SHELTER OF THE WOODS.
BUT OUR PRECIOUS LEAD DWINDLED AS MY MATE ARRIVED, SPIED OUR MOONLIT TRAIL --
-- AND WHIPPED HIS POOR PONY INTO A FROTH, SWIFTLY OUT-STRIPPING HIS MEN.
ANOTHER WOMAN MIGHT HAVE BEEN FLATTERED BY SUCH HEATED PURSUIT --
-- BUT NOT I. TO MY HORROR, THE GAP BETWEEN US CLOSED FAST, PLACING MY ELF FRIENDS WELL WITHIN HIS DEADLY ARROWS' RANGE.

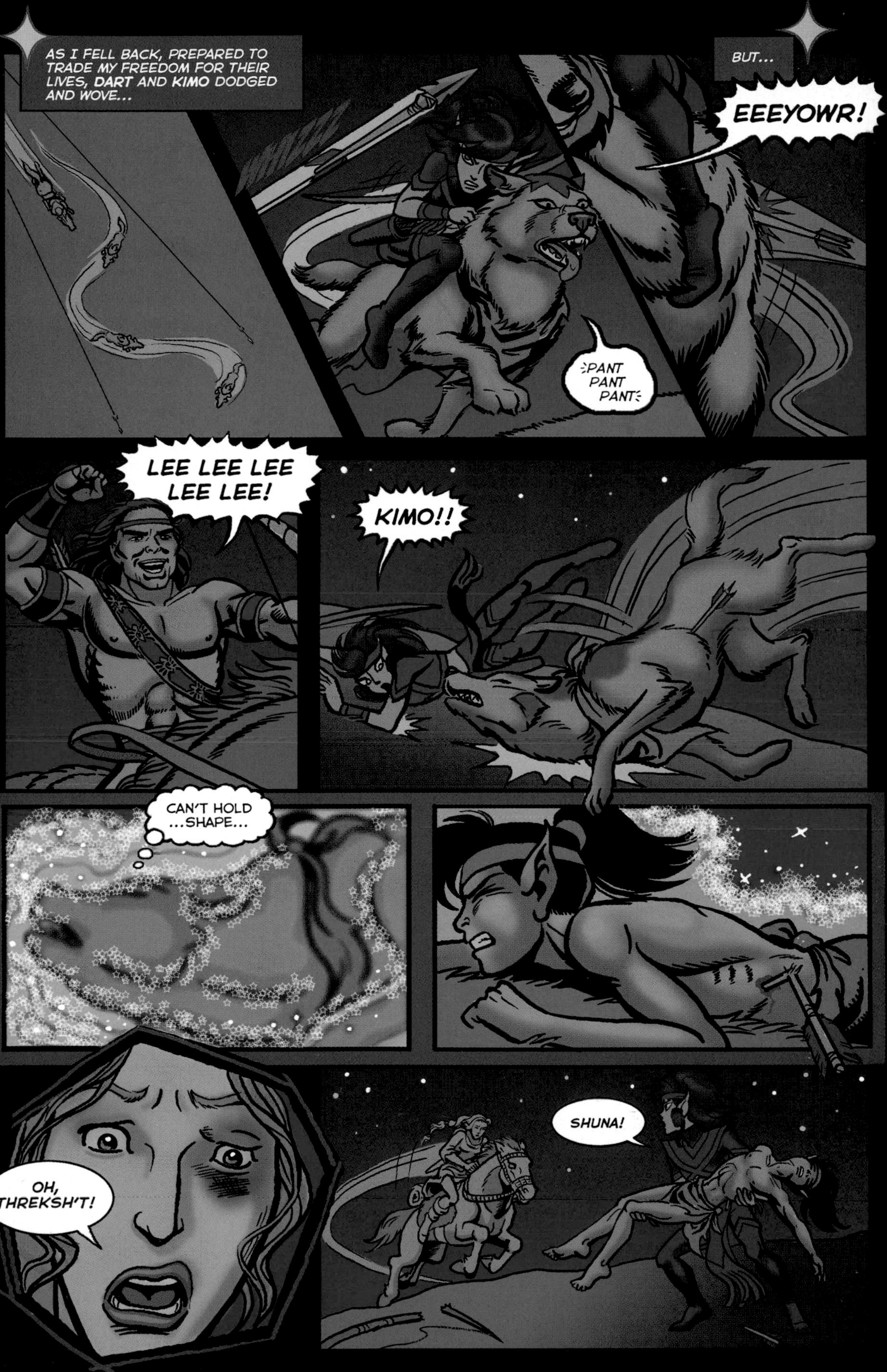
AS I FELL BACK, PREPARED TO TRADE MY FREEDOM FOR THEIR LIVES, DART AND KIMO DODGED AND WOVE...
BUT...
EEEYOWR!
PANT PANT PANT
LEE LEE LEE LEE LEE!
KIMO!!
CAN'T HOLD ...SHAPE...
OH, THREKSH'T!
SHUNA!

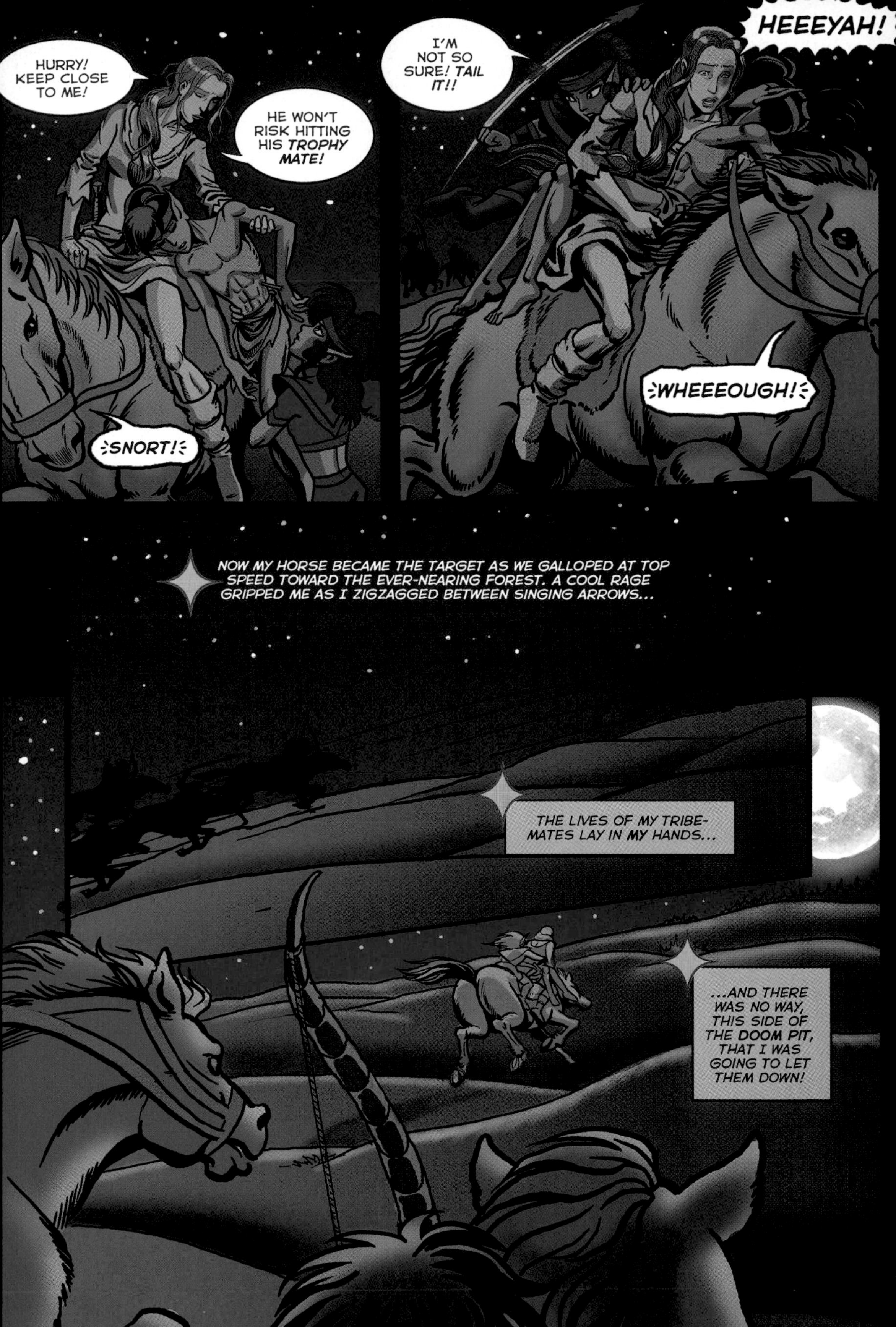
HURRY! KEEP CLOSE TO ME!
HE WON'T RISK HITTING HIS TROPHY MATE!
SNORT!
I'M NOT SO SURE! TAIL IT!!
HEEEYAH!
WHEEEOUGH!
NOW MY HORSE BECAME THE TARGET AS WE GALLOPED AT TOP SPEED TOWARD THE EVER-NEARING FOREST. A COOL RAGE GRIPPED ME AS I ZIGZAGGED BETWEEN SINGING ARROWS...
THE LIVES OF MY TRIBE-MATES LAY IN MY HANDS...
...AND THERE WAS NO WAY, THIS SIDE OF THE DOOM PIT, THAT I WAS GOING TO LET THEM DOWN!

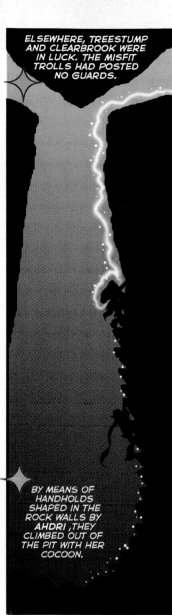

ELSEWHERE, TREESTUMP AND CLEARBROOK WERE IN LUCK. THE MISFIT TROLLS HAD POSTED NO GUARDS.

BY MEANS OF HANDHOLDS SHAPED IN THE ROCK WALLS BY *AHDRI*, THEY CLIMBED OUT OF THE PIT WITH HER COCOON.

KNOWING THEIR CAPTORS WERE NEITHER QUICK NOR BRIGHT, THEY DID WHAT ELVES DO BEST...

...STEALING SWIFTLY AND SILENTLY...

...THROUGH THE LABYRINTHINE HALLS THEY HAD COME TO KNOW SO WELL...

...IN SEARCH OF A PASSAGEWAY LEADING TO THE SURFACE.

AT THE SAME TIME, CUTTER'S DESCENDING BAND, BEARING A FRESH KILL, CAME UPON THE FALLEN BOULDERS BLOCKING THE STAIRS.

WELL WELL! WHEN DID *THIS* HAPPEN?

⁖SNIFF⁖ WHAT'S THAT STRANGE, *SICKLY* SCENT?

SMELLS LIKE *TROUBLE!*

TREESTUMP? CLEARBROOK? WHERE ARE YOU?

ANYTHING WRONG?

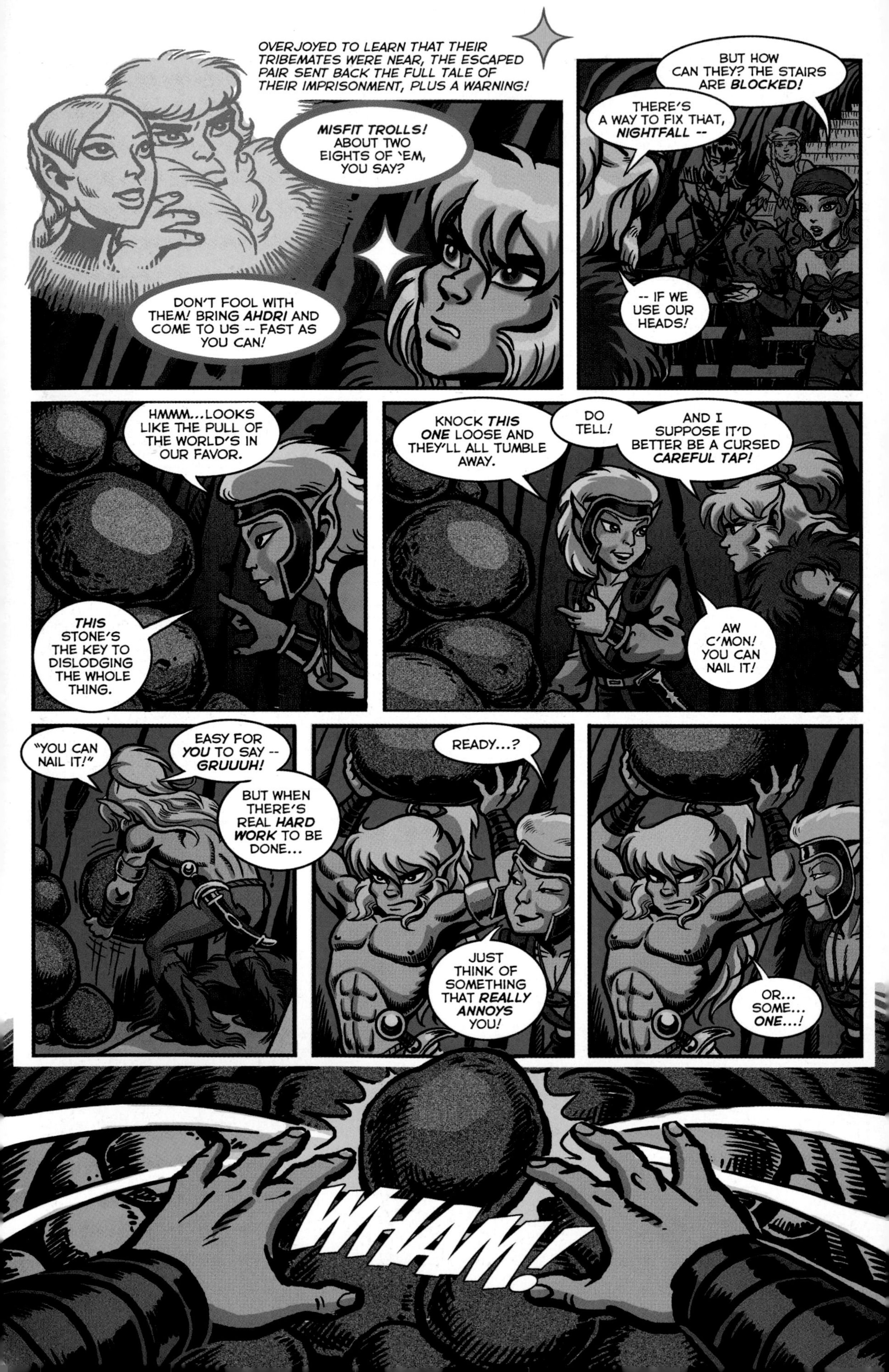
OVERJOYED TO LEARN THAT THEIR TRIBEMATES WERE NEAR, THE ESCAPED PAIR SENT BACK THE FULL TALE OF THEIR IMPRISONMENT, PLUS A WARNING!
MISFIT TROLLS! ABOUT TWO EIGHTS OF 'EM, YOU SAY?
DON'T FOOL WITH THEM! BRING AHDRI AND COME TO US -- FAST AS YOU CAN!
BUT HOW CAN THEY? THE STAIRS ARE BLOCKED!
THERE'S A WAY TO FIX THAT, NIGHTFALL --
-- IF WE USE OUR HEADS!
HMMM...LOOKS LIKE THE PULL OF THE WORLD'S IN OUR FAVOR.
THIS STONE'S THE KEY TO DISLODGING THE WHOLE THING.
KNOCK THIS ONE LOOSE AND THEY'LL ALL TUMBLE AWAY.
DO TELL!
AND I SUPPOSE IT'D BETTER BE A CURSED CAREFUL TAP!
AW C'MON! YOU CAN NAIL IT!
"YOU CAN NAIL IT!"
EASY FOR YOU TO SAY -- GRUUUH!
BUT WHEN THERE'S REAL HARD WORK TO BE DONE...
READY...?
JUST THINK OF SOMETHING THAT REALLY ANNOYS YOU!
OR... SOME... ONE...!
WHAM!

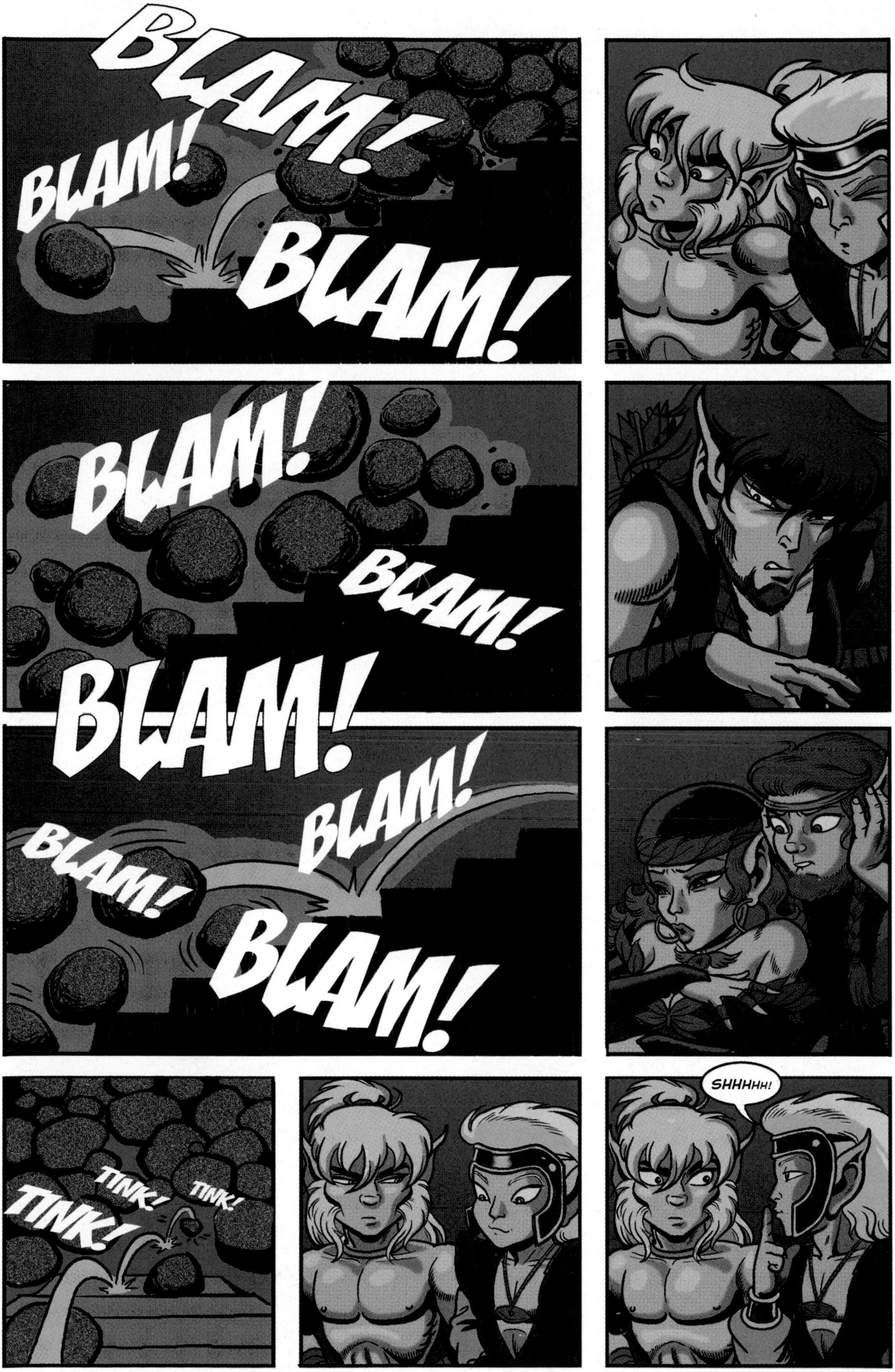
BLAM!
BLAM!
BLAM!
BLAM!
BLAM!
BLAM!
BLAM!
BLAM!
BLAM!
TINK!
TINK!
TINK!
SHHHHH!

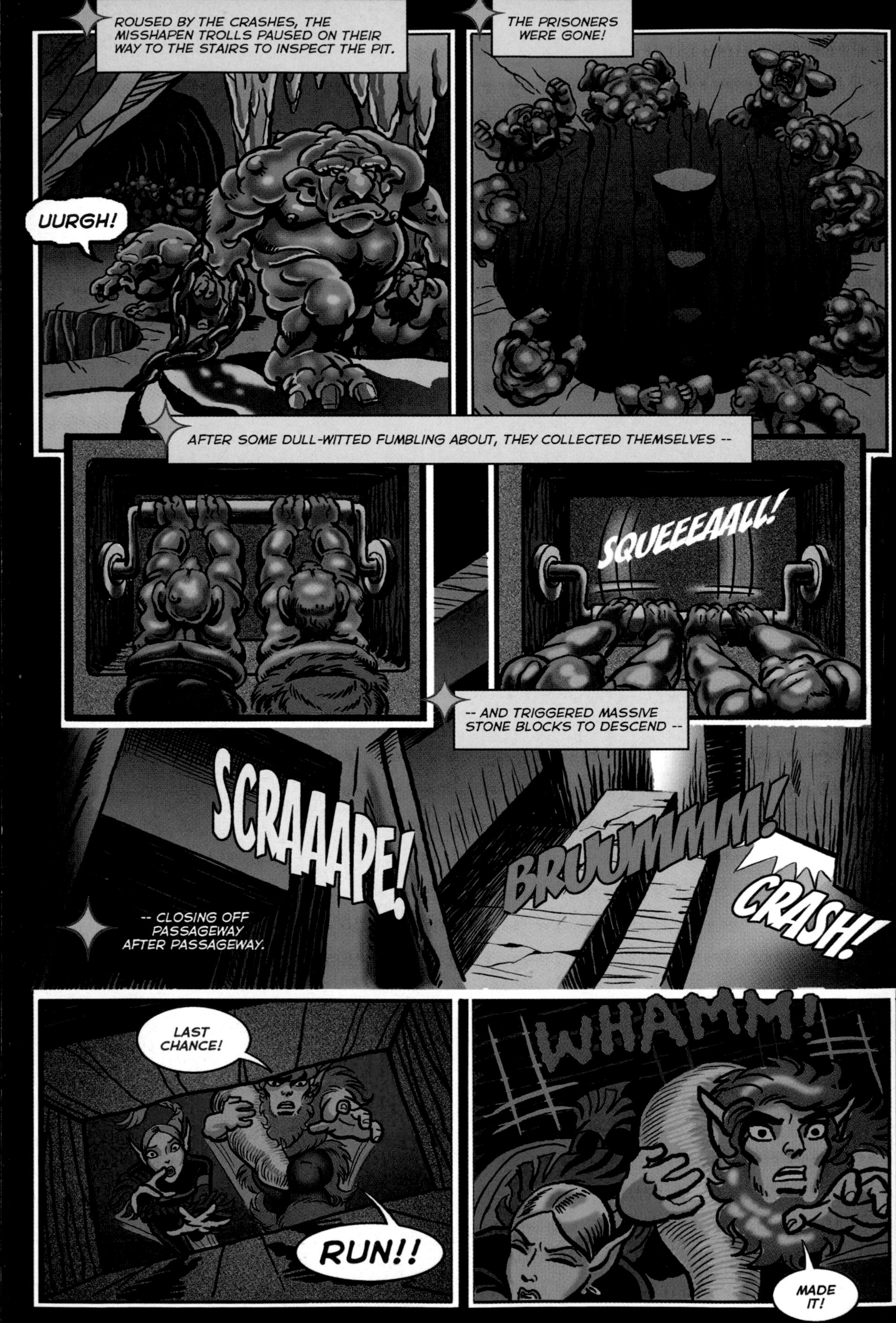
ROUSED BY THE CRASHES, THE MISSHAPEN TROLLS PAUSED ON THEIR WAY TO THE STAIRS TO INSPECT THE PIT.
UURGH!
THE PRISONERS WERE GONE!
AFTER SOME DULL-WITTED FUMBLING ABOUT, THEY COLLECTED THEMSELVES --
SQUEEEAALL!
-- AND TRIGGERED MASSIVE STONE BLOCKS TO DESCEND --
SCRAAAPE!
BRUUMMM!
CRASH!
-- CLOSING OFF PASSAGEWAY AFTER PASSAGEWAY.
LAST CHANCE!
RUN!!
WHAMM!
MADE IT!

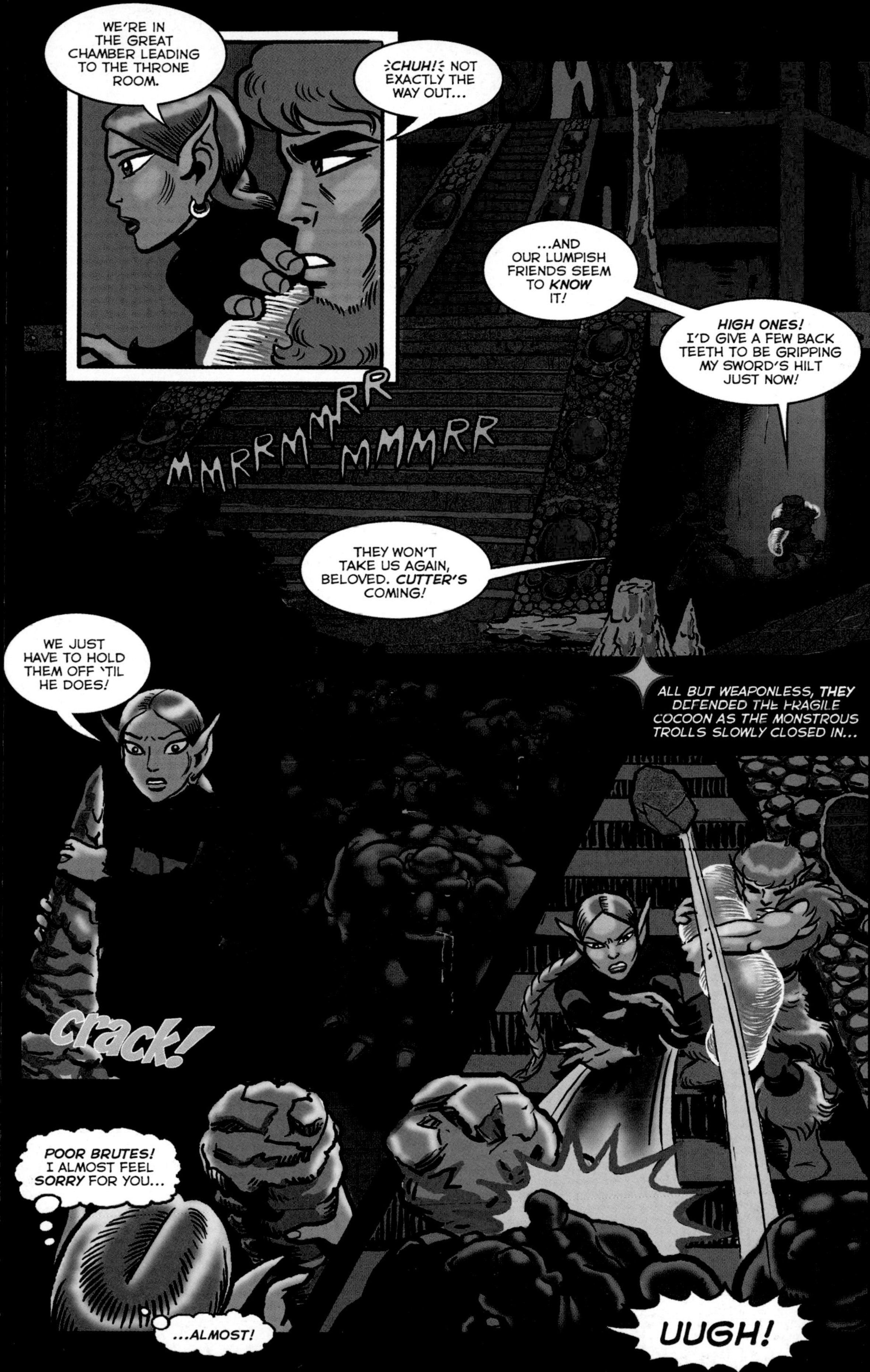
WE'RE IN THE GREAT CHAMBER LEADING TO THE THRONE ROOM.
CHUH! NOT EXACTLY THE WAY OUT...
...AND OUR LUMPISH FRIENDS SEEM TO KNOW IT!
HIGH ONES! I'D GIVE A FEW BACK TEETH TO BE GRIPPING MY SWORD'S HILT JUST NOW!
MMRRMMMRR MMMRR
THEY WON'T TAKE US AGAIN, BELOVED. CUTTER'S COMING!
WE JUST HAVE TO HOLD THEM OFF 'TIL HE DOES!
ALL BUT WEAPONLESS, THEY DEFENDED THE FRAGILE COCOON AS THE MONSTROUS TROLLS SLOWLY CLOSED IN...
CRACK!
POOR BRUTES! I ALMOST FEEL SORRY FOR YOU...
...ALMOST!
UUGH!

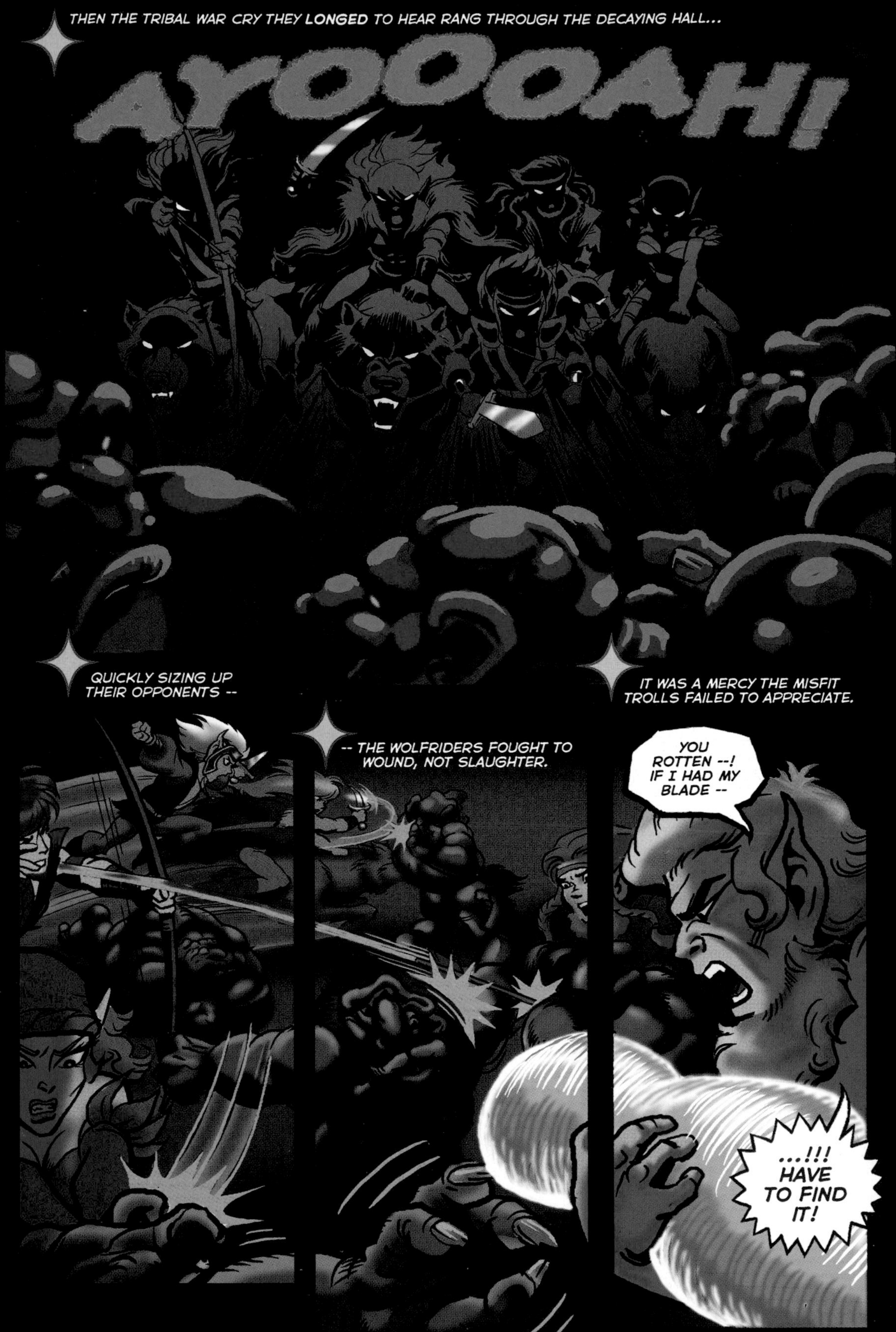
THEN THE TRIBAL WAR CRY THEY LONGED TO HEAR RANG THROUGH THE DECAYING HALL...
AYOOOAH!
QUICKLY SIZING UP THEIR OPPONENTS --
-- THE WOLFRIDERS FOUGHT TO WOUND, NOT SLAUGHTER.
IT WAS A MERCY THE MISFIT TROLLS FAILED TO APPRECIATE.
YOU ROTTEN --! IF I HAD MY BLADE --
...!!! HAVE TO FIND IT!

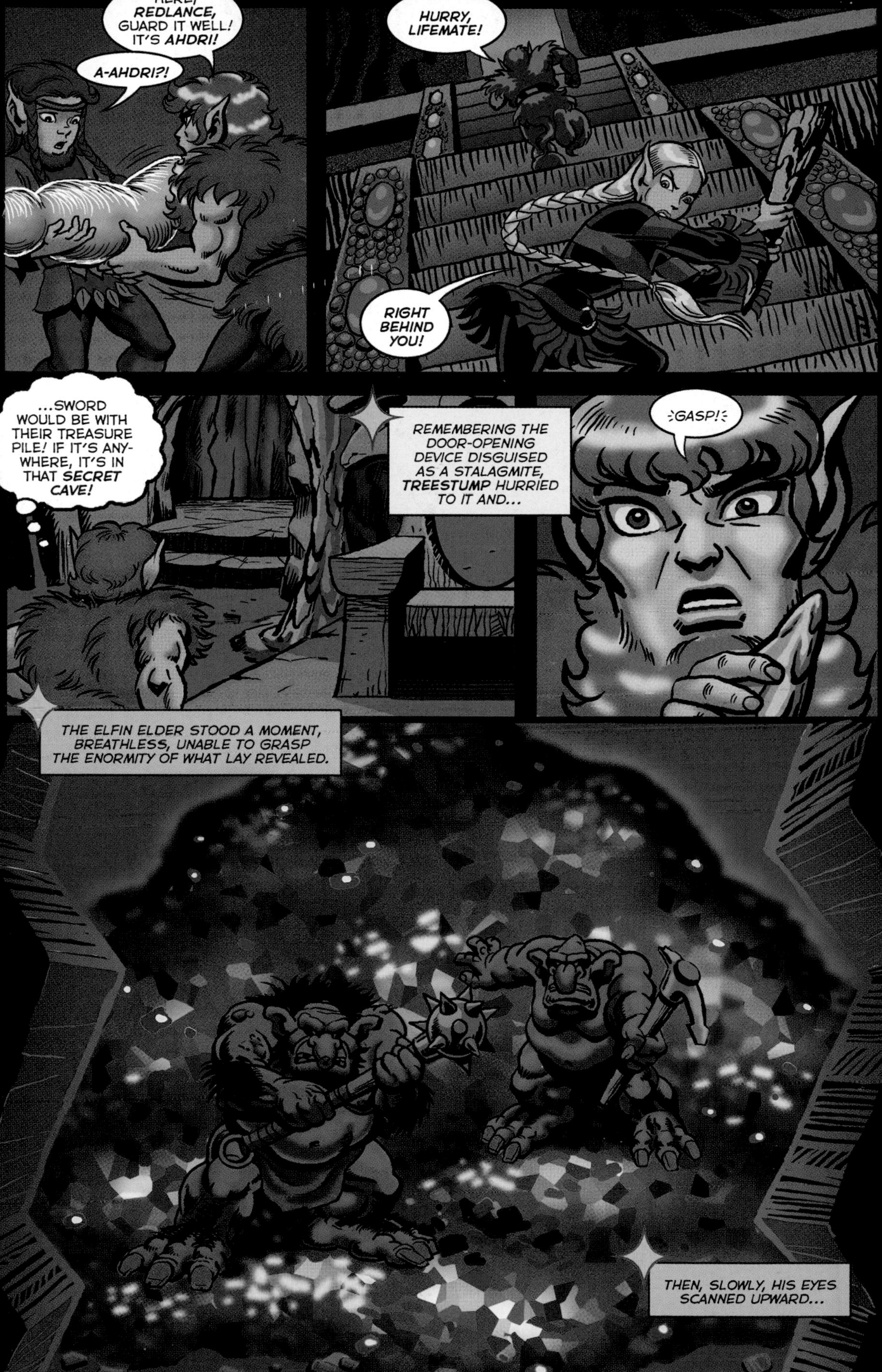
HERE, REDLANCE, GUARD IT WELL! IT'S AHDRI!
A-AHDRI?!
HURRY, LIFEMATE!
RIGHT BEHIND YOU!
...SWORD WOULD BE WITH THEIR TREASURE PILE! IF IT'S ANY-WHERE, IT'S IN THAT SECRET CAVE!
REMEMBERING THE DOOR-OPENING DEVICE DISGUISED AS A STALAGMITE, TREESTUMP HURRIED TO IT AND...
GASP!
THE ELFIN ELDER STOOD A MOMENT, BREATHLESS, UNABLE TO GRASP THE ENORMITY OF WHAT LAY REVEALED.
THEN, SLOWLY, HIS EYES SCANNED UPWARD...

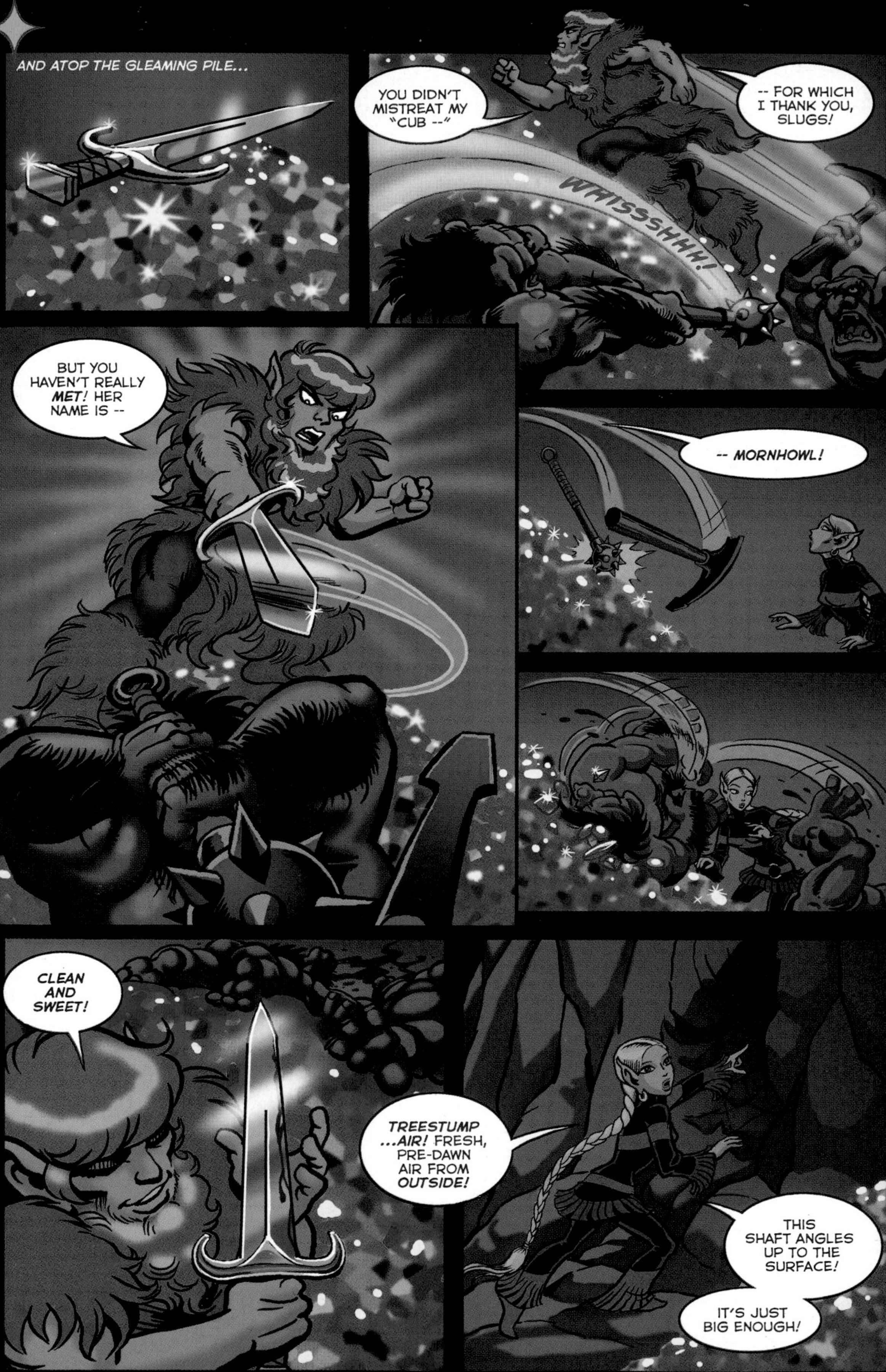
AND ATOP THE GLEAMING PILE...
YOU DIDN'T MISTREAT MY "CUB --"
-- FOR WHICH I THANK YOU, SLUGS!
WHISSSHHH!
BUT YOU HAVEN'T REALLY MET! HER NAME IS --
-- MORNHOWL!
CLEAN AND SWEET!
TREESTUMP ...AIR! FRESH, PRE-DAWN AIR FROM OUTSIDE!
THIS SHAFT ANGLES UP TO THE SURFACE!
IT'S JUST BIG ENOUGH!

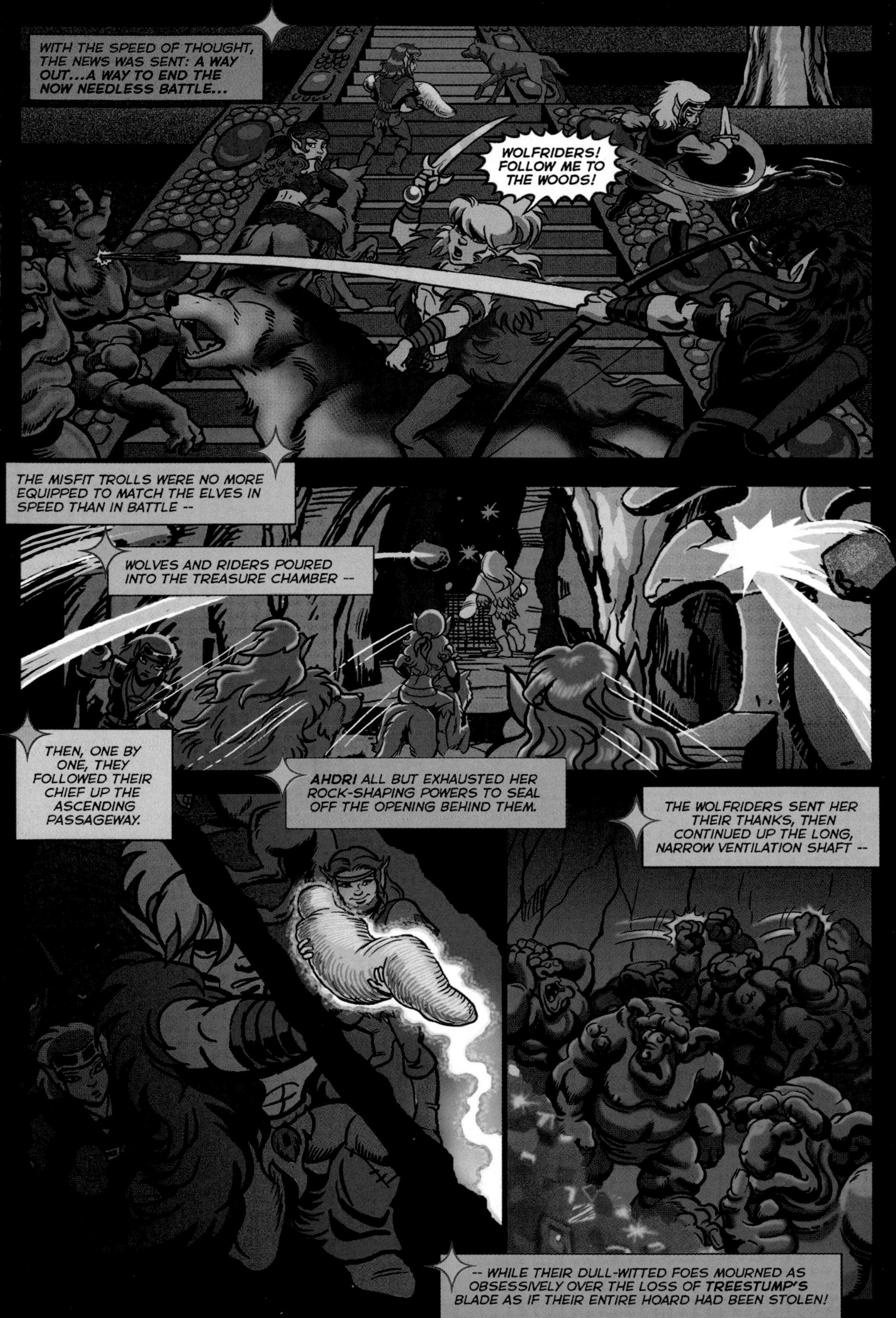
WITH THE SPEED OF THOUGHT, THE NEWS WAS SENT: A WAY OUT...A WAY TO END THE NOW NEEDLESS BATTLE...
WOLFRIDERS! FOLLOW ME TO THE WOODS!
THE MISFIT TROLLS WERE NO MORE EQUIPPED TO MATCH THE ELVES IN SPEED THAN IN BATTLE --
WOLVES AND RIDERS POURED INTO THE TREASURE CHAMBER --
THEN, ONE BY ONE, THEY FOLLOWED THEIR CHIEF UP THE ASCENDING PASSAGEWAY.
AHDRI ALL BUT EXHAUSTED HER ROCK-SHAPING POWERS TO SEAL OFF THE OPENING BEHIND THEM.
THE WOLFRIDERS SENT HER THEIR THANKS, THEN CONTINUED UP THE LONG, NARROW VENTILATION SHAFT --
-- WHILE THEIR DULL-WITTED FOES MOURNED AS OBSESSIVELY OVER THE LOSS OF TREESTUMP'S BLADE AS IF THEIR ENTIRE HOARD HAD BEEN STOLEN!

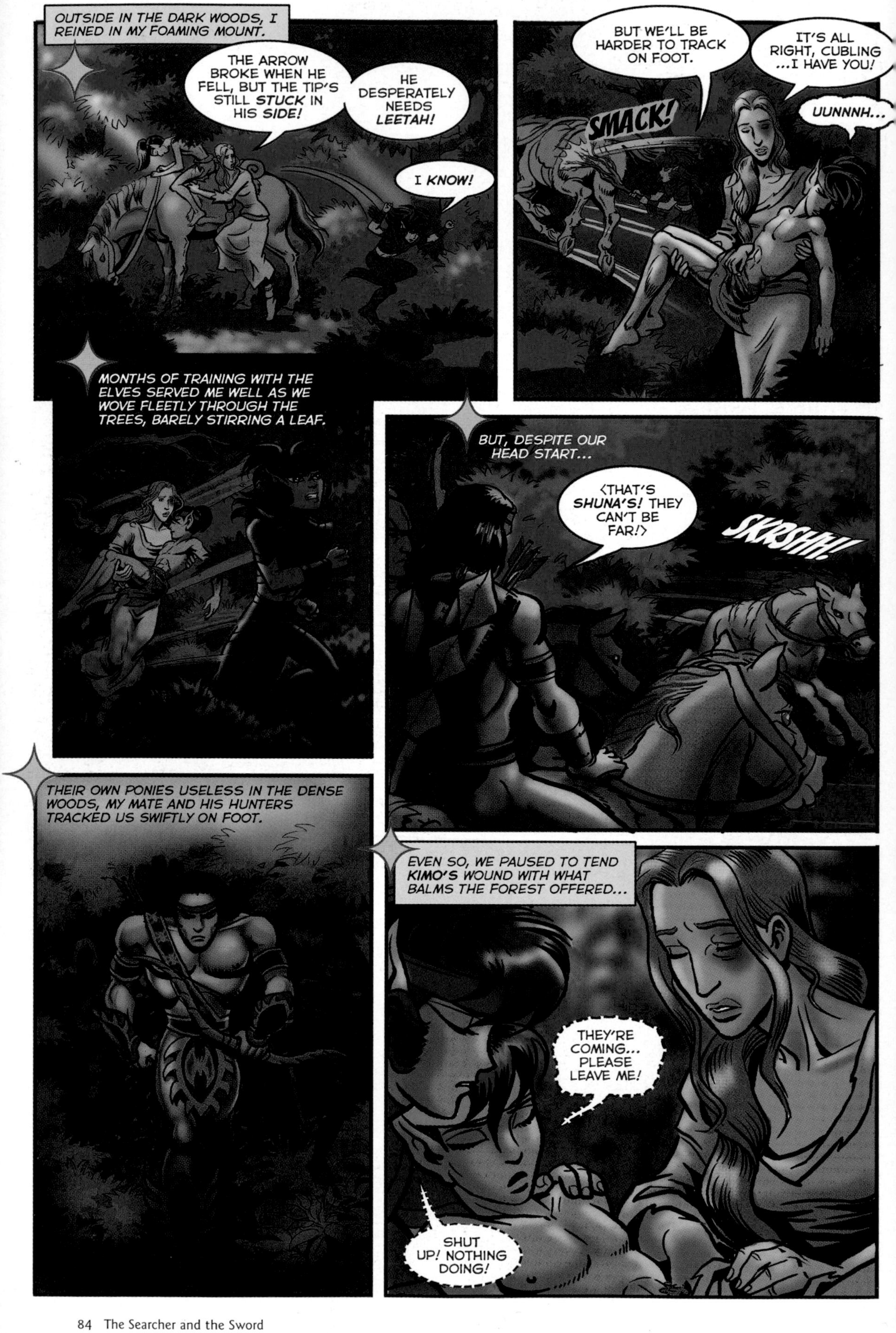
OUTSIDE IN THE DARK WOODS, I REINED IN MY FOAMING MOUNT.
THE ARROW BROKE WHEN HE FELL, BUT THE TIP'S STILL STUCK IN HIS SIDE!
HE DESPERATELY NEEDS LEETAH!
I KNOW!
BUT WE'LL BE HARDER TO TRACK ON FOOT.
IT'S ALL RIGHT, CUBLING ...I HAVE YOU!
SMACK!
UUNNNH...
MONTHS OF TRAINING WITH THE ELVES SERVED ME WELL AS WE WOVE FLEETLY THROUGH THE TREES, BARELY STIRRING A LEAF.
BUT, DESPITE OUR HEAD START...
<THAT'S SHUNA'S! THEY CAN'T BE FAR!>
SKRSHH!
THEIR OWN PONIES USELESS IN THE DENSE WOODS, MY MATE AND HIS HUNTERS TRACKED US SWIFTLY ON FOOT.
EVEN SO, WE PAUSED TO TEND KIMO'S WOUND WITH WHAT BALMS THE FOREST OFFERED...
THEY'RE COMING... PLEASE LEAVE ME!
SHUT UP! NOTHING DOING!

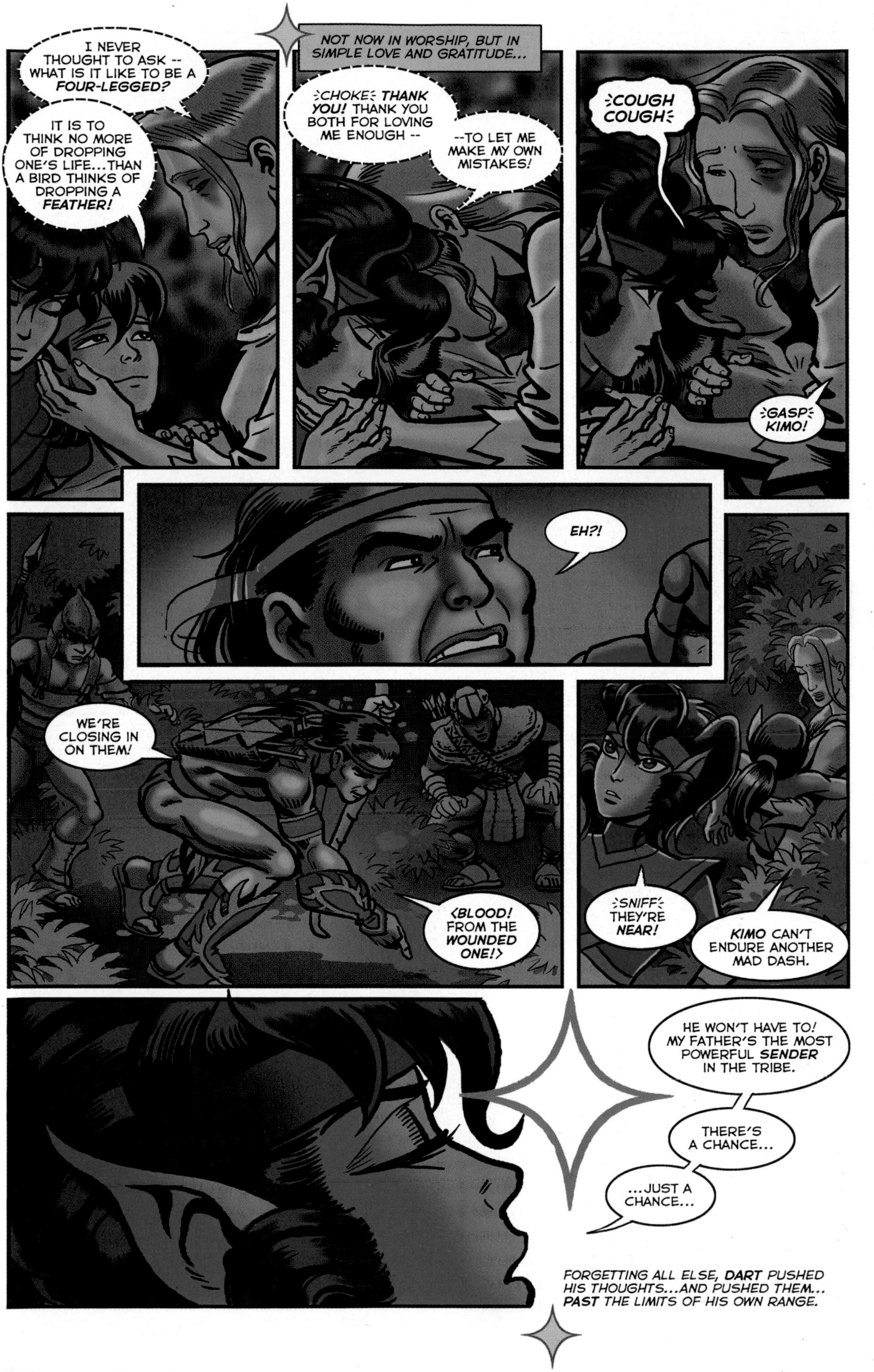
I NEVER THOUGHT TO ASK -- WHAT IS IT LIKE TO BE A FOUR-LEGGED?
IT IS TO THINK NO MORE OF DROPPING ONE'S LIFE...THAN A BIRD THINKS OF DROPPING A FEATHER!
NOT NOW IN WORSHIP, BUT IN SIMPLE LOVE AND GRATITUDE...
CHOKE THANK YOU! THANK YOU BOTH FOR LOVING ME ENOUGH --
--TO LET ME MAKE MY OWN MISTAKES!
COUGH COUGH
GASP KIMO!
EH?!
WE'RE CLOSING IN ON THEM!
<BLOOD! FROM THE WOUNDED ONE!>
SNIFF THEY'RE NEAR!
KIMO CAN'T ENDURE ANOTHER MAD DASH.
HE WON'T HAVE TO! MY FATHER'S THE MOST POWERFUL SENDER IN THE TRIBE.
THERE'S A CHANCE...
...JUST A CHANCE...
FORGETTING ALL ELSE, DART PUSHED HIS THOUGHTS...AND PUSHED THEM... PAST THE LIMITS OF HIS OWN RANGE.

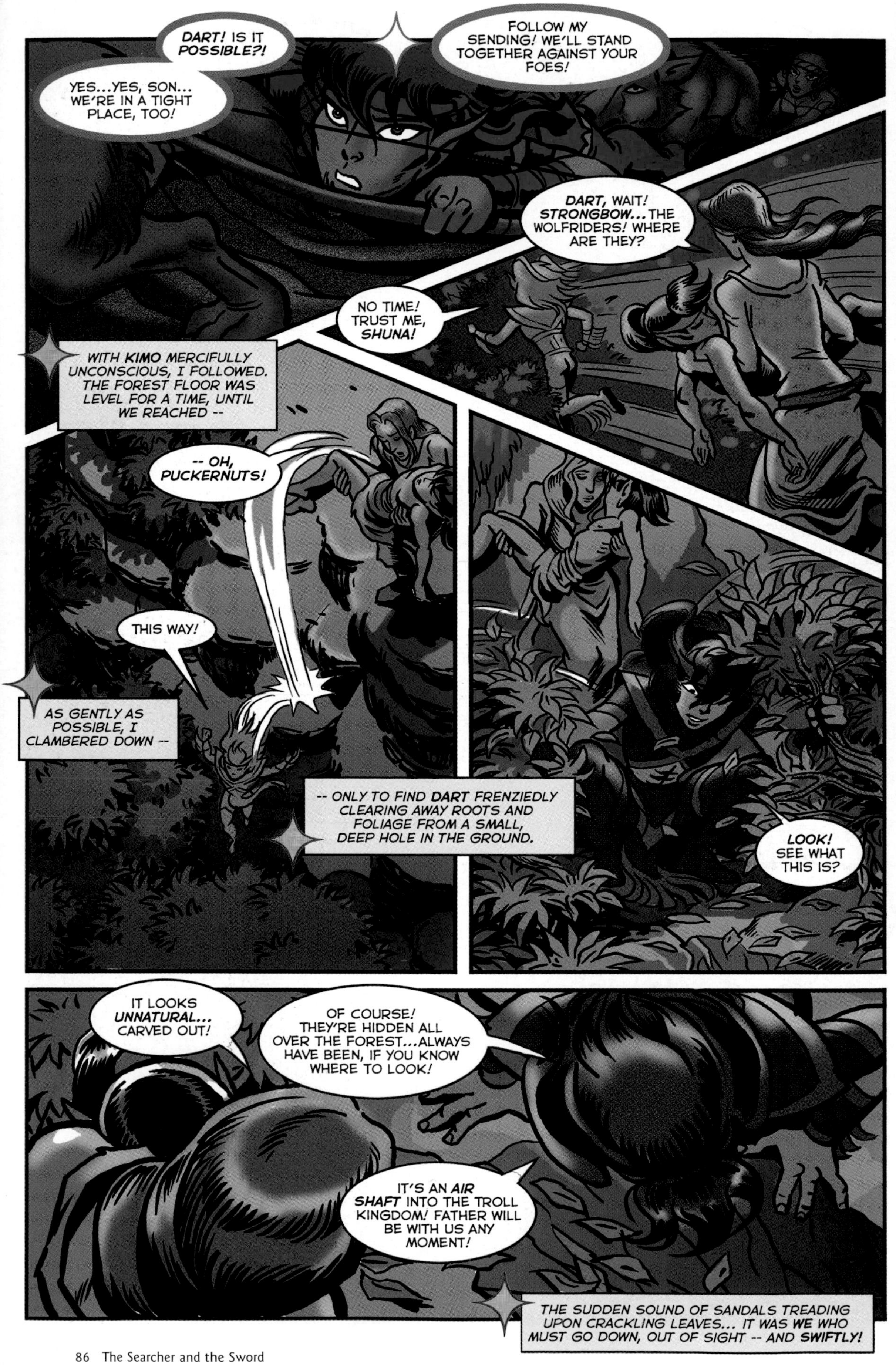
DART! IS IT POSSIBLE?!
YES...YES, SON... WE'RE IN A TIGHT PLACE, TOO!
FOLLOW MY SENDING! WE'LL STAND TOGETHER AGAINST YOUR FOES!
DART, WAIT! STRONGBOW... THE WOLFRIDERS! WHERE ARE THEY?
NO TIME! TRUST ME, SHUNA!
WITH KIMO MERCIFULLY UNCONSCIOUS, I FOLLOWED. THE FOREST FLOOR WAS LEVEL FOR A TIME, UNTIL WE REACHED --
-- OH, PUCKERNUTS!
THIS WAY!
AS GENTLY AS POSSIBLE, I CLAMBERED DOWN --
-- ONLY TO FIND DART FRENZIEDLY CLEARING AWAY ROOTS AND FOLIAGE FROM A SMALL, DEEP HOLE IN THE GROUND.
LOOK! SEE WHAT THIS IS?
IT LOOKS UNNATURAL... CARVED OUT!
OF COURSE! THEY'RE HIDDEN ALL OVER THE FOREST...ALWAYS HAVE BEEN, IF YOU KNOW WHERE TO LOOK!
IT'S AN AIR SHAFT INTO THE TROLL KINGDOM! FATHER WILL BE WITH US ANY MOMENT!
THE SUDDEN SOUND OF SANDALS TREADING UPON CRACKLING LEAVES... IT WAS WE WHO MUST GO DOWN, OUT OF SIGHT -- AND SWIFTLY!

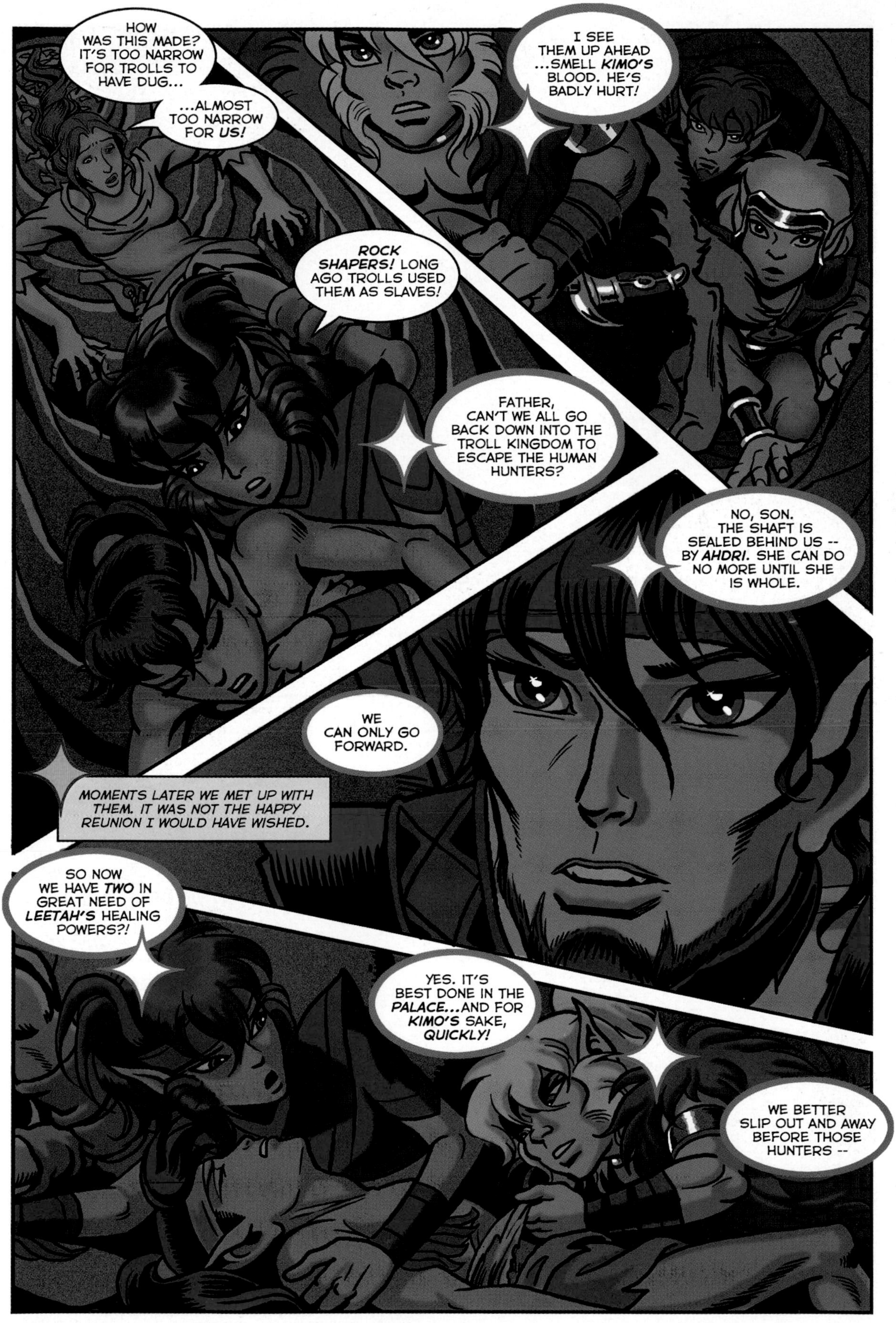
HOW WAS THIS MADE? IT'S TOO NARROW FOR TROLLS TO HAVE DUG...
...ALMOST TOO NARROW FOR US!
I SEE THEM UP AHEAD ...SMELL KIMO'S BLOOD. HE'S BADLY HURT!
ROCK SHAPERS! LONG AGO TROLLS USED THEM AS SLAVES!
FATHER, CAN'T WE ALL GO BACK DOWN INTO THE TROLL KINGDOM TO ESCAPE THE HUMAN HUNTERS?
NO, SON. THE SHAFT IS SEALED BEHIND US -- BY AHDRI. SHE CAN DO NO MORE UNTIL SHE IS WHOLE.
WE CAN ONLY GO FORWARD.
MOMENTS LATER WE MET UP WITH THEM. IT WAS NOT THE HAPPY REUNION I WOULD HAVE WISHED.
SO NOW WE HAVE TWO IN GREAT NEED OF LEETAH'S HEALING POWERS?!
YES. IT'S BEST DONE IN THE PALACE...AND FOR KIMO'S SAKE, QUICKLY!
WE BETTER SLIP OUT AND AWAY BEFORE THOSE HUNTERS --

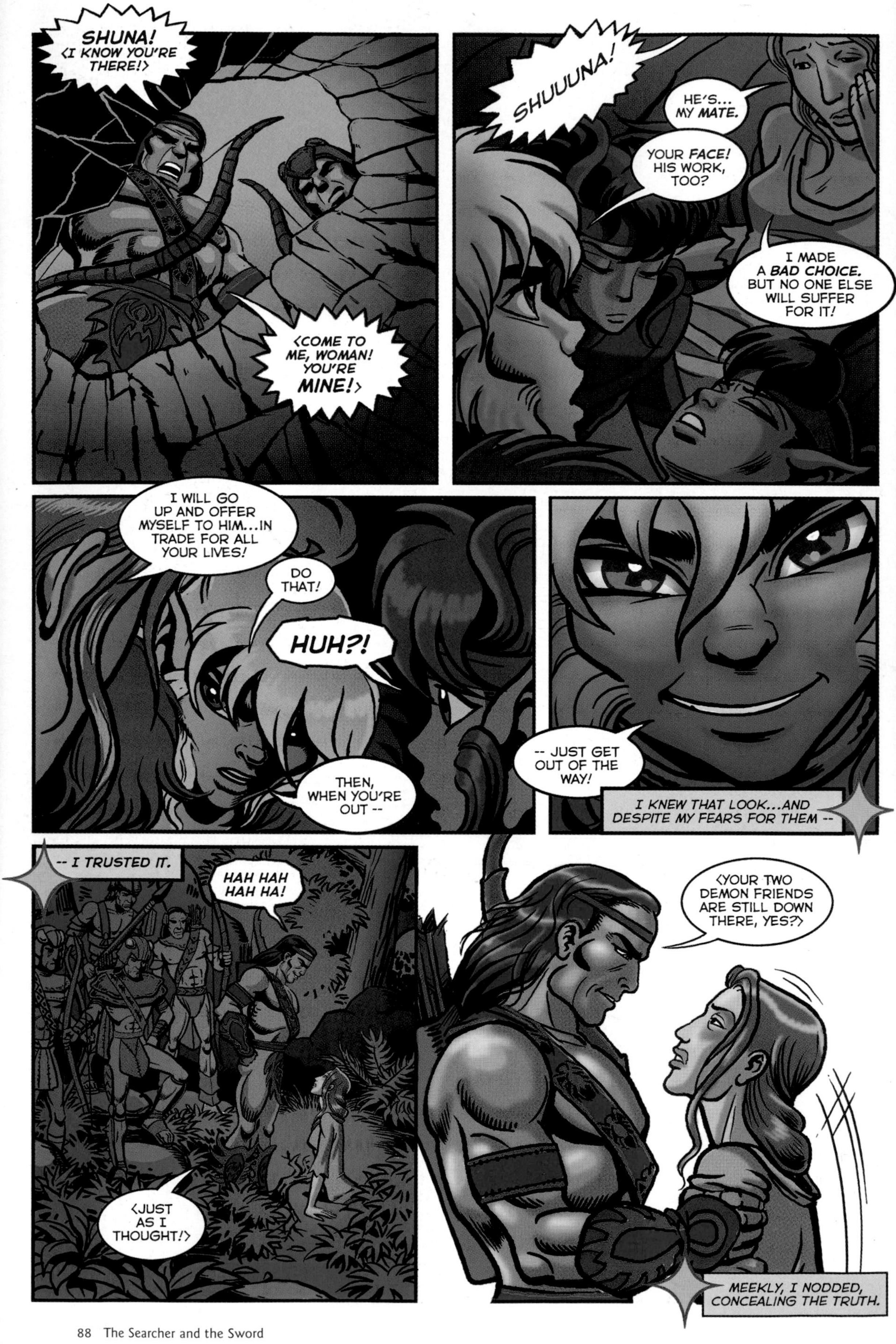
SHUNA! <I KNOW YOU'RE THERE!>
<COME TO ME, WOMAN! YOU'RE MINE!>
SHUUUNA!
HE'S... MY MATE.
YOUR FACE! HIS WORK, TOO?
I MADE A BAD CHOICE. BUT NO ONE ELSE WILL SUFFER FOR IT!
I WILL GO UP AND OFFER MYSELF TO HIM...IN TRADE FOR ALL YOUR LIVES!
DO THAT!
HUH?!
THEN, WHEN YOU'RE OUT --
-- JUST GET OUT OF THE WAY!
I KNEW THAT LOOK...AND DESPITE MY FEARS FOR THEM --
-- I TRUSTED IT.
HAH HAH HAH HA!
<JUST AS I THOUGHT!>
<YOUR TWO DEMON FRIENDS ARE STILL DOWN THERE, YES?>
MEEKLY, I NODDED, CONCEALING THE TRUTH.

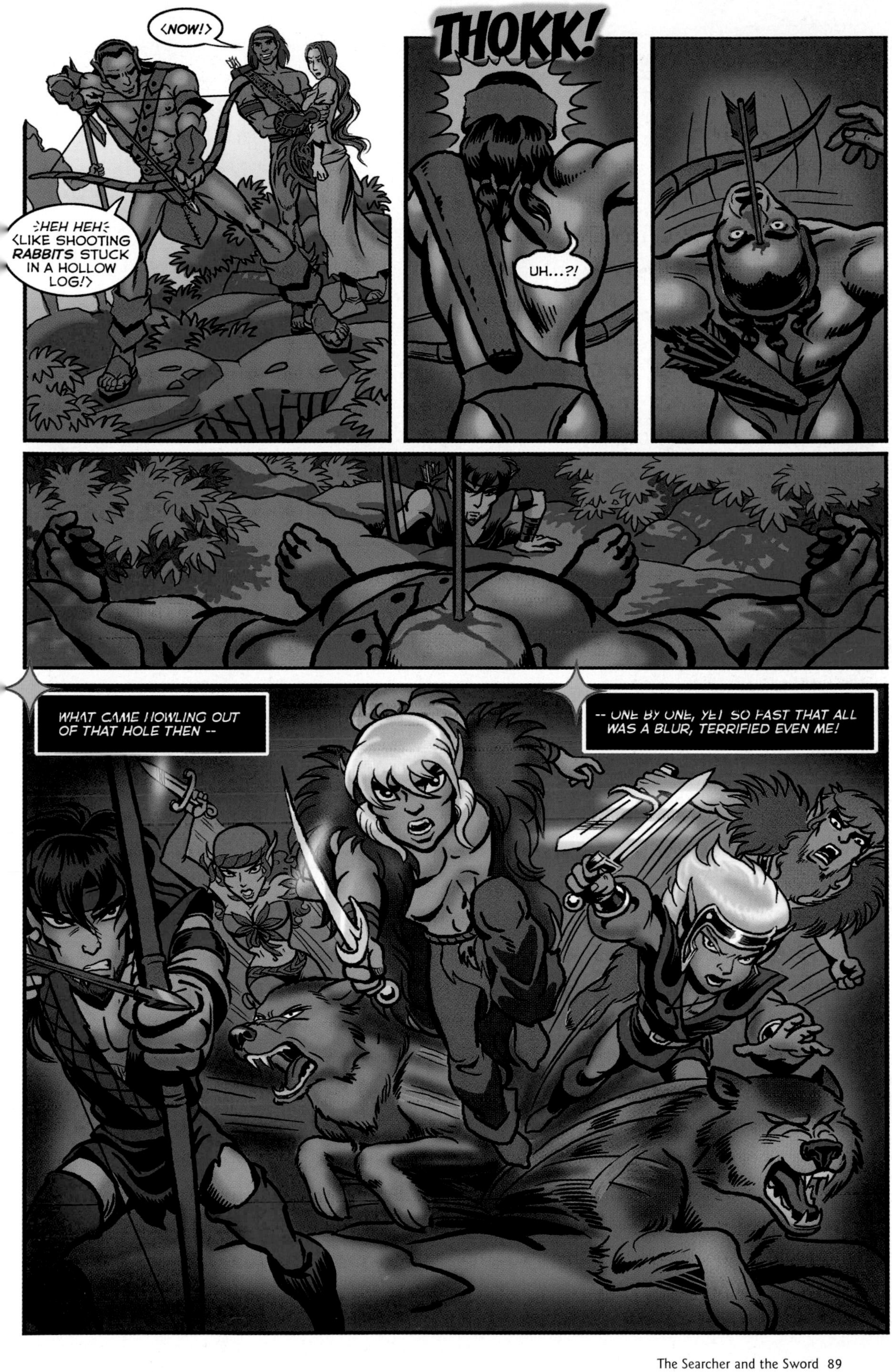
<NOW!>
:HEH HEH: <LIKE SHOOTING RABBITS STUCK IN A HOLLOW LOG!>
THOKK!
UH...?!
WHAT CAME HOWLING OUT OF THAT HOLE THEN --
-- ONE BY ONE, YET SO FAST THAT ALL WAS A BLUR, TERRIFIED EVEN ME!

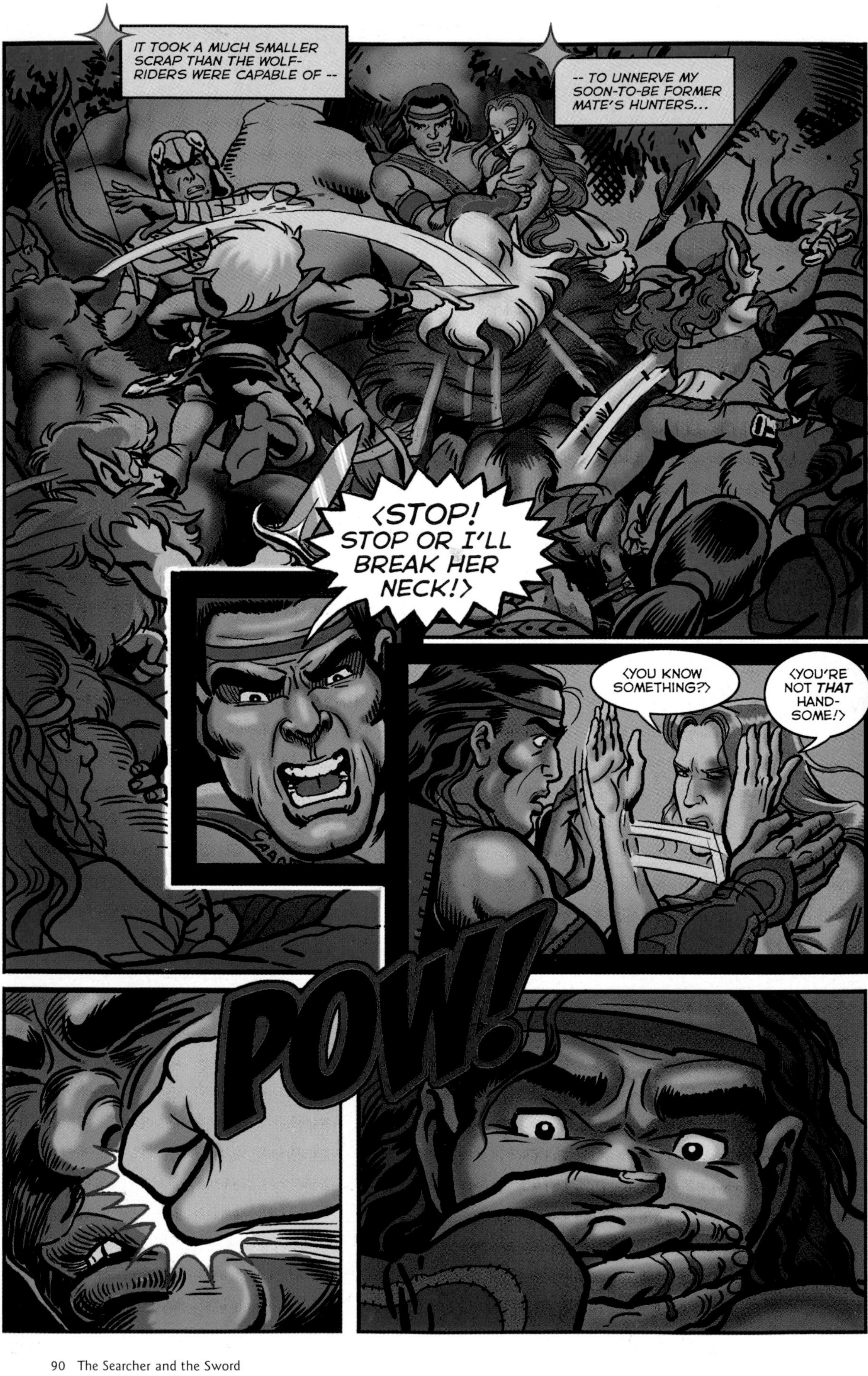
IT TOOK A MUCH SMALLER SCRAP THAN THE WOLF-RIDERS WERE CAPABLE OF --
-- TO UNNERVE MY SOON-TO-BE FORMER MATE'S HUNTERS...
<STOP! STOP OR I'LL BREAK HER NECK!>
<YOU KNOW SOMETHING?>
<YOU'RE NOT *THAT* HAND-SOME!>
POW!

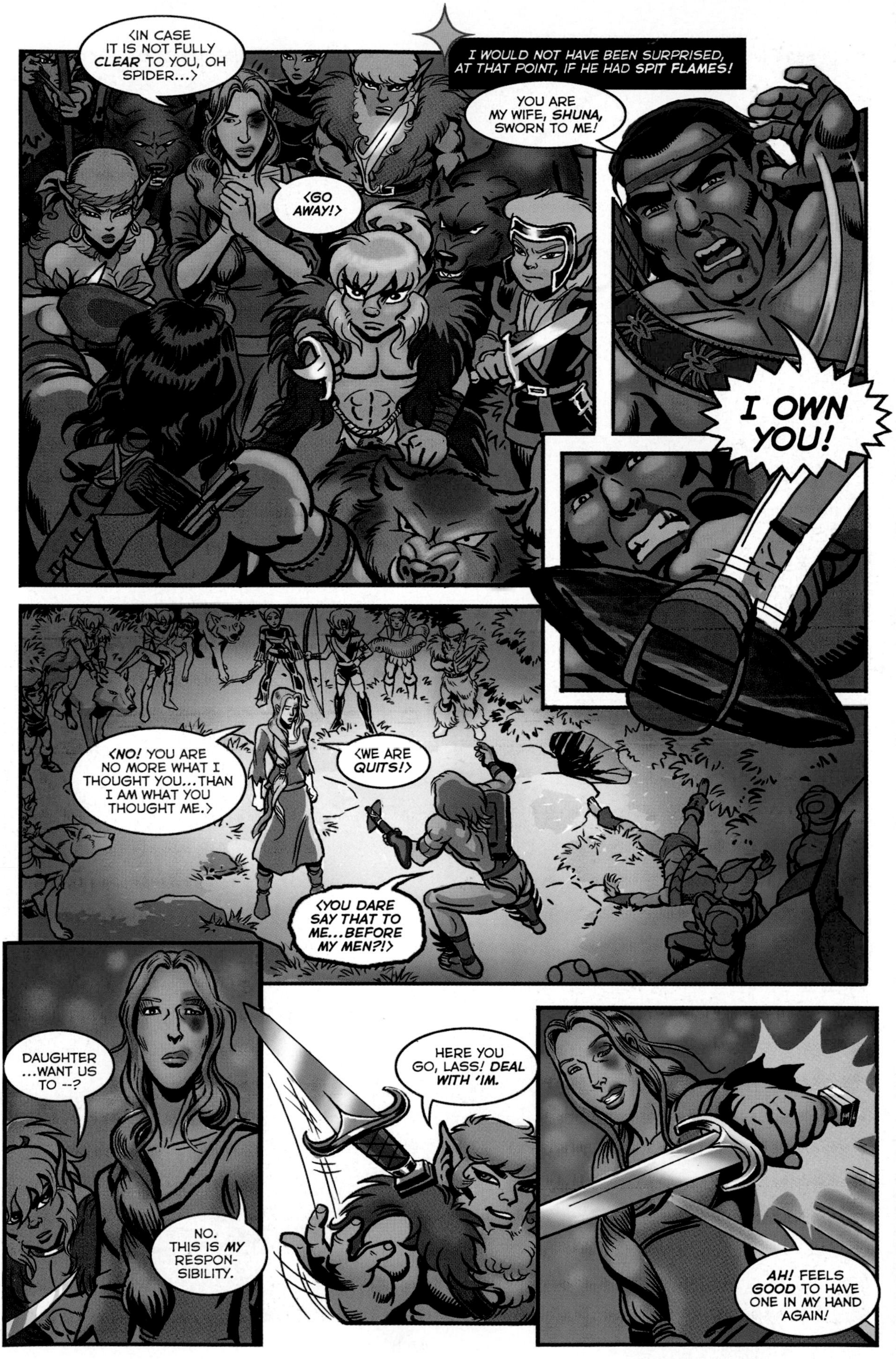
<IN CASE IT IS NOT FULLY CLEAR TO YOU, OH SPIDER...>
<GO AWAY!>
I WOULD NOT HAVE BEEN SURPRISED, AT THAT POINT, IF HE HAD SPIT FLAMES!
YOU ARE MY WIFE, SHUNA, SWORN TO ME!
I OWN YOU!
<NO! YOU ARE NO MORE WHAT I THOUGHT YOU...THAN I AM WHAT YOU THOUGHT ME.>
<WE ARE QUITS!>
<YOU DARE SAY THAT TO ME...BEFORE MY MEN?!>
DAUGHTER ...WANT US TO --?
NO. THIS IS MY RESPON-SIBILITY.
HERE YOU GO, LASS! DEAL WITH 'IM.
AH! FEELS GOOD TO HAVE ONE IN MY HAND AGAIN!

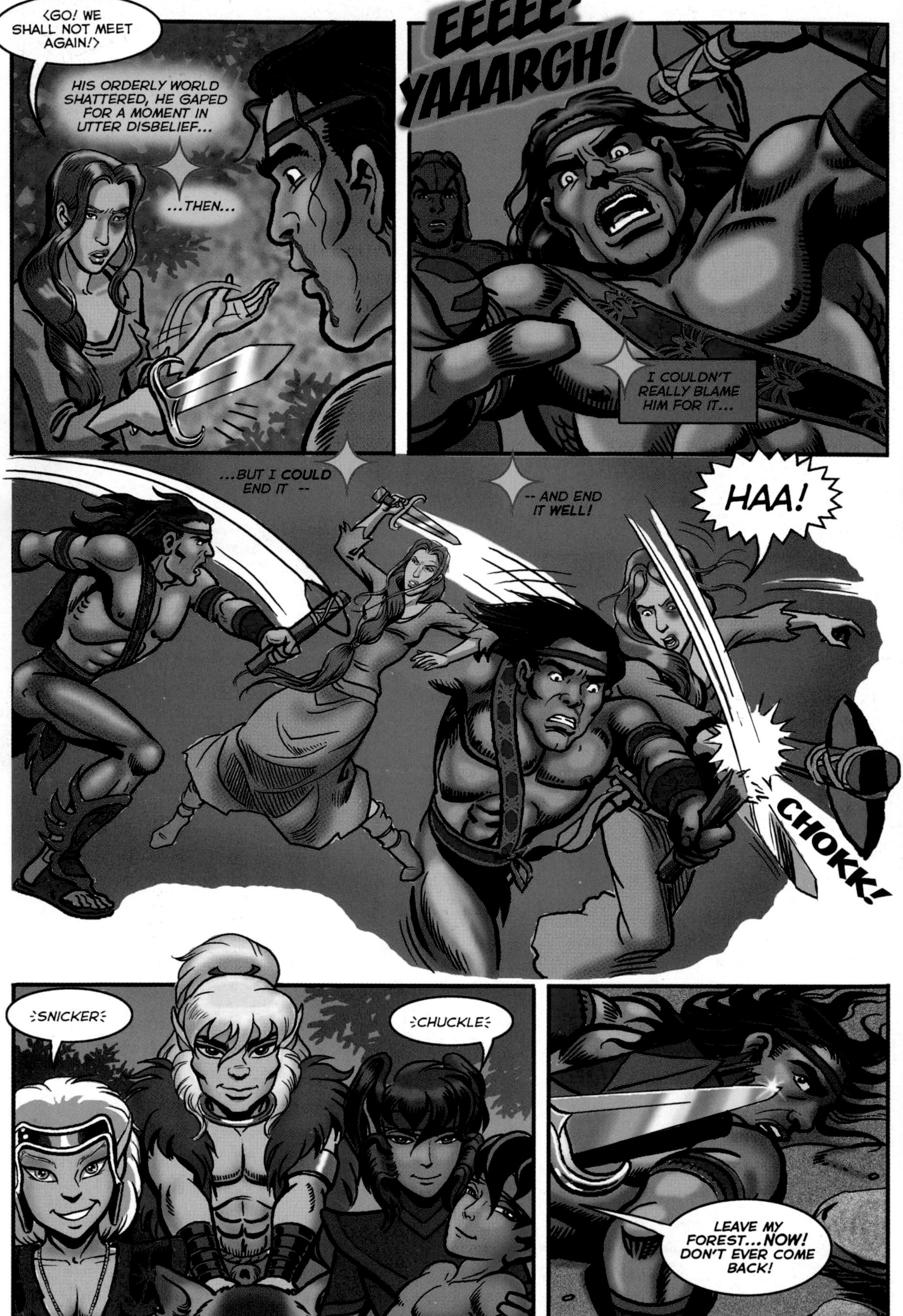
<GO! WE SHALL NOT MEET AGAIN!>
HIS ORDERLY WORLD SHATTERED, HE GAPED FOR A MOMENT IN UTTER DISBELIEF...
...THEN...
EEEEE-YAAARGH!
I COULDN'T REALLY BLAME HIM FOR IT...
...BUT I COULD END IT --
-- AND END IT WELL!
HAA!
CHOKK!
SNICKER
CHUCKLE
LEAVE MY FOREST...NOW! DON'T EVER COME BACK!

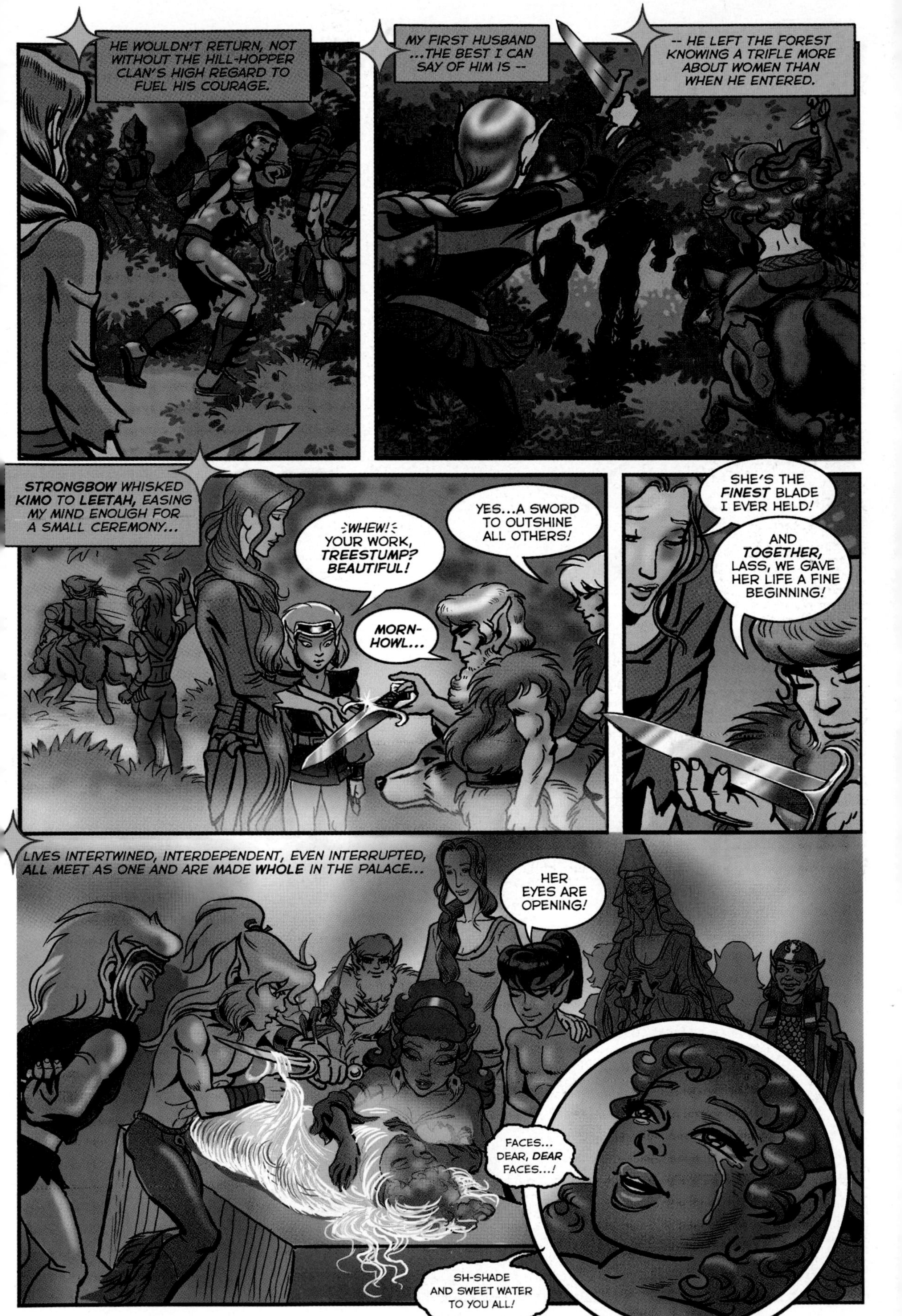
HE WOULDN'T RETURN, NOT WITHOUT THE HILL-HOPPER CLAN'S HIGH REGARD TO FUEL HIS COURAGE.
MY FIRST HUSBAND ...THE BEST I CAN SAY OF HIM IS --
-- HE LEFT THE FOREST KNOWING A TRIFLE MORE ABOUT WOMEN THAN WHEN HE ENTERED.
STRONGBOW WHISKED KIMO TO LEETAH, EASING MY MIND ENOUGH FOR A SMALL CEREMONY...
WHEW! YOUR WORK, TREESTUMP? BEAUTIFUL!
YES...A SWORD TO OUTSHINE ALL OTHERS!
MORN-HOWL...
SHE'S THE FINEST BLADE I EVER HELD!
AND TOGETHER, LASS, WE GAVE HER LIFE A FINE BEGINNING!
LIVES INTERTWINED, INTERDEPENDENT, EVEN INTERRUPTED, ALL MEET AS ONE AND ARE MADE WHOLE IN THE PALACE...
HER EYES ARE OPENING!
FACES... DEAR, DEAR FACES...!
SH-SHADE AND SWEET WATER TO YOU ALL!

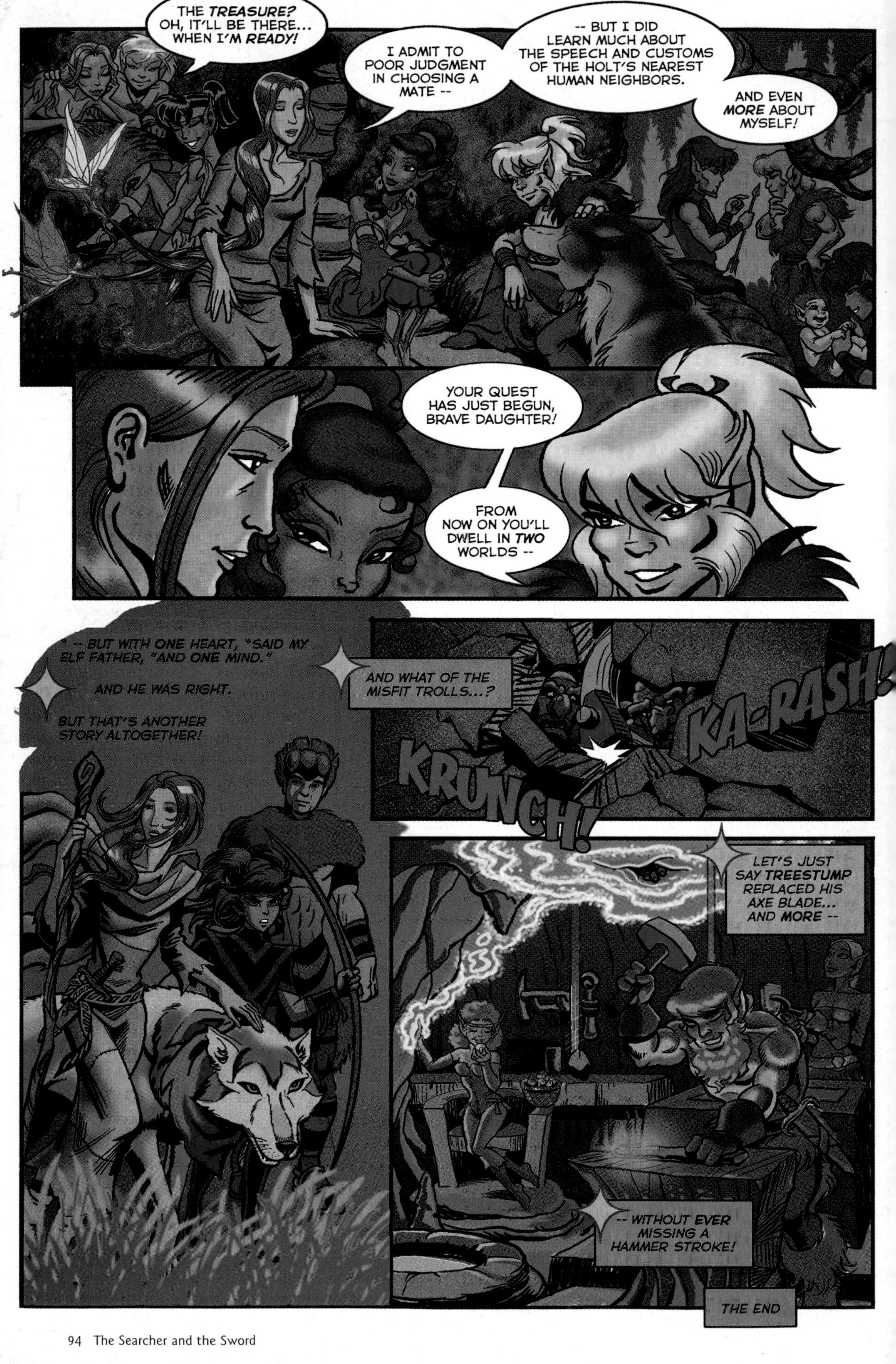
THE TREASURE? OH, IT'LL BE THERE... WHEN I'M READY!
I ADMIT TO POOR JUDGMENT IN CHOOSING A MATE --
-- BUT I DID LEARN MUCH ABOUT THE SPEECH AND CUSTOMS OF THE HOLT'S NEAREST HUMAN NEIGHBORS.
AND EVEN MORE ABOUT MYSELF!
YOUR QUEST HAS JUST BEGUN, BRAVE DAUGHTER!
FROM NOW ON YOU'LL DWELL IN TWO WORLDS --
" -- BUT WITH ONE HEART, " SAID MY ELF FATHER, "AND ONE MIND."
AND HE WAS RIGHT.
BUT THAT'S ANOTHER STORY ALTOGETHER!
AND WHAT OF THE MISFIT TROLLS...?
KA-RASH!
KRUNCH!
LET'S JUST SAY TREESTUMP REPLACED HIS AXE BLADE... AND MORE --
-- WITHOUT EVER MISSING A HAMMER STROKE!
THE END

WENDY PINI

Born Wendy Fletcher in San Francisco, her imagination was fueled by all forms of fantasy and mythology. At an early age she began spinning her own tales of elves, monkey-gods, aliens and sorcerers, her artistic and storytelling talents influenced by everything from Japanese manga to TV animation, from Shakespeare to the Ramayana.

A largely self-educated artist, Wendy began exhibiting her artwork in fanzines and at science fiction conventions in the mid 1960s, garnering awards and recognition. In 1972 she married Richard Pini and in 1974 she began her professional career as an illustrator for science fiction magazines.

In 1977, a deeply personal project called *ElfQuest* was born. As the first continuing fantasy/adventure graphic novel series in America to be co-created, written and illustrated by a woman, *ElfQuest* became a phenomenon in the comics industry.

In the late 1980s Wendy wrote and illustrated two critically praised graphic novels based on the cult hit TV series *Beauty and the Beast*. Wendy has also done work for Marvel Comics, First Comics, Comico, *Frazetta Fantasy Illustrated* magazine, and DC Comics.

Following her bliss, she continues to produce new *ElfQuest* stories and art, from graphic novels to coloring books to fine art prints.

RICHARD PINI

Richard Pini was born in 1950 in New Haven, Connecticut. Educated in Boston and Cambridge, he concentrated in astronomy, which prepared him ideally for careers in planetarium entertainment, teaching high school science, programming computers for IBM, and publishing comic books and graphic novels.

A longtime comics fan, Richard met Wendy through the letters page of Marvel Comics' *Silver Surfer*, and the two developed a lifelong relationship. When Wendy set out to create ElfQuest, Richard was by her side, and together they formed Warp ("Wendy and Richard Pini") Graphics. When the series took off, he found himself acting as editor and publisher, occasionally writing material for both the comics and prose stories as well. Over the course of Warp Graphics' 25-year life span, Richard has taken on nearly every possible *ElfQuest*-related task, including writing, editing, publishing, marketing, and administrating.

THE ELFQUEST LIBRARY
FROM DC COMICS
COMPACT EDITIONS

WOLFRIDER
VOLUME 1

WOLFRIDER
VOLUME 2

THE GRAND QUEST
VOLUME 1

THE GRAND QUEST
VOLUME 2

THE GRAND QUEST
VOLUME 3

THE GRAND QUEST
VOLUME 4

ARCHIVE EDITIONS

VOLUME 1

VOLUME 2
(NOVEMBER 2004)

FIND THESE AT YOUR LOCAL BOOKSTORE OR VIA DCCOMICS.COM